My Dream and Beyond

A Pilot's Journey

The Little Aviator

Boys had boats, their favourite toy,
Not I—when I was just a boy
I dreamt of wings for soaring high
And cutting wake in yonder sky.
And where my hero's footsteps went—
I'd follow in the firmament.

(Author Unknown)

My Dream and Beyond

A Pilot's Journey

Don McKay

GENERAL STORE PUBLISHING HOUSE
499 O'Brien Road, Box 415
Renfrew, Ontario, Canada K7V 4A6
Telephone 1.613.432.7697 or 1.800.465.6072
www.gsph.com

ISBN 978-1-77123-013-1

Cover art, design, formatting: Magdalene Carson
Printed by Custom Printers of Renfrew Ltd., Renfrew, Ontario
Printed and bound in Canada

Cataloguing data available from Library and Archives Canada.

To all those who did not make it—I often think of them.

Contents

Acknowledgements

My children often asked me to write about some of my flying experiences. What started as a brief outline turned into what is now my book. I was encouraged by a friend, Richard Latreille, who has a publishing background and had read all the chapters, to have my book published. Family and friends also encouraged me. I thank each and every one of them.

Jane Karchmar was selected by Tim Gordon, the publisher of General Store Publishing House, to evaluate my book. I was given Jane's e-mail address and sent a copy to her. Soon a message arrived stating "undelivered." I thought it a bit strange but in the cyber world strange things happen, so I sent it again and received "undelivered" once more. My immediate thought was, "Wow, quickest rejection in history." Jane advised me that her Kindle had been full but she could now receive. Once Jane realized that the book was all capitals and double spaced, I do believe I filled her Kindle again. Being a computer-savvy editor, she soon had all the words reduced to lower case and was able to proceed in evaluating the book. Her remarks were positive, and now I had to contact the publisher. I cannot thank Jane enough for her patience and positive feedback; she put me on the right track, or should I say airway.

My conversations with Tim Gordon were positive and a decision to proceed was made. Tim assigned Lesley Murray to be my editor.

Lesley and I conferred via e-mail. She would ask a question and I would provide the answer. Lesley would then say, "Are you sure?" and so it went. I do believe editors have a soft spot for budding authors. Lesley proved to be patient and offered very good advice for a better book. I had the privilege of meeting Lesley in her office in Renfrew. We discussed the book and she was kind enough to show me the tricks of her trade. She has my heartfelt thanks for her quiet and insightful input. Thanks to Tim Gordon, of General Store Publishing House, for his support, and Magdalene Carson, for the great layout of the book and photos.

Judy, my long-suffering wife, is a happy lady now that the book has reached its final destination—published. Judy is happy I no longer spend endless hours writing and re-writing on the computer. Without her support and understanding of what I was trying to accomplish, this book would never have been completed.

I would be remiss if I did not thank all the instructors and line pilots I flew with over the years: the Fundy Flying Club, RCAF, Trans-Canada Airlines, and Air Canada. Many are in the book. Names have been changed because I could not get in touch with individuals for permission to use their names. They will no doubt recognize the event they were involved with. Memories shared are both happy and sad.

In addition, I want to acknowledge the men and women, both military and civilian, who work in fair weather and foul to ensure aircraft have a safe departure. There are many behind the scenes who work to make the system function. They have my respect and admiration. I salute them all for a job well done.

Unless credited, all photographs are from my own collection.

Any mistakes are mine and mine alone.

Foreword

Don McKay, in my opinion was, and still is, an officer and a gentleman. He also is every inch a pilot *par excellence*. From the time he decided to get his pilot's license until he retired, he has managed to fulfil his every dream from start to finish.

It is a personal pleasure to count him as a very good friend. Don was a pilot from the age of seventeen until he was sixty. During this time, he acquired 25,000 flying hours or nearly three years in the air. When he graduated as a pilot in the RCAF, he was selected as a pilot instructor on the T-33 Silver Star aircraft. He flew many aircraft in his ten-and-a-half years in the air force. This included breaking the sound barrier in the F-86 Sabre, and flying twice the speed of sound in the CF-104 Starfighter.

Don has flown everything from single-engine aircraft to 747 jets, with the responsibility for people's lives. I personally enjoyed his instant recall of his adventures in aviation, both in the RCAF and his thirty-one years of flying for Trans-Canada Airlines (now Air Canada).

This book is a good read. It also explains the dedication Don had to further his dreams, never for a moment forgetting his wife and family. His book, I believe, will be full of hope and an inspiration to students wanting a career in aviation.

It will also explain what it means to endeavour to persevere towards your dreams.

— Richard Latreille

Richard Latreille served as an airman in the RCAF working on the F-86 Sabre in the European Theatre. He also worked on the Avro Arrow. Richard also spent time in the Canadian Army and attained the rank of captain. After he retired from the service, he worked with major book publishers in both Toronto and Ottawa.

Chapter One

The Early Years

"Daddy, someday I will be in one of those." My dad told me years later that I made this statement as we walked along Stanhope Beach, Prince Edward Island, on a warm sunny day. A twin-engine aircraft had passed overhead. The year was 1942, and World War II was being fought in Europe and the Far East. Aircraft were frequently seen along the east coast. My journey into aviation began at the tender age of five years.

I never wavered in my dream.

Before I continue with my story, perhaps some information on my life growing up might prove interesting.

I was born October 5, 1937, in Sydney, Nova Scotia. Mum never made it to the hospital. I guess I was anxious to start, so I was born at home. I was the third child; Lorne was the oldest, born in 1932, and Shirley was born in 1934. Mum was a stay-at-home parent. Dad was the assistant manager of the local F.W. Woolworth's store.

Dad was born and brought up in Truro, Nova Scotia. His dad was an engineer for Canadian Pacific Railways.

Mum was given to a family out of an orphanage in 1916. Over the years, I spent many hours in the Halifax archives trying to piece together her background. I was just curious and wanted to know more about our family background. The only item I found was Mum's parents' wedding certificate, but it made her very happy. The overall information is patchy at best.

I believe Mum's father was probably killed on the Halifax docks. He was a teamster, driving horses and wagons. Accidents were frequent on the docks. I have surmised that if, indeed, he had been killed, there would have been no income for Mum's mother. As often happened in those long-ago days, Mum, age four, along with her older sister, Hilda, age six, were placed in the St. Joseph orphanage in Halifax. Speaking with Mum over the years, I always tried to get her to talk about her time in the orphanage, but the only thing she ever said was that her older sister gave her a bad time and she never wanted to see her again. The girls were given to separate families in the Mulgrave area of Nova Scotia. Mum's last name at birth was Carmichael, but she was given to the Tait family, who were good to her, and she adopted the Tait name.

I never did learn how Mum and Dad met.

One day, when Mum was home alone with her first baby, Lorne, she went to answer the door. Standing before her was Hilda, her older sister, and another lady, who introduced herself as her mother. Mum was terrified. The Lindbergh kidnapping in March 1932, and the death of the young Lindbergh baby, had been all over the papers and radio. In Mum's mind, they were going to take her baby. She told them to go away and slammed and locked the door. Mum told me that she often wondered if she did the right thing. To my knowledge, she never saw or heard from either woman again. My search for Hilda also proved fruitless. I was hoping I would find her and have them reconcile after all the passing years.

Dad was transferred to Charlottetown in 1938, when I was a year old.

In Charlottetown, we lived on Grafton Street. There was a park directly across from where we lived. Down the street was the lieutenant-governor's residence on a point of land overlooking Northumberland Strait. I have many memories of our time in Charlottetown. In 1939, the King and Queen of England visited, on their first Canadian visit. People say I was only two-and-a-half and should have no memory of the visit but likely saw pictures. They are probably correct. During the winter months, a neighbour had a large dog hooked up to a small sleigh; it was great fun being pulled around the park.

One spring, probably 1940, my older sister, Shirley, along with many others, was down near the lieutenant-governor's mansion, watching others jumping from one piece of ice to the other. Somehow, Shirley fell, or perhaps, in the excitement of others, was pushed into the water. She was struggling to get out without much success. Luckily, there was an individual who saw her plight, jumped into the harbour, and saved her. His name was "Booby" Mills, one of the very few African Americans who lived on the island. Shirley became very sick, coming down with one illness after the other. My older brother, Lorne, and I came down with whatever Shirley had, but not to the same degree. We were housebound, and a quarantine sign was placed on the front door. I often later thought, "Poor Mum," having to put up with all the sickness for three months.

On another occasion, a neighbour had just finished painting his fence and house white. I guess I did not like the colour, so the neighbour's daughter and I found some yellow paint in their garage, and we proceeded to repaint every place we could reach. Dad had to help the neighbour repaint what we had painted. I was four years old at the time. On another occasion, when I was probably four-and-a-half, I was invited to a birthday party. I was all dressed up and wore a small hat. On my way to the party, one of the older kids took my hat and put it high up on a telephone pole. Naturally, I climbed the pole to retrieve my hat. I had climbed up 10 to 12 feet, and when I looked down, "down I came." On my descent, my leg ripped on one of the steel climbing rungs and caused quite a mess. I spent seven months in a baby carriage. I was not allowed to walk until my leg healed.

Dad's boss came to supper one evening. He was really the first person I had seen who was practically bald. I sat and stared at him for the longest time. Finally he spoke to me, and I told him, stuttering I might add, "but, but, but, you got no hair." He laughed and said, "I do not have much, do I?"

One afternoon the doorbell rang. Mum peeked out the window and told me to tell the person she was not home. I opened the door and told the man, "My mum told me to tell you she is not home." Mum later told me she did not think I would take her literally; well, I did.

Wherever Mum went, I was always hanging onto her. One morning, when Mum was doing a wash with the old roller washing machine, she had just left to do something when she heard a very loud scream. Realizing I was not with her, she ran back into the kitchen. I had climbed up on a chair, somehow getting the rollers turning and putting my arm, elbow first, between the rollers. Mum had the presence of mind to hit the release mechanism, releasing my arm. I still have a scar on my left elbow to remind me of the incident.

One Saturday morning I was not to be found. Everyone was looking for me. Eventually, I was found in a tent, sitting in the front row singing my heart out. The tent had been erected that morning by "holy rollers" for a service. I was five.

I wasn't a bad kid; I was just curious.

Ann, my younger sister, was born in 1941. Dad was transferred to Saint John, New Brunswick, in late 1942. He proceeded to Saint John ahead of us, looking for a place for us to live. We followed a month or so later. The only way off the island was by boat, and Mum was terrified. Here she was with three young children and a baby; World War II was on, and it was well known that German submarines often took a short-cut through Northumberland Strait. There was a picture of us taken on board the ferry, all in life jackets for the crossing. No wonder Mum was terrified; she thought we would be attacked and killed. We arrived in New Brunswick without incident.

Our new home was the end unit of a very large house that was once part of a private girls' school, known at that time as "the Wilkinson Estate." The building overlooked what is now Rockwood Court. The house was close to woods and just over a hill from Lilly Lake, a favourite spot for the entire city, with year round access and sports of all kinds. My new friends and I spent many hours playing in the woods and climbing trees. I recall jumping for a branch, which I caught, but it broke and I fell, breaking my arm when I fell onto some rocks.

In 1943, I was six. It was time to start school, so hand-in-hand with Mum, we arrived for day one at Saint Vincent's Boys' School. The teacher took my hand and we entered the classroom. I was told to sit at a desk. I spotted a red bench under the side blackboard, sat on it, and cried until my mother came to pick me up. The next day, Mum promised to take me to the movies if I behaved myself during my day at school. The movie was a musical. I was enthralled with the music and the singing. I was a good lad the rest of my time at school, honestly.

My most vivid memory of Grade 1 is going to the washroom and not being able to re-button my pants; there were no zippers at that time. Sister Ann, my teacher, came to my rescue on more than one occasion and buttoned my fly. She was a very kind and gentle person and always had a smile.

Mum had a great friend, Mary McGrattan. She was a character, and Mum was always happy to see her. I was always going around the house singing, usually the same song; "I Am a Lonely Little Petunia in an Onion Patch". I would sing the song over and over. Mary finally told Mum, "That kid of yours should be locked up in a cell all by himself." She was probably right.

I remember visiting relatives in Truro, Nova Scotia, when I was probably six or seven. My uncle managed a soft drink plant in Truro. I remember travelling with him to Debert, Nova Scotia, where we would deliver soft drinks to the different messes. Debert was a staging area for troops waiting to ship overseas, via Halifax, and convoy to Europe. There were quite a few twin-engine aircraft coming and going, and I could not keep my eyes off them. The aviation bug was biting even harder.

During the war years, we would sit by the railway track watching the seemingly endless procession of freight trains heading for Halifax. The flat cars were loaded with trucks, tanks, Bren-gun carriers, and a myriad of other equipment that we had no clue about—either what they were called or what they did.

A boyhood friend, Daryl Lorette, and I would build balsam models. These models had an elastic band attached to the propeller and to a point near the rear of the model. We would wind the propeller until the elastic was tight, release the model and it would fly a few feet and then come crashing down. We would repair them and off they would go again. When we thought the model was repairable for only one more flight, we would stuff the model with paper and light it with a match. Once the plane was airborne, the smoke and flames were very evident and down it came burning to a small heap of ashes. This "flaming" probably came from watching *The World Today* at the movie theatre that showed German / Allied aircraft being shot down in flames.

Daryl and I also made dozens of parachutes, usually out of one of Dad's handkerchiefs or any material we could put our hands on. We would tie metal toy soldiers to the chute, roll them into the chute, and either toss them up as far as we could, or throw them off barn and shed roofs, even from tree limbs that stuck out from the trunk. Most of the time they worked well.

Sandy Johnson operated a stable just down the hill from our home, and I spent many hours there mucking out stalls. My reward was a free horse ride. I got pretty good at riding, so much so that Sandy let me escort paying customers around the park. The horses were docile and easy to control. Many years later, while visiting Saint John, Judy and I visited with Sandy and his wife. They were both in their late 80s at the time. I was very glad to have seen him again after so many years. He was thrilled and proud that I was a military pilot.

During the war years in Saint John we had a boarder. The gentleman was a sea captain, who was sent over to Canada to complete acceptance trials on each new Corvette, a convoy escort ship. The trials were conducted in the Bay of Fundy before release to the navy. He spent nearly a year with us.

Just prior to VE day, there was a merchant ship loaded with war material, mail, and parcels, destined for Europe. The ship was tied to the dock at the bottom of King Street. Someone, during the night, released the hawsers holding the ship, and it drifted into the middle of Saint John harbour and became hung up on rocks. The harbour was full of floating mail and parcels that had escaped from a hole in the ship. It was nearly two years before the ship was finally refloated, unloaded, and then taken out to sea and sunk.

I remember the day that the war in Europe ended. It seemed the whole city of Saint John headed for King's Square. A military band was playing and smiles were on every face. King Street was the main shopping street and quite steep. All the stores closed for the day but they left their awnings in the out position. Every awning was ripped off the store fronts before the day was finished.

In August 1945, a German U-boat, U889, arrived in Saint John. The U889 had surrendered to the Canadian Navy in May of 1945, off Shelburne, Nova Scotia. The sub was a trophy and was doing the rounds of Maritime ports for all to see. During its visit to Saint John, it was accompanied by HMCS *Juliette*. Every school kid in the city had a tour through the boat. I recall going down one hatch walking perhaps 20 to 30 feet and going back up on deck. The one thing that always stuck in my mind was the smell. I encountered the same smell on the Moscow subway system, and realized the smell was body odour. Even into the '60s and '70s many Europeans or Russians did not use deodorant.

After the war, Uncle Ross stayed with us for a few weeks. He was married to Dad's sister and had a daughter, Barbara. Looking back, I think he just wanted to unwind before he approached his family. Ross had landed at Normandy and was a pipe major in the North Nova Scotia Highlanders. Imagine, you are a pipe major, on the beach with the Germans shooting at you. He did what he was trained to do; he stood up and started playing the bagpipes to get the lads moving inland and off the beach. The Germans, in World War I, called those in kilts, "Ladies from Hell."

Every evening, Ross would walk the woods behind our home and play the pipes. This was his way of unwinding. People would come out of their homes and listen to him play. Ross was instrumental in setting up the Halifax Military Tattoo. The Halifax Tattoo is considered the second best in the world, after Edinburgh, Scotland. Barb, his daughter, played the pipes in the tattoo for years. Ross died in his early 40s, no doubt as a result of his wartime experiences. He was a nice man.

One beautiful, sunny, warm day, two of my friends and I decided to play in the Fisher Lake area near Lilly Lake. It was hot, and my friends elected to go for a swim. I could not swim, so I sat on a rock and watched them. They kept egging me on to jump into the water, so I finally said okay. I stripped to my shorts, dangling my feet in the water. I stood up and slipped on a rather steep, slimy rock ledge and went straight to the bottom. There I was, sitting at the bottom of the lake, not having a clue what I should do or what was going on. I looked up at my friends, who were looking down at me. I doubt if they had a clue that I was in trouble and near drowning. I have read that when you are drowning you see your whole life pass by like a movie. It's true. Even though mine was a short clip, that is exactly my memory.

I was in a bad way when, out of nowhere, a man walking his dog arrived. He immediately recognized the situation, jumped into the water, and pulled me to the surface. He administered artificial respiration and brought me back to the land of the living. He took me home; for some reason, he seemed to know who I was and where I lived. He explained to Mum what had happened. Mum checked me over and turned around to thank the man, but he was not there. We never knew his name. Personally, I have always thought that he was my guardian angel. It was just not my time to leave this beautiful earth. I was seven years old.

I had always wanted a Red Ryder BB gun. Mum and Dad agreed and I received my rifle for Christmas. I was a happy camper. One beautiful warm spring day, we were all sitting around the veranda. I was playing with my BB gun and fired a BB, which hit a purse on a small table, ricocheted, and hit Mum on the ear lobe. I was up and running like hell, with Mum in hot pursuit. I threw the rifle over my head, ran down the hill, and headed for the woods. I never saw my Red Ryder rifle again.

Dad was not happy with his advancement with Woolworth's. He was offered employment, as manager, of a "federal store" in Saint John, New Brunswick. The new store carried the same merchandise as Woolworth's but on a smaller scale. He was happy, and we were eventually transferred to a federal store in Sackville, New Brunswick.

Near the end of our first year in Sackville, Dad had an opportunity to open his own store. He had always wanted to be his own boss. The store became locally known as "Mac's." Mac's was a variety store, a little bit of everything; clothing, toys, candy, etc. I often helped in the store, filling in for Dad when he went home for lunch or attended business meetings around town. All was going well.

My younger brother, Michael, was born in Sackville in 1949. Mum was very sick during her pregnancy. Dad was given the choice of saving Mum or the baby. Mum kept saying, "Save the baby." Dad abided with Mum's wishes. Mike was born healthy, and, by another one of those family miracles, Mum survived. I remember running home from school to see my new brother. I took a shortcut, fell, and ripped my new rubber boots on a piece of barbed wire.

We lived in Sackville for about four years. I really enjoyed the small town. I attended the new Catholic Holy Rosary School. The teachers were all nuns, and the pastor was Father Michael Louis Lafontaine of the Dominican Order. He later became a navy chaplain. I communicated with him when I was stationed at Gimli, Manitoba. He died at a relatively young age.

Lorne and I became altar boys. The Dominican Order wore white cassocks, as did we, when serving mass. The cassock had a hood and a waist rope or tie to keep it from dragging; it was hot to wear. Lorne and I were known as "the big pope and the little pope." Lorne ended up marrying a Baptist, Barb Steadman, and remained in Sackville after we moved back to Saint John. Holy Trinity only went to Grade 6, and I started Grade 7 in a brand new public school. It was my first time away from a religious school. I thoroughly enjoyed myself with sports of all kinds. I was a reasonable basketball and baseball player, but I loved track. I was very good in the high jump as well as running; not many could catch me. I was thin, gangly, and fast.

In the winter months, we played a lot of hockey. I was either left wing or centre. During one game, I had the puck and was close to the boards heading for the opposition net. I was checked pretty hard and ended up in the opposition's bench. I shook the check off and skated to our bench, but I was not feeling very well. Our coach told me to go to the dressing room and relax, as the period was just about over. The team arrived and the coach took one look at me and saw my sweater was raised over my left shoulder. He thought something might be broken and he sent me to the local clinic, which was across from the rink. The doctor helped me remove my sweater and shoulder pads and stated that my collarbone had popped out of its socket. He told me to take a deep breath and then he pushed the collarbone back into position. My shoulder felt okay, so I put my gear back on, returned to the rink, put my skates on, and played the rest of the game, none the worse for wear.

During the winter festival we did square dancing on ice. Great fun. I only learned how to dance after we moved back to Saint John. Our neighbour in Sackville was Dr. Weldon, a dentist. I often babysat for him and his wife. He had a great collection of encyclopaedias and world history books. I always loved history and I looked forward to my babysitting task so I could read from his books. I actually completed what was the Grade 11 history course by grade 8, all because I had access to Dr. Weldon's books.

In 1951, Princess Elizabeth, soon to be queen, visited Canada. (My wife and I visited Kenya, Africa, in 2010, and we actually stayed in the same lodge that Elizabeth and Philip stayed on the historic day she was advised that her father had died and she was now Queen of England and the Dominions.) The train stopped at Sackville and the whole town and surrounding area was there to see her. I would later rub shoulders with royalty during my military days and with Air Canada.

Another activity I became involved in was the reserve army in 1952. I lied about my age (I was 15) and many of the new recruits did the same. I became a member of the Princess Louise (NB) Hussars, a tank regiment. We paraded at the local armoury once a week, and during the summer we had full basic training at Camp Utopia, near St. Stephen, New Brunswick. We had rifle and bayonet drill, using the old Lee Enfield rifle and firing the Sten semi-automatic weapon, as well as the Bren machine gun. In addition, we unpacked hand grenades, armed them on the range, and tossed them over the safety position. It was all great fun. They even paid us for having a great time.

A group of us headed for Calais, Maine, one weekend when there was a circus in town. I travelled with another chap from Sackville and we proceeded to view the circus. We approached a tent where an older gentleman was verbally advertising a great show. One dollar a peek. We paid our money and were directed to walk between tents that had another piece of canvas attached to form a path. We could see two holes in the tent and looked in. There was an older woman sitting in a chair, bare breasted. She looked at us, cupped her breasts, and said, "What do you want, honey, chocolate or vanilla?" We scrambled to vacate the place as fast as our legs could carry us. We had never seen a bare-breasted woman before. I imagine she chuckled about us the rest of her life.

During Easter break we proceeded to Camp Sussex, near Sussex, New Brunswick. Because the Hussars were a tank regiment, we got to ride in Sherman tanks and shoot the tank guns, both cannon and 30mm machine guns. In addition, there was a "Honey" tank. It was a reconnaissance vehicle that could do 30 mph on a paved road. The tracks were large rubber pads rather than the large steel tracks on the Sherman.

One exercise we were given was to drive what the military called a 60-hundredweight truck. Luckily, one of our group had a driver's licence. The truck had to be double-clutched to change gears. It was interesting to watch the driver's spurts, stalls, and more spurts, but he soon got the hang of it. Our job was to get the truck stuck; we certainly tried. We would sit in streams, turn the engine off, and wait for the vehicle to settle. After a while, we would start the engine, put it in gear and away we would go. We even tried sitting in mud, but always managed to get out. We never did get stuck.

In 1952, I was selected to be part of the cenotaph guard on Remembrance Day; standing at the corner of the cenotaph, head bowed, hands resting on the rifle. We thought it was a great honour to be selected, especially since the war was still fresh in everyone's mind.

My older brother, Lorne, was a sergeant in the air cadets. Lorne wanted to become a pilot; I guess every boy did during the war years. After the war, Lorne remained in the air cadets and, when he was eighteen, went to Moncton to join the RCAF. He wrote all the necessary Stanine, or Standard, tests. These were initiated by the U.S. military during World War II. The tests were used to test the aptitude of those wishing to join the military. The tests included questions on mathematics, science, language skills, and trade skills. Lorne passed all the required medical examinations. Unfortunately, he was unable to complete his eye examination as no doctor was available. He made the trip to Moncton three times. During his third visit, he was able to get the required eye exam but to his surprise and disappointment, he was colour-blind. He was one very sad lad when he returned to Sackville.

Several years later, while I was at the Fundy Flying Club and, having obtained my private pilot's licence, I arranged with my brother to meet me at the Amherst, Nova Scotia, airport. I would take him up in a Fleet Canuck for his first trip in an aircraft. I told Lorne that I would not do anything foolish—no steep turns, just a comfortable, easy ride. I strapped him in and started the engine. We taxied out and took off. We were not in the air two minutes when Lorne grabbed my arm quite tightly with both hands and said, "Get the aircraft down, now." I turned back and landed. Lorne never flew again. Perhaps it was a good thing he was colour-blind.

It was about this time that the province instituted a sales tax. Sackville was very close to Amherst, Nova Scotia. That province had no sales tax, so everyone drove to Amherst to shop. Consequently, Dad's business suffered and he was forced to close the doors, losing everything in the process. Dad was able to return to federal stores in Saint John. I was about fifteen, in Grade 9 at this time, and was back at Saint Vincent's. I remember being pleasantly surprised to see the same faces that I started with in Grade 1. Grades 10 and 11 were completed at another new high school, St. Malachy's. I graduated in 1955. Mr. Fred MacMurray was the principal of the school. I visited with him when I was in the air force and on leave in Saint John. He told me he always wanted to be a pilot and was envious of my being able to wear pilot wings. Mr. MacMurray was truly a nice man.

I met Judy at a Saint Peter's High School dance during my Grade 10 year. I was immediately attracted to her and we started dating soon after the dance. We have now been married for 53 years.

Chapter Two

My Dream Takes Flight

I had my first flight at the Fundy Flying Club on February 26, 1955. My student pilot permit was QM-1661, issued April 6, 1955. The aircraft was a Fleet Canuck, CF-DPC, with side-by-side seating. Jack Woodley was the pilot. He was not an accredited instructor, but he had quite a lot of experience. The club often asked him to do the "fam-flight," (familiarization flight), over the city of Saint John and surrounding area. Jack was a Saint John police detective. Don MacLaren was the chief flying instructor and club manager, with whom I did most of my initial flying. I had a grand total of nine hours and fifteen minutes when I completed my first solo April 17, 1955.

The first time alone in an aircraft is an unforgettable memory. I felt confident. I completed my take-off check, which basically was a good look around at the instruments and making sure the doors were closed. I pushed the throttle to the stop, accelerated, and became airborne off Runway 05, straight out to 1000 feet. I levelled out, turned right for the downwind leg, turned right again on the base leg, turned to line up on final on Runway 05, landed, and taxied into the flying club. I had a grin that has lasted throughout my forty-three-year flying career.

Don MacLaren was killed while landing on water. He hit a hidden log, causing the aircraft to flip. He either broke his neck or was unconscious from the crash and drowned.

Saul Clark was another instructor, from Tillsonburg, Ontario. His family was in tobacco farming. I completed most of my instrument flying with Saul, who was a patient and very nice man, in contrast to Don, who was hyper and, at times, had a quick temper.

Alice was the secretary of the flying club. I never could figure out how she typed. She could not see the keys due to her rather large breasts. She eventually married the new chief instructor, Bruce Carter. He was from New Zealand. I was near the end of my flying club training when he came along. Bruce eventually became an MOT (Ministry of Transport) inspector.

I had never told Mum or Dad that I was taking flying lessons. While I was growing up, we never had a car. As luck would have it, my parents and younger brother were out for a drive with a friend one day. They stopped at the airport to watch the aircraft, and, at the very time they arrived, I was finishing lunch at the terminal restaurant. I paid my bill and walked out of the terminal, across the tarmac, to a parked Fleet Canuck. I started the engine, taxied out, and took off. Both of my parents were rather surprised, to say the least, to see me go flying. It was not until I got home that night that I was asked, "What were you doing in that airplane?" I explained my desire to learn to fly, and they reluctantly finally said, "Okay, but be careful."

I recall one solo flight when I was on final for Runway 23 when I noticed a TCA (Trans-Canada Airlines, which later became Air Canada) DC-3 aircraft, on final for Runway 05. Knowing he had passengers I broke off my approach; heck, I was in no hurry to land. I turned right, away from the DC-3. The TCA captain felt I was too close or something and broke off his approach, turned left, and lost sight of me. At the same time, I could clearly see him as I had completed my turn. I manoeuvred to fit myself behind him for landing. In any event, the captain was rather upset and charged me with a violation for being too close to him. I wasn't, but I was required to present myself for a hearing by the Ministry of Transport, in Moncton, New Brunswick. I thought my budding flying career was about to come to a rapid conclusion.

I entered the assigned room at the assigned time. The TCA captain was seated in the room and gave me quite a stare. The MOT supervisor convened the board of inquiry, and I was asked to give my side of the story. I mentioned to the board that after the TCA DC-3 elected to go around, the aircraft turned left. At that point, the board chairman turned to the captain and asked him if my statement was correct. He said, "Yes, sir. That little shit made me overshoot and I turned left to rejoin the circuit." At this point, the chairman looked at me and said, "Young man, you were correct in your actions by turning right when you meet another aircraft, as per the MOT rules." He told me I was excused, and the violation against me from the TCA captain would go no further. As I was leaving the meeting room, I heard the chairman say, "Captain, you should know better." I closed the door and left. I heard later the captain was given a lecture and told to review the rules of the air. I was home free and my budding career was still on track.

I was in Grade 11 when I started flying. The teachers soon got wind of my weekend activities. Class on Monday started with them asking me how the flying was going. My classmates were happy about the teachers' questions; it delayed the class for a few minutes.

Throughout my high school years I worked at the federal store, a local department store, usually in the stockroom. Friday evenings I became a floor walker, helping customers and getting change for the different cashiers. The money I made paid for my flying lessons. In those days, the stores closed Saturday at noon. I would hitchhike to the airport for instruction; a dual lesson (with an instructor), was $11 per hour, while a solo flight cost $9 per hour.

One day, when I was about to go on a solo trip, another student, whose name escapes me, told me he was going to fly to a Girl Guide camp on the Saint John River and buzz his girlfriend. He asked me to follow him and buzz the place as well. Naturally, I jumped at the idea. We found the camp with no problem and we both buzzed the camp a few times. Then we broke off and I followed the other aircraft away from the camp. The other aircraft had no problem clearing a hill, but the closer I got to the hill the more certain I became that I was not going to make it over. I could not turn the aircraft away from the hill; I was committed. I slowly reduced my airspeed, trying to gain a bit of altitude. I barely cleared the top of the trees, and was very near the stall speed. I was happy to see the other side of the hill had a downslope. I was able to get the airspeed back up quite easily. I later learned that there were different kinds of propellers; one good for cruising and another for climb capability. Needless to say, I was not the one who had the climbing capability. Live and learn.

During my last year in high school, I applied for a summer job with TCA as a ramp rat, and, to my delight, I was accepted. Basically, my job was loading and unloading passenger luggage, unloading used food containers from the galley, and loading new meals from the airport restaurant. I worked on DC-3/DC-4 as well as the Bristol freighter.

One hot Saturday afternoon, we were attempting to get a DC-3 tire and hub out the door of a DC-4. We got it to the door okay, but then we lost it. The tire rolled down the conveyer belt as people scrambled out of the way. Then it rolled across the infield, across Runway 14/32 and up a small incline where it finally ran out of steam and fell over. We were all laughing so hard it was a wonder anything else was accomplished that day.

The airport was a great place to work. I was around aircraft on a daily basis. Working on the ramp made me appreciate the ramp staff, particularly after I started to fly for Air Canada. I knew both sides of the business of getting an aircraft into the air. I would be called into work on long weekends, Christmas, Easter, as well as the summer months. My whole reason for taking flying lessons was that someday I might fly for what was then TCA, later Air Canada.

On many occasions, crews taxiing out for takeoff would call into the radio room and state that there were deer at such-and-such place. Everyone would jump on an old fire truck. One of the mechanics always had a rifle handy, and we would bounce our way to the designated area, making so damn much noise that by the time we arrived the deer were long gone. The mechanic with the rifle frequently hunted on the airfield. One of the ramp attendants suggested we place a dummy deer near the button of Runway 05, a fair distance from the terminal building. Everyone thought it would be a great idea. We got some old steel barrels, drilled a couple of holes, and stuck mop handles in the holes to represent antlers. We had arranged with a DC-3 crew to call in, stating, "Deer, vicinity of 05." The mechanic jumped on the fire engine and headed out on his own. He spotted the "deer" and it sounded like a war zone, he was firing so much. But the deer would not fall over. A short time later he returned, not in a very good frame of mind, cursing at one and all. We got a great kick out of it, but he never went hunting on the airport property again.

TCA had two mechanics stationed in Saint John: Jim MacMillan and Ernie Crawley. Jim served in the RCAF and worked on Lancaster Bombers in the UK during the war. He also worked at the flying club as a mechanic. Ernie Crawley was senior mechanic. One night, a DC-3 was required to remain overnight due to heavy snow. TCA regulation required that the engines be started every hour and run up to maintain warm oil temperature. I elected to stay and help Ernie. I would lie awake waiting for each scheduled hour to arrive, wake Ernie, and off we would go to start the engines. Ernie showed me the start-up procedure and we would complete a run-up. After a couple of sessions, Ernie let me start the engines on my own. What a thrill. On one session, the snow let up a bit and Ernie said, "Let's taxi around a bit." He gave me a few hints on how to taxi. After about three hours of waking Ernie up and going out to the aircraft, Ernie said, "You go do it," and went back to sleep. I was gone in a flash. I started the engines and noticed the snow had let up a bit, so I released the brakes and taxied down the runway. As I was returning to the ramp, it started snowing heavily. I knew exactly where the terminal was, but I could not see it! Again and again I strained to see the terminal when it suddenly dawned on me that I was too far down the ramp and was heading for K.C. Irving's hangar. Mr. Irving practically owned Saint John, including the radio station, the bus service, and many service stations, to name a few. He had several aircraft parked in his hangar.

I quickly shut down the engines and the aircraft came to a stop about 10 feet from K.C.'s hangar. I was sweating bullets. I left the aircraft and retrieved a small tug, a small but powerful gasoline operated runabout. I hooked up the tow bar to the tail wheel, which made it easy to steer the aircraft, and placed the aircraft back in front of the terminal. It was snowing so hard my tracks were soon covered up and no one was the wiser. The next hour I told Ernie I was too tired to go out with him. He never knew how close I came to damaging a TCA DC-3.

Years later, after I retired, I called Ernie while I was visiting Saint John, and we had coffee together. I told him the story and he got a good chuckle out of it. He said he often wondered why after my being so keen to start the engines with him, I begged off the last couple of starts. Now he knew.

One aircraft that K.C. owned was a twin-engine Mallard amphibian; it could operate on land or water. On several occasions, K.C.'s pilot took me along for a trip to Loch Lomond Lake, where we would land and wash the aircraft. I was no doubt brought along because of my agility in climbing up on the wings and washing them. I really enjoyed these flights. I later heard he was in the Caribbean flying between the islands, where, I'm certain, he was enjoying himself. He is now retired and living in Saint John, New Brunswick.

Harold Titus, owner of a popular Saint John bakery, had a Sea-Bee aircraft, also amphibian. I would often go with him and land on Loch Lomond and wash his aircraft. He allowed me to take the aircraft off the lake on a couple of occasions. It certainly required a different flying technique.

The Bristol freighter usually arrived during the evening. The main cabin was designed to carry freight, so it was necessary to climb a ladder to access the flight deck. The cockpit sat above the large bulbous doors, which opened to allow large articles to be placed on board. The lighting in the cargo area was not the best. One evening, as I was about to leave the aircraft, I noticed a coffin strapped down and on its way to Montreal. When I approached the coffin, a body rose up from behind the coffin and said, "Boo!" I was out of the aircraft like a shot, only to be greeted by the rest of the ramp crew laughing their heads off. Jimmy Heighten was the culprit who set me up and hid behind the coffin. On another occasion, Jim threw a box at me. I read the address label and discovered it contained the cremated remains of a Norwegian sailor going home. I got rid of the box in a hurry.

I received my private pilot's licence number, QMP-2963, on August 10, 1955, with a grand total of thirty hours and forty minutes of flying in my log book. I was now qualified to carry passengers, assuming they were brave enough to come for a ride. During the time I worked on the ramp for TCA, I also got a job with the Fundy Flying Club. My duties included keeping the hangar clean and tidy, as well as refuelling and tying down aircraft for the night. I would also help Joe Ellis. Joe was a jack of all trades, and the nicest man you would ever want to meet. He was very good at repairing the all-fabric Fleet Canuck. I would help him measure, cut, and dope the area that needed fixing. Joe had a son, Paul, who was also taking flying lessons.

On one occasion we had a flour-bombing contest. A club member used his hardtop jeep as a target, and we would fly over it and throw our flour bomb out the window. Closest to the jeep or a hit on the jeep won. Paul was not like his father; he was a bit of a show-off and a hot-dogger. He decided he was going to do anything to win the bombing contest. He flew very low and, as he approached the jeep, the aircraft door opened, followed by a hand with a bag of flour. Paul's intention was to place his flour bomb smack on the middle of the jeep roof. He missed, but he did manage to hit the jeep with his left wheel collapsing the jeep roof and nearly losing control of the aircraft. After he landed, he walked towards the group with his tail between his legs. Joe and everyone else present were not impressed. Paul eventually joined the RCAF (Royal Canadian Air Force) and received his pilot's wings. He was assigned to Sabres and an overseas posting. He did not do well on squadron and was taken off flying duties. He became a simulator instructor. Later, he was transferred back to Canada and I lost complete track of him.

I had graduated from high school and now had two jobs. I was making what seemed pretty good money so, since I was seventeen with a pilot's licence, I thought it was about time that I received my driver's licence and purchased a car. I was tired of hitchhiking to the airport. I elected to buy a 1952 Ford Meteor. The price was $1,200. The first night I had the vehicle, two school buddies, Gerry Byrne and Joe Finnegan, and I drove around the city. After we stopped for the famous cherry coke, the car would not start. I stood outside and pushed while steering and my buddies pushed from the rear. Once we reached the top of a hill, we all jumped into the car and, as soon as we had a little speed, I popped the clutch and away we went. This happened to us three or four times. I took the car back the next day and a new battery was installed, which solved the problem. My girlfriend, Judy Semple, now my dear wife of over fifty years, started calling the car "Nelly Bell." The name stuck.

Naturally, I was keen to go flying at any time, to build up my hours towards a Commercial Licence. One Saturday afternoon, a gentleman arrived at the club and asked if he could have a ride over the city. The manager, knowing I was keen for hours, asked me to take him up for an hour. He was paying, so I leapt at the opportunity. We took off and as we circled the city, the passenger stated that he used to fly but it had been a while and asked me if he could have the controls. I was quite happy to let him "have a go." It was obvious to me, at my stage of flying that he could really fly. His actions were smooth and well controlled. I asked him where he learned to fly, and he told me he was in the German Luftwaffe during the war; captured, released, and eventually immigrated to Canada in the early '50s. He told me he was working as a salesman, at Calps', a local department store in Saint John, in the lingerie department. We both got a chuckle out of that. We returned to the airport and landed; he thanked me, paid the bill, and left. I often wondered what became of him.

On another occasion, I was asked to fly a businessman to Bathurst, a grass strip in northern New Brunswick. I was to drop him off and fly back. Again, someone else was paying the bill. The gentleman in question showed up on time and away we went. It wasn't long before I realized he was drunk. He hauled out a bottle, took a drink, and offered me one as well. I declined. I was not certain what I should do, because I did not know what he might do. My problem solved itself; he fell asleep. I woke him on arrival and we went our separate ways.

George Legere was a fixture around the club. He had learned to fly in the '20s and loved it. Many times he would drive to Moncton, rent a Cornell aircraft from the Moncton Flying Club, fly back to Saint John, and give his friends a ride over the city. When finished, George would fly the aircraft back to Moncton and drive home.

Often, George would see me and invite me along for a ride. Of course, I always jumped at the chance. George asked me if I had ever done any aerobatics. I had not. He proceeded to show me how to loop the Fleet Canuck. I never did know if the aircraft was stressed for aerobatics, heck, at my stage of the game all I really knew was; pull back you went up, push forward, you went down. But that did not stop George. He would place his felt hat on the forward pedestal and, as we looped, he would go for negative "G." His hat would start to float and George, laughing the whole time, would move his head trying to put his hat back on. He was good at it.

I was busy refuelling an aircraft one day when George taxied by, waved at me, and said he was just doing a quick trip around the harbour and told me to jump in, which I did. I strapped in and said to George, "There is no control column on my side." He mumbled that someone must have taken it out to fix it. I thought nothing more of it and away we went. We circled the city and as we got to the middle of the Saint John Harbour, at about 2,000 feet, George said, "You have control." I said, "How? I have no control column," at which point he opened the door, and said, "Neither do I." In his hand he had a control column, which he tossed into the harbour.

I did not have a clue what to do. I placed a pen I had into the control column insert position and tried to move the control surfaces, but that was a lost cause. George was roaring with laughter. I thought he had gone off the deep end and we would end up in the bay. About this time he stretched out and laughed even more, and as he stretched out I could see his control column was still in place. The bugger had set me up, removing my control column before he asked me to go with him on his "quick trip." Over the years, George and I had many chuckles over the incident.

George was very proud of the fact that I had gone on to join the RCAF and received my pilot wings. Whenever I saw him over the years, he was always telling everyone he taught me to fly. He was a wonderful man. George, well into his 70s, continued to fly a converted Avenger aircraft spraying for bud worms in New Brunswick. I was told he landed for a refill of chemicals, told the ground crew he felt a bit tired and was going to have a quick nap. When they came to tell him his aircraft was ready he did not respond. George was gone. It was the end of an era, but he died doing what he loved to do, fly.

"Bunker" McDevitt was another ramp worker with TCA. He had his pilot's licence and acquired quite a few flying hours. The crews of the DC-3 encouraged him to apply to the company for a pilot's job, but he never did. No explanation was ever given. One summer, Bunker flew the converted Avenger during the bud worm season. The Avenger was a big machine and when loaded with chemicals and fuel it was heavy. Bunker was doing a run when he hit the tops of some trees; the aircraft cart-wheeled, crashed, and exploded, killing Bunker.

It had always been my dream to fly for TCA, so to that end I asked what a commercial licence would cost. I was told $1,500, but if I paid cash, I would receive a 20 percent discount. That was still more money than I ever had or seen. I mulled over in my mind how I could get that much money. The federal store had a soda fountain. Most large stores and pharmacies had a soda fountain where you could buy sandwiches, doughnuts, and cold drinks. Mrs. Bizzo was the manager of the fountain. She heard about my dilemma, and said, "Go ask the bishop." I never thought the bishop would ever extend a loan to a seventeen-year-old, just out of high school.

Mrs. Bizzo persisted in encouraging me to "go see the bishop." I got my courage up and walked into the bishop's palace (his residence and offices). I explained to the secretary that I wanted to talk to the bishop. I was asked to sit and wait. Soon, Monsignor Cronin arrived. He always scared us kids to death. I explained to him my desire to become a commercial pilot, but neither I nor my parents had the money to pay for the training. He listened to my proposal, asked if I intended to pay it back, and naturally, I said, "Yes." I was told my request was one he had never heard before, but he would present my request to the bishop. I was told to come back in a week, which I did. To my delight, I was given a cheque in the sum of $1,200, made out to the Fundy Flying Club. The total amount payable to the course was paid in full. I thanked the monsignor and everyone else I could think of. I was literally on cloud nine.

I paid the club and started my commercial program; Mrs. Bizzo, God bless her soul, said, "Told you so." I was told by the monsignor that there was no need to make payments and no interest would be charged, but when I finished all my training and when I was able, I was to repay the loan. I was not in a position to repay the loan with interest until I joined the RCAF. I knew that if I did pay off the loan, someday some other seventeen-year-old would probably ask for money for a dream, and the experience I had with the bishop might just help his dream along.

I was required to have so many hours in night flying for a commercial licence. I did a couple of night flights with Saul Clark to prove my proficiency, and I was given permission to go night flying any time I wanted. I already had a key to the flying club hangar. My girlfriend, Judy, and I would drive to the airport, open the hangar doors, push an aircraft out, close the door, fly up the river to Fredericton, land, have a coke and a chocolate bar, then fly back to Saint John. It became our Saturday night date, weather permitting. Judy's dad learned of our Saturday night dates and was not impressed with me flying his daughter. He relented, once it was explained that I now had a pilot's licence and was allowed to take passengers. He did say that when he was courting his wife he had to walk or ride a bike on dates. Dating now had a whole new meaning for him.

Although I had been using the aircraft radios, I was required to obtain a radio operator's licence. I was given an address of the office in Saint John, so I made an appointment and arrived at the scheduled time. The gentleman told me I was to go into the next room and that the phone would ring. I was to repeat everything he said back to him. I entered the room, sat down, and the phone rang.

He said, "Hello."

I said "Hello," and he said, "Now we begin."

I said, "Now we begin."

He said, "No, no."

Naturally, I said, "No, no."

Then he said, "You don't understand," so I repeated, "You don't understand."

I guess I put him off his feed; he opened the door shaking his head and said, "That's enough," and gave me my licence. As I look back I think he must have been completely exasperated with me. He never thought I would take him that literally. I imagine he told the story to his co-workers, who probably got a kick out of it.

I was also required to be qualified on instrument flying. There was a "Mickey Mouse" setup in front of me, situated so that I could only see the instruments and not outside, although, if you put your head in a certain position you could see a bit of the outside, which helped. I was required to do turns, climbs, and descents, all on instruments. I was then introduced radio range flying. Wearing headsets you would listen for an "A" or an "N" in Morse code. I was required to find my position using the "A" and "N" signals, identify the quadrant I was in, track towards the station, and, on arrival, complete an approach to the runway—all on instruments. It was very challenging, but Saul, my instructor, was easy to get along with and I progressed. Eventually, I came to love instrument flying; it was very satisfying to go from point "A" to "B" never seeing the ground, make an approach, descend to limits, and then look up and see the runway straight ahead. Throughout my flying career, I never tired of making instrument approaches. It was always very satisfying.

I managed to get to the Moncton Flying Club and fly their Link trainer. The Link was a holdover from World War II. Once in the Link, better known as "The Beast," you lowered a hatch-like device over your head, so all you could see was the instruments. No peeking in this machine. Mr. Norm Caruthers was the instructor and he talked me through climbs, turns, and descents. When you were flying the Link it felt as if you were on the point of a pin; it was very easy to over-control. The Link was definitely a challenge, but it certainly helped my proficiency in instrument flying.

The Fundy Flying Club acquired a Piper Cruiser (PA-22)—a tail dragger—and a Tri-Pacer with a nose wheel. Naturally, I had to get checked out on both aircraft. The Cruiser was quite a bit faster than the Fleet Canuck, and in the winter months we attached skis to the aircraft. I managed to get a rating on skis as well.

The Tri-Pacer was faster than the Cruiser, and you could take three passengers rather than the one in the Fleet and Cruiser. Judy's uncle, a retired army officer, was anxious to go flying with me. I took him, his wife, and Judy on a sightseeing flight over the city and along the coast. It was a beautiful day and everyone enjoyed the flight.

The local newspaper called the club with a request to rent the Tri-Pacer for a trip to Penfield, an old wartime airport. There were reports that thousands of deer were gathering and the paper wanted some pictures. I was lucky enough to fly the photographer—more hours paid by someone else. Neither of us could believe the number of deer. There were literally thousands of them covering nearly the whole airport. The pictures were printed in the local paper; no one could give an adequate explanation as to why the deer gathered as they did. To my knowledge, they have never gathered in such large numbers again.

Chapter Three

The Long Cross-Country

I was anxious to complete the 150 hours required for a commercial licence as soon as possible. I started to plan a trip through the United States, back up into Ontario and home. I needed someone to come with me to help pay for food and lodging. The hours we flew would be paid for out of my payment from the bishop. Eventually, Doug Fifield, a chap I had never met before, said he would come along. The deal was, I paid for the flying, he paid for meals and lodging. Off we went.

We left Saint John and flew to Old Town, Maine, where we cleared U.S. customs. Then off for Augusta and Portland, Maine, where we spent the night at a motel within walking distance of the airport. The next day we landed at Worcester, Massachusetts, and Flushing, New York. After we landed, an airport employee said he was heading for town and would drop us off at the YMCA. We took him up on his offer and managed to see a bit of the downtown. In the morning, we were able to catch a subway back to Flushing Airport. Today, Flushing Airport no longer exists; it is now known as Flushing Meadows, home of the U.S. tennis championships.

We headed north out of Flushing, enjoying a beautiful view of New York. It was quite a sight. We followed the Hudson River and landed near Albany, on a grass field at Whitford, New York, where we refuelled and headed for Buffalo. We circled Niagara Falls before we landed in Buffalo for the night. We were required to file a flight plan for each flight leg, and normally, on landing, the tower or radio station would advise, "Flight plan closed." I assumed on landing at Buffalo that our flight plan had been cancelled like all the other times we had landed. The next day I filed a flight plan for London, Ontario. The gentleman who took our flight plan took one look at the aircraft registration and asked where we came from. We told him, and he said that there was a search being organized to look for us, because we had not cancelled our flight plan the day before. Lesson learned: never assume things are done for you. I always made certain in the future that I cancelled my flight plans. The gentleman who took our flight plan called someone and said, "Call off the search, I have the missing pilots." We had a little lecture and off we went.

After takeoff, we again had a good look at Niagara Falls. The day was very hot and hazy. I was not instrument rated so I was required to fly VFR (visual flight rules), which means "in sight of the ground at all times." We looked and looked for the London airport. We looked for any airport we could land on because we were getting low on fuel and it was starting to get dark. I spotted a race track. We flew low and slow over it and I decided to land. We touched down okay, but what I missed seeing on the fly-by was a white quarter pole, used in measuring distance in horse racing. The pole threatened to take the wing off. I hit the brakes and turned sharply; we came to an abrupt halt in a little ditch with our propeller in the ground and our tail sticking high in the air. I turned off all the switches and Doug and I vacated the aircraft. By this time we had a bit of an audience, mostly teenagers, who we learned were from a local First Nation's band. I had them help us get the tail back on the ground. Once the aircraft was in its normal position, I could see that the propeller was damaged and the engine cowling had a few dents; otherwise the aircraft looked okay.

Prior to leaving Saint John, Saul Clark had mentioned that if we had any problem in Ontario, to call the Goderich Flying Club, which I did. I explained our problem and where we were. I had learned from our audience that we were at the Melbourne racetrack, and it was now pretty dark. They said they would be down tomorrow. I warned them about the quarter pole, assuming they would fly to Melbourne. The evening turned into a long one as several teenagers hung around the aircraft and I was reluctant to leave to go to a hotel, not knowing what they might do to the aircraft. Doug and I took turns catnapping in the aircraft.

The Goderich Flying Club's chief pilot and a mechanic arrived midday by car. The mechanic checked the airframe over and said we only required a new prop. Luckily, they had brought a new prop. A few dents were banged out and all was accomplished in good time. The chief instructor from the Goderich Flying Club started the engine, ran it up, checked the magnetos, and declared the engine was okay. He taxied to the end of the racetrack and took off. In the meantime Doug, the mechanic, and I piled into the vehicle and drove to Goderich, about two-and-a-half hours north of Melbourne.

On arrival at Goderich, we were informed that the aircraft operated normally and that Goderich had been in touch with the Fundy Flying Club and we were free to go. I elected to do a local test flight for my own satisfaction and found everything was working the way it should.

Doug and I then departed for Toronto Island Airport. The aircraft performed beautifully and we landed at the island in the late afternoon. We cancelled our flight plan, and had the aircraft serviced. The island folks told us we were welcome to sleep on the terminal benches if we wanted to. We accepted; it would save Doug a few dollars. We then proceeded, via a shuttle ferry, into the big city of Toronto for dinner and sightseeing. The past day had been a long one, considering we had little sleep the night before, so we elected to return to the island early. It was shortly after eight in the evening and the ferry to the island was there but it was deserted. We checked around and found a sign that said ferry service terminated at 8 p.m., so we snuck on board and spent the night on the ferry benches.

The next morning, we flew the Lake Ontario shoreline to Kingston, refuelled, and headed for a small strip near Montreal, where we spent the night. On September 1, we flew to Megantic, Quebec, and remained overnight. The next day we were homeward bound; landing in Fredericton, refuelling for the final leg into Saint John. After a twenty-nine-hour, ten-minute cross-country flight, we were home. Both Doug and I thoroughly enjoyed the experience, and I was well on my way to having the required hours for my commercial licence.

Life returned to normal after our cross-country flight. I was still working on the ramp for TCA and the flying club. Judy and I resumed our Saturday night flights to Fredericton. All was proceeding as planned.

One afternoon, while I was working at the flying club, the control tower reported an overdue aircraft travelling from Shearwater, Nova Scotia, to Saint John. The aircraft was a Naval Harvard with only the pilot on board.

The club was asked to assist in the search. The government would reimburse for gas. I jumped at the opportunity of more free flying. We searched along the coast for most of the afternoon, sighting nothing. We thought he might have ended up in the Bay of Fundy; if so, game over. The radio range station advised us that the aircraft had been found farther up the coast and the pilot was waving to aircraft overhead. Being curious, we proceeded to the crash site where we waved to the downed pilot. He was waiting for a helicopter to pick him up.

We saw the Harvard, nose in with its tail to the sky; shades of Melbourne. The sky was becoming crowded with other aircraft, so we headed back to Saint John. We never did hear the reason for the crash. Helicopters were few and far between in those days. I remember a rescue by helicopter in Saint John at the MacVitty plant. They made manhole covers; somehow one of the men cleaning the chimney was unable to climb down. It was quite something to see him rescued by a basket dangling from the helicopter.

One bright morning, Judy and I were going to do a flight over the city. I checked the aircraft over and saw from the fuel indicator that we had enough for our flight. The fuel indicator was a wire attached to a float. As the fuel burned off, the wire would lower into the fuel tank, situated on the top of the engine cowling and visible to the pilot.

We took off on Runway 14 and almost immediately the engine started to sputter. I was uncertain as to why, so I made a quick left turn, followed by a right, pushing the primer pump all the time. We lined up and landed on Runway 32 sputtering all the way to the flying club. The only thing I could think of was that the float indicator was not working and that we were actually low on fuel. Further investigation showed that the wire for the fuel float had actually been bent and therefore stuck in position. How it became bent was never found out, but I learned a good lesson; visually check that fuel is actually on board, regardless of what the indicator was showing.

I also worked for Household Finance (HFC) during my flying

club days. One of the club members, who worked for HFC, approached me and asked if I wanted to make a few extra dollars. I was keen to listen to his proposal, as I was always willing to make extra dollars to pay for flying lessons. He explained that one of his jobs was to repossess vehicles from individuals who had delinquent accounts. I agreed to help him.

We would not contact the person directly, but after dark we would park and stake out a home, ensuring the auto to be picked up was in the driveway. After we were certain everyone was asleep, I would stay in the "getaway" car. He would sneak towards the home and open the car door, and then start the engine, with a technique he knew, and we would hightail it away, with me driving the getaway car. Usually the lights would come on in the home as we made our escape.

I recall on one mission we approached a home in mid afternoon. No one was home. The car to be repossessed was in the driveway, but would not start, so we pushed it back, tied a line to the other vehicle and headed for town, which was about an hour away. The problem was that I steered the towed car and the temperature was well below zero with no heat. By the time we arrived in the city I was as cold as I can ever remember. The money was good but I always felt bad taking the cars, so I soon ceased this activity.

I was rapidly approaching the required 150 hours for a commercial licence; however, it was necessary to write a set of examinations for the Ministry of Transport. The flying club did have some ground-school classes but it was very basic navigation; rules of the air and meteorology. All the information was from a publication called, "From the Ground Up." Our instructor would just read a passage and then explain it the best he could.

It was obvious I was on my own. I learned that the pass mark was 60 percent and if you failed an examination the next time you wrote it you had to have 70 percent. I felt confident about all the exams except for navigation. There really was no one qualified at the flying club who could give me the proper instruction, although they were all instructors, with instructor licences. None of them, to my knowledge, aspired towards commercial aviation, which was my goal at the time.

The Fleet Canuck at the Fundy Flying Club after I received my commercial pilot's licence.

My exam marks arrived in the mail and, as I expected, I passed all the exams except for navigation. The exam had been full of questions concerning weight and balance, which I had never done; four-engine aircraft, which I knew nothing about; and requirements for trans-Atlantic crossings, of which I had no clue. At least I now had some idea what the exam was all about, so I studied, wrote the navigation exam a second time, and failed again. The next time I would have to make 80 percent.

I was now really concerned, so I studied even harder. I drove to Moncton and sat for the exam, with pen in hand for the third time, knowing I had to now pass the exam with a minimum of 80 percent. I handed in the exam, and the MOT inspector said that if I wanted to wait he would review my exam right away. He started to correct my paper, with me nervously watching him and praying. Finally he looked up and said, "Passed, 85 percent." I was on cloud nine once again.

I had now passed all my exams and had the required hours. I completed a flight check ride with an MOT inspector without any difficulty. On August 17, 1956, I received my commercial pilot's licence, QMC-7066. The flying club was happy for me and advised the local paper of what they called "my accomplishment." Apparently I was

Judy and me at a Fundy Flying Club function.

the youngest, at that time, to have received a commercial licence. I never knew if this was true or not. It was now time for step three; apply for a pilot's job with TCA.

During August 1956, Bill Hegan, the TCA station manager, helped me fill in the application form. The form was sent via company mail to TCA headquarters in Montreal. I waited.

Approximately six weeks after submitting my application, I received a letter from TCA inviting me to Montreal for an interview. I was authorized to fly TCA with a return to Saint John.

On the day of departure, the flight crew of the DC-3 was told by the ground crew of my trip, and I was invited to sit in the jump seat to Montreal. Needless to say I was excited. I knew how to start the aircraft, but I was not going to tell them of my taxiing experience. The trip was uneventful and the crew answered my many questions. We started our descent into Montreal and as we entered cloud at about 8,000 feet, there was a bang. The flight crew had a problem with the left engine and elected to shut it down. Air Traffic Control and the TCA radio operator were advised and we landed in Dorval with a group of fire trucks to greet us. I admired the calm approach of both pilots and was now keener than ever to become a TCA pilot.

I had my interview, wrote the Stanine tests, and had a medical. In all I spent two days in the "big city." I recall after the eye examination, I was walking back to the YMCA, my place of residence for my stay. I noticed that everything was appearing diffused and double. I was very careful crossing the street; cars seemed to be approaching from every direction. Lunch was a bit of a disaster; the plate looked double and as I went to cut a piece of meat I hit the mashed potatoes instead. Whatever the optometrist put in my eyes gradually wore off and I was back to normal by late afternoon. It was quite an experience.

In early September, I was advised by TCA that my application had been accepted and I was scheduled for a course in October. I was one happy lad. Not more than three weeks went by when another letter arrived stating my course would now start in December. Oh well, another month or two to wait. At least I was on the list. One week prior to the starting course date, I was advised my course would now start in April 1957. I was very disappointed, but help was close at hand. Judy said, "If you want to fly that badly, join the air force." So I did.

Chapter Four

Royal Canadian Air Force Selection

I now found myself at the military recruiting unit in Saint John. I was required to write a Stanine exam again, fill out a multitude of forms, and then was sent to have a medical. I passed all the requirements and was advised I would be notified in about two weeks of my status. True to the promise, the letter arrived stating I was to report to RCAF Station Crumlin, which is now London International Airport, in Ontario. I would finally arrive at the London airport, which Doug Fifield and I were looking for when we ended up on the racetrack at Melbourne.

It was January 1957.

I left Saint John by train, with all my family and Judy bidding me *bon voyage*. Mum said, "I don't mind you joining the air force but promise me you won't get into any more airplanes." It was one promise I failed to keep.

Candidates from all over Canada arrived at Crumlin Field to complete the Personnel Selection Unit (PSU) activities. There were probably 150 of us in all. The stay at Crumlin was relatively short. We were subjected to a myriad of physical and mental tests such as aptitude tests—EEGs, ECGs, and flying aptitude tests. We were pushed, pulled, and prodded the whole time at Crumlin. One candidate was Dave Segee, from Saint John. Neither of us knew until we were introduced at Crumlin that we were both from Saint John. We chummed together throughout the rest of our training.

We were also required to complete a sheet of multiple choice questions about our background. An example of the questions was, "Do you like girls?" Duh. One of the questions was, "Do you stutter?" I answered yes, because as a kid in the lower grades there were times when asked what my name was, I could not get it out, stuttering, "I, I, I." In any event, I was called into an office to meet with a psychiatrist. He reviewed my answers, stating, "You checked off that you stutter." I said, "Yes, sir." He then went on to tell me that we had been chatting for thirty minutes and I had not stuttered once, and that what I had was crowd fear. He further stated that I had a mind that worked so fast that my mouth could not get things out fast enough. He advised me to slow down before I spoke. He said with my mind I would make a good pilot because I think so fast. I thanked him, and since that day, I have always tried to be aware of the fact that I have to slow myself down before I speak. Eventually, I volunteered for positions where I would have to get up in front of a group of students and teach, thus acquiring more confidence in myself.

When the testing was completed, we all gathered in a large room and were called into an office one at a time. I was told I was selected for pilot training. I was elated! Several did not pass and were given a ticket home.

Successful candidates were loaded onto a bus and driven to the Institute of Aviation Medicine (IAM) in Toronto. We were put through all kinds of stress tests. For example, we were put on a swing structure and moved back and forth at a set rate. Then we were blindfolded and the exercise was repeated. The swing would stop quickly and the blindfold removed quickly as well. Most of the group immediately lost their breakfast. I was one of the few who were not sick. At the time, we had no idea what the tests were intended to prove. I did learn many years later that the tests were part of an American test program for future astronauts and I was a participant in the program.

Chapter Five

Ground School and Chipmunk Aircraft

Things happened rather fast after the initial selection. We were given a uniform and lots of accessories, a military haircut, and sent to RCAF Centralia, Ontario, the home of Pre-Flight School (PFS), where we officially became course 5702. Our course director was Flying Officer Danny Turner, who was our "mother hen" and was responsible for some of the courses as well as reviewing exams.

In the next twelve weeks, we were subjected to what seemed to be a complete review of our high school subjects. We also had training in principles of flight, aero-engines, navigation, meteorology; the list goes on. Every Friday morning we wrote an exam, failing which, we were given a ticket home. Our numbers dwindled rapidly. Every Friday afternoon we usually had a batch of needles, then physical training, usually a cross-country run. Saturday saw everyone sore from the needles and tired from the mental and physical strain of the week.

One Friday afternoon, we were all lined up with nothing on but shorts, waiting our turn to be "stuck." John Stefynation, a course mate, kept telling everyone there was nothing to worry about, it was only a needle. My turn arrived and there were two people administering the needles. I held both arms out and they went to work. John was next in line; he fainted and received his shots where he lay. We teased him about it later, particularly after all his bravado talk.

Another cadet with the last name of Harris literally stank. We told him to take a shower, but he never would. Finally, we had had enough. We threw him into a shower with his uniform on and threw all his clothes in with him. We did not let him out until he and everything else was washed.

Our drill instructors were Sergeant Collins and Corporal Knolls. A cadet was assigned, on a weekly basis, to parade the course to and from classes as well as back and forth to the mess hall. Corporal Knolls would conduct daily drill and parade inspection. We made certain our uniforms were pressed and boots shined so you could see your face in them. When things were not to the corporal's liking, you usually felt his swagger stick. We called it his "rectum stretcher."

After lunch on one warm beautiful day, we were receiving a lecture from the officer in charge of base discipline. The heat was still on in the building and we were all having a hard time trying to stay awake. Larry Mattson was sitting next to a radiator and fell asleep with his head against the wall. A blackboard eraser flew through the air and hit him. He tried to focus and compose himself as the officer asked, "Cadet, are you tired or bored?" Larry, in his half-asleep state, said, "Bored, Sir," which was the wrong answer. Class was cancelled and we marched and marched. Next, we put on gym clothing and were told to run ten miles. Some of us completed the run; others did not. Larry was not very popular for a day or two.

In May 1957, after twelve weeks at the Pre-Flight School those of us selected for pilot training were assigned to Primary Flying School (PFS), also located at Centralia, Ontario. Those chosen as navigators were sent to Winnipeg for training at the navigation school. It was at this point in training that we were joined by our NATO course members, who were from England, Belgium, Denmark, and Norway. All were excellent representatives of their countries. We all had the same goal, to become pilots. Initially we all got along beautifully. We later had some problems with two Brits.

We were about to get our hands on the Chipmunk, but not before a week of ground school so that we could learn about the aircraft. It seemed that the air force made us build the aircraft before we were allowed to fly it.

My instructor was Flying Officer Mike Thomas, quiet but efficient. He asked me if I had ever flown before. I explained my journey before joining the RCAF. After six hours and fifteen minutes of training, I had my solo in the Chipmunk. My previous flying had certainly helped.

The flap selector on the Chipmunk was a ratchet affair; you

squeezed the handle then selected the flap by placing the lever into a slot for the desired degree of flap. On one flight, I selected the landing flap and went to release the handle; I could not. My flying glove was stuck in the ratchet. Here I was on final with only one usable hand. After some struggle, I managed to get my hand out of the glove and landed. I retrieved my glove after returning to the ramp.

I wore flying gloves throughout my air force career. The gloves were of soft leather and were considered a safety feature in the event of an onboard fire. We all thought we would just burn that much faster.

One of our NATO trainees was Jim Van Roy, a real character. During a solo flight, Jim decided to fly over Detroit, Michigan, because he wanted to see what the big city looked like. Needless to say, the American Air Traffic Control was not amused. They recognized the Chipmunk and called Centralia. Jim was notified and reluctantly returned to Centralia. He received a lecture about not penetrating American air space because it made them nervous.

On another occasion, Jim, again solo, decided it was hot and landed the aircraft on a long stretch of beach near Grand Bend. He set the parking brake, left the engine running, and went for a swim. He took off with no problem; however, a report was submitted by a local, who spotted the aircraft on the beach and thought the airman was in trouble. Jim was given another lecture. I actually saw the aircraft Jim had been flying. Seagrass was wedged into the tail wheel assembly and there was sand in the cockpit. How he got away with his stunts is a miracle.

I thoroughly enjoyed flying the Chipmunk. We did all our flying visually, which means the ground is visible at all times. One thing the air force trained you for was to fly the aircraft to its limit, and by so doing you learned your own limits. This training served me well over the years.

After breakfast, one bright Saturday morning, Dave Segee and I decided to spend the day at the base swimming pool. The week had been long and hard and we needed a distraction. We certainly enjoyed the pool. However, our week caught up to us and we both fell asleep. When we woke, we were both badly sunburned. We proceeded to the local base hospital, where we were attended to, but not before receiving a lecture on "self-inflicted wounds." We managed to get back to the barracks and slept the sleep of death, only waking for a run to the bathroom. We missed our Sunday meals. When Monday arrived we were sore, but able to carry on.

Our Chipmunk training was now complete. I had a grand total of twenty-seven hours, fifty-five minutes on this initial trainer. We were now posted to Number 3 Flying School (3FTS), RCAF Station at Claresholm, Alberta. It was June 1957.

Chapter Six

Claresholm and Harvard

Keith McConnell owned a 1956 Ford. Keith, "Spike" Milligan (one of the Brits on our course) and I elected to travel together to Claresholm and share the car expenses. We had a blast. Each took a turn driving, and the miles rolled together in a series of wonderment as we travelled westward. Our travels took us through Yellowstone National Park as well as the badlands of Montana and the Wild Bill Cody "Buffalo Bill" museum. All were historical and interesting. We crossed the "Great Divide," where we stopped. I am not certain what altitude we were at, but it was June and there was a rather steep incline covered with snow. We decided to race—last one to the top loses. We raced to the top huffing and puffing, trying to catch our breath. I think at that time we came to the realization that the higher one goes the less oxygen one gets. Another lesson learned.

Claresholm was nestled in the foothills of the Rocky Mountains, roughly 100 kilometres south of Calgary. We arrived as scheduled, ready to face the "Yellow Peril," as the North American Harvard airplane was affectionately called. First, it was back into the classroom to learn all about the yellow beast. In addition, there were more navigation and meteorology lectures. Exams were written, after which we were now to be turned over to our flight-line instructors. Our course director, "Mother Hen," was Flying Officer Neil Murray.

Shortly after our arrival, there was a fatal accident involving a student and his instructor. A telephone repair man was up a pole and heard the aircraft. He described the aircraft as being in a flat spin and saw the wing of the Harvard hit the pole next to him. The aircraft corkscrewed around the pole, crashed, and caught fire. He got down the pole faster than he went up it. He reported that he could see the pilots were still alive but obviously badly hurt. He was unable to render any help due to the heat from the fire. It was quite an experience for the poor man.

Throughout our training, any time there was a fatal accident, the military made all the students get back into the air as quickly as possible. The logic was to get the students concentrating on their own flying and not dwelling on the accident. Prior to reporting to the flight line, we were all equipped with parachutes. I recall the "parachute lady," for the lack of a better term. She was a rather large girl, called "Bimbo," who would help you strap the chute on. She would have you sit down, and then she would grab you by the crotch and ask if the chute was comfortable. Everyone stated in a loud voice that it was just fine. Bimbo was quite a character. Our paths would cross again in a few short years. The parachute was a seat type; that is, you put the chute on prior to entering the cockpit and the chute fit nicely into the bucket seat of the Harvard.

My first flight in a Harvard was on July 15, 1957, and my instructor was Flying Officer "Mo" Martin. My first impression of the Harvard was how large it was in comparison to the Chipmunk. The cockpit was also huge in comparison. Initially, we did clear-hood flying to get used to the new machine and, after six hours and twenty minutes, I had my solo in Mark IV Harvard 20397. Another milestone.

After you went solo, it was a tradition that you were hosed down by the other cadets and your tie was cut in half. Yes! We flew with flying suits, but were required to wear a shirt and tie underneath. I still have the cut tie.

As cadets, we had our own mess, where we could have a beer, or play darts. After everyone had gone solo, we had a "solo party." Our instructors attended, as well as many senior officers including the base commander, Group Captain Joe McCarthy. When I went into the washroom, adjacent to the cloak room, several of my coursemates were trying on the base commander's "scrambled egg hat." Naturally, I had to have a go. I placed his hat on my head and at that moment the wing commander in charge of flying entered. He took one look at me and said, "You can take his hat, but don't take mine." We all scrambled back to the party. One of our cadets was from Vancouver and he did not get along with his instructor. As luck

Going solo in the Harvard.

would have it, he had one beer too many. He confronted his instructor and pulled a knife on him. He was quickly subdued and the MPs took him to the base lockup. The next morning he was handed over to the RCMP and we never saw him again.

"Jim" Van Roy, our Belgium coursemate, had more than a few beers in him. At some point in the evening he was no longer with us. We probably thought he was going to bed to sleep it off. He did sleep it off, but when he was found the next morning he was sound asleep in a Harvard with the engine running, in the holding area used for run-ups prior to takeoff. Jim apparently wanted to go flying. How he started and taxied the aircraft without being heard is a mystery to me. He received another lecture and was assigned cadet duty officer for a week or so. We wondered what he would do next.

We did not have long to wait. There was an incident where a student had part of the undercarriage "hang-up": one wheel would not lower. An instructor was called to the tower and the student was talked into landing the aircraft on the one gear down with enough force to see if the other wheel would loosen its grip and lower. It worked. The student overshot, left the gear down and landed normally. All the students were given a briefing on the incident so we would be prepared in the future. Jim took off that very day, did his assigned air work, and on final reported one wheel would not lower. The tower put the binoculars on his aircraft and could easily see that all gears were down and locked and advised him that all looked normal. Jim just wanted to do a low pass and get a little attention. Everyone liked Jim and enjoyed his company. Years later, while flying a CF-104 with the Belgian air force, something happened right after takeoff. Jim had no time to eject and was killed in the crash.

Another student on our course was a Brit, named Ricky Hogarth. Ricky sported a handlebar moustache. He was a pompous, overbearing SOB. He referred to the Canadians as "colonials." As the story goes, he got his comeuppance. One evening in our barrack block, which was one large room with upper and lower bunks for the whole course, a scheme was hatched. I mentioned Ricky had a handlebar moustache that was his pride and joy. He would play with it and look down his nose at us. So, before lights out we jumped him and held him down. I held one leg as he kicked and thrashed. One of our Canadians shaved off "half" his moustache. When he was finally released, he cursed and swore vindictive remarks to one and all. Ricky's thrashing caused him to bugger up his back and he ended up in the veteran's hospital in Calgary. He was re-coursed to 5705. Good riddance.

The next time I saw Ricky was at our course's 40th reunion, in London, England. He was still very bitter towards the Canadians over his "incident" and blamed us all for hurting his career advancement. Even the Brits had had enough of him and told him as much. He was never invited to a reunion again. No loss. He now lives in Belgium.

Now we were Senior Course and moved from the barrack block to another building, where we were assigned two to a room. My first roommate was Torkil Jensen, a tall blond Dane, who was quiet. We got along very well. Over the years, I have tried to get in touch with him but was not successful. I did learn from other Danes that he had joined Lufthansa, the German airline, and had been pretty well blackballed by the rest of the Danes, who remembered the German occupation.

Harvard formation flying.
RCAF

One day, years later, I was boarding an elevator at Dorval airport. I was in uniform and flying for Air Canada, when out of the elevator stepped Torkil, in a Lufthansa uniform. We chatted for a minute or two. I was operating a flight to the Maritimes and was running late. I gave him my address and phone number, but he never followed up on my request to keep in touch.

Another Brit, Tommy Moran, was a nice enough guy, but he would stand in front of a mirror, on a daily basis, and flex his muscles à la Charles Atlas. We all got a bit tired of this. One of our Canadian cadets had one beer too many and decided he was going to beat Tommy up. He snuck into Tom's room and in his drunken state proceeded to pound Tommy, who happened to be asleep at the time. The racket brought most of the course members awake and to the rescue. Our Canadian cadet did not remember his actions of the previous evening and Tom wisely let it pass.

Tom returned to the UK on graduation. His fellow Brits lost track of him, until one day he knocked on one of their doors asking for a loan. I heard he approached most of his fellow course members. Tom died alone in the streets of Liverpool—a very sad ending.

Archie Kaye, a Canadian, joined our course in Claresholm. He had completed some flying the previous summer and was completing his training to Wings Standard. Archie was on a university training program sponsored by the military and had just completed his engineering degree. Archie was older than most of the men on the course, but gave freely of his time and knowledge whenever we had an academic problem.

One day on a layover in London when I was with Air Canada, I was with a large group of pilots having a beer. I was talking to a very senior captain, who mentioned he and his friend Archie Kaye had just bought a sailboat together. Once I heard the name I asked a few questions, and it was the Archie from our course at Claresholm. The senior captain's name was George McKay; I always called him "Uncle." He arranged to have Archie meet him for lunch at their yacht club in Toronto. I was the surprise. Archie walked into the dining area and knew me immediately. He had not changed very much over the past twenty-five years. Naturally, we talked and talked. Poor George was very quiet and we stuck him with the bill. As a result of our meeting, Archie now joins in our reunions both in Canada and the UK. He and his wife were involved in an automobile accident; sadly, his wife was killed and Archie spent nearly three months in hospital. We are in frequent contact via the Internet.

The flying proceeded quickly. We did lots of aerobatics and instrument flying, during which the instructor sat in the front seat and the student sat in the back, with a hood that covered the cockpit. Cheating by looking out was next to impossible. We soon learned to depend on our instruments. On many occasions, the instructor would take control and put the aircraft in all kinds of different, so-called "unusual positions." It was hard to keep a good view of the instruments with the wild gyrations of the aircraft, in order to have some idea what position the aircraft was in. The instructor would shout, "Recover!" You would take control and, by interpreting and depending on your instruments, execute a recovery. Initially it was difficult but we soon got the hang of it. We practiced recovering from unusual positions on most of the aircraft I flew in the air force.

Another aspect of instrument flying was instrument takeoffs, under the hood. When power was applied on takeoff, the Harvard had a strong tendency to swing, so opposite rudder was applied to compensate for the swing. Initially we would over-control, with the instructor hollering, "Keep it straight!" I imagine it was quite a sight for those in the control tower to see the Harvard weaving left and right down the runway. With continuous practice, and patience from our instructors, we soon mastered the technique.

Eventually, we became quite proficient in flying the Harvard on instruments, so radio range and cross-country flying was introduced. I now had a new instructor, Flying Officer Chris Oliver. He was British by birth and had immigrated to Canada, specifically to join the RCAF. His father was a high-ranking military officer in the Royal Air Force; he just wanted to get out from under his influence. Chris, in a word, was a "character." I recall taking off to do a cross-country to Lethbridge, south of Claresholm, and making an approach to the airfield utilizing radio range procedure. I was fully prepared to apply the power and go around when Chris took control, landed, and we taxied to the parking area. He shut the engine down and told me to amuse myself for a few hours. At this point, his girlfriend arrived in a car. He hopped in, waved, and I was left to fend for myself. It was August and the weather was beautiful, so I spent my time walking around the airfield and stretching out on the grass in the shade.

We had probably landed about ten thirty in the morning, and Chris showed up at about four that afternoon. We retrieved a battery cart to start the Harvard and off we went back to Claresholm. I thought we would fly the airway back, but Chris was in a hurry, so we went direct. He was anxious to be back by five to go to the officers' mess for a beer. Character indeed!

On another occasion, we were doing a cross-country flight to Penhold, another Harvard station north of Calgary. I was in the back seat trying to fly the radio range with "dit-dahs" and "dah-dits." As we flew along, Chris stated over the intercom that he was hungry. He wanted me to get a clearance for a radio range approach into Calgary, followed by a full-stop landing. I received the clearance and proceeded to the range station to complete a full radio range approach, including the procedure turn. As we approached the range station, I was listening for the "cone of silence," indicating we were right over the station so I could then continue to bracket the beam to the airport. As we approached the "cone," Chris came on the intercom again. "McKay," he said, "I have just written a poem and I want you to tell me what you think of it." Here I am listening for the "cone," flying the aircraft, and having to listen to his poem. I managed to recognize the "cone" and we approached the field with Chris still talking. We landed and taxied to the terminal. Chris set the parking brake and told me to wait with the engine running until he had breakfast. He was kind enough to get a window seat and wave at me as he sipped his coffee. Character, yes, but he had a method to his madness and I learned a lot from him. Our paths would cross again over the coming years.

Christmas fell on a Wednesday in 1957, and as the date approached, it was obvious we would be finished flying on the Friday before the holidays. There were a few of us who were anxious to be home for Christmas. I had already bought an engagement ring and was anxious to get home to propose to Judy. Four of us; Keith, Dale, Carl, and I had the greatest distance to travel, so we made the necessary airline reservations with TCA. The commanding officer, Group Captain Joe McCarthy, dictated that all flight cadets would attend a children's party on December 24. This order really screwed up our plans. We would not make it home for Christmas. I was delegated to approach our course director to have him intercede on our behalf. I explained that we already had our tickets for Friday evening and would he please ask the commanding officer to excuse us from attending the children's party. Our course director approached the CO, and he told us the CO gave him a resounding "No," to our request, stating that all cadets would attend the children's party. Naturally, we were disappointed and wondered what we could do. We decided the hell with the CO and his planned children's Christmas party; we would go home anyway. Friday arrived and we, as cadets, were required to attend an airman beer Christmas party in one of the hangars. Once again, I was elected to approach our course director and ask him to present our case to the CO who was at the party. Our course director refused to approach the CO, with words like, "I am not that crazy," so I informed him that cadets McConnell, Northrup, Sandelin, and McKay were leaving for Calgary to catch our flights to the east. Our course director was a bit shocked to say the least. Before he could say anything, I was already mixing with the crowd and heading for the exit where the other three were waiting. I told them what transpired and then we left for Calgary, knowing we would be in for some trouble when we returned

When I arrived home, my mother informed me that there was a telegram for me. Basically it said, "Consider yourself under open arrest. Return to Claresholm immediately." I later learned the other fugitives received the same telegram. We all ignored it.

Christmas at home was great. Judy said yes to my engagement proposal and I got to see my family and some high school friends. Now it was back to reality and what was waiting for us at Claresholm. My flight arrived in Montreal on schedule, but I had about a five-hour wait for the connection to Calgary. I read and talked to the ticket agents, who even bought me coffee. I began to feel drowsy; the past week was catching up to me. I lay on a bench and fell asleep. When I woke up, my connecting flight was taxiing out; I had missed it. The agents said they announced my name over the intercom and even looked for me, but I was out of view, sound asleep. The next flight was three hours away and I made sure I was on it. I managed to get a bus to Claresholm and a cab to the base, but it was now about ten in the evening.

The only entrance to the base was through the guard house, at the main gate. I signed in and the corporal on duty recognized my name and told me to wait for an escort. I was now under "close arrest." The CO had set the wheels in motion to make certain we were not going to defy him and get away with no punishment. In "open arrest" you were on your own, but "close arrest" meant that I was escorted by another cadet wherever I went until my status was resolved by the CO. Unbeknownst to us, the CO had called training command headquarters, explained what we had done, and stated that he wanted us "CTd" (ceased training). Command apparently reviewed our files and the circumstances surrounding our departure and, on reflection, told the CO there were no grounds for us to be CTd. We were all doing well on course, both in flying and on the academic side. Group Captain McCarthy was not a happy CO, but he had other plans for us.

We were marched into his office and told we were going to have a summary trial, using his authority as commanding officer. We were given a stern lecture about obeying orders. Each was fined $100, a fortune to us at that time, and told that our promotions to flying officer, after receiving our wings, would be delayed. At the same time, the CO ordered our pay to be withheld for two consecutive pay periods, so we had to borrow money from the rest of the cadets on course. We did not complain; we had no desire to bring the ire of the

CO back down upon us. Once we finally got paid, we paid off all our creditors. The station personnel soon heard of our punishment and expressed their opinion of the unfair treatment we received—all because we did not attend the children's Christmas party. Even the officers were ticked and, to the CO's disappointment, we were even invited to different officers' homes for dinner.

We were told that after a period of time our records would have the "summary trial" removed from our files. Prior to my leaving the RCAF, I was stationed at headquarters in Ottawa. I was in position to access my file, which I did. The summary trial had been removed all right, but in true military fashion the whole write-up had red lines through it and, naturally, was the first thing you saw on opening the file. The punishment never hurt my career one bit; I received a permanent commission and was promoted as if nothing had ever happened.

We were halfway through our Harvard training. We had mastered the beast pretty well and had a grand time doing solo cross-country flights. We were told that if we ever were unsure of our position, to go low, past a grain elevator. Each town had its name painted on the elevator. The name was there, but too small to read, but in large letters was "Purina." The joke was all the towns were called "Purina."

Station Claresholm printed a newsletter every now and then, including promotions, and notices of upcoming events. The editor elected to do a write-up on our course, and said that we were the first course ever to go through Claresholm without having one aircraft incident or accident. The ink was hardly dry when we made up for lost time by having one incident after the other. Most of the incidents coincided with the fact that we had just started night flying.

I was solo one dark evening, when the wind really picked up on the ground. No general recall of aircraft was issued, but, since I was nearing the end of my exercise, I elected to return a bit early. All went well until I started my round out to land and I was hit with a gust of wind. I was probably a bit slow to react. In any event, I hit the wing tip on the ground, bending a few things. I recovered okay and taxied in, only to find I was not the first to break our "record." Two other coursemates had beaten me to it, both having bent wing tips on landing.

One evening, an instructor had completed checking out a fellow coursemate for his first night solo. The instructor jumped out of the Harvard and sent the fearless airman on his way. I should mention that when taxiing the Harvard you had to do a series of "S" turns. It was impossible to see straight ahead over the large engine cowling. The taxiing procedure was drilled into us on a daily basis—"remember S turns." In his excitement to go night solo, our fearless airman forgot this point and headed for the runway for his trip. As luck would have it, there was another Harvard sitting at the button waiting for take-off clearance. This student was also on his first night solo and he had just dropped off his instructor. You guessed right. The second Harvard plowed smack into the other parked Harvard. The propeller cut up the wing, as well as the fuselage and the rear seat position, where the instructor had just left. The lad in the parked Harvard saw the propeller spinning towards him. He shut his Harvard down and jumped out and ran to the infield, where he had a good view of the other Harvard coming to a rather quick stop. Both pilots were unhurt, and the next day we were all given a stern talking to about what could have been a very serious accident. Someone could have been killed all because a student, in his excitement to go night flying, forgot what he was trained to do. Neither Harvard was repairable; they were scrounged for parts and junked.

I don't recall ever seeing another station newsletter.

One of our favourite things to do, while solo, was to meet other cadets over an area called Clear Lake. Here, we would twist and turn trying to get on each other's tail, dogfighting. It was great fun. On one flight, as I twisted my Harvard into position behind another Harvard, I ended up in a spin, and down I went. I recovered from the spin and climbed back up. I pulled again, to get behind another Harvard only to end up spinning down again. I could not figure out why I kept entering spins. Then it dawned on me. There were two marks of Harvard, or versions, Mark II and Mark IV; the Mark IV being the later, updated model. In the Mark II it was necessary to push a round handle called a "power push," which gave you hydraulics and the gear would retract after takeoff. In the cockpit the "three finger" undercarriage position indicators would still move to their up position indicating the undercarriage was up. If you failed to push the "power push" the "fingers" would move to the up position anyway but the gear would stay down, no hydraulics. My previous many flights had been in a Mark IV, where all you did was select the gear up, hydraulics were automatically energized, and the "fingers" would move to the up position indicating the gear had retracted. My spin problem developed because I had failed to select the "power push." Live and learn. This happened quite frequently. It was great fun watching someone trying to get on your tail with his gear down and then entering a spin.

Throughout our training we had periodic check rides that were completed by a flight commander or someone from what we called "the standards flight." These pilots were usually quite senior instructors. Many were wartime retreads and did not have a regular student but went flight-to-flight doing check rides. When one of these pilots flew with you, you knew you were being tested to ensure your progress was at an acceptable standard. It also reflected on your instructor.

One of our NATO students was "Spike" Milligan. Spike was RAF; he had great difficulty flying the Harvard and was eventually CTd. He returned to the UK and transferred to administration. Spike did well in his new duties and retired as an air commodore. Another RAF student, Dick Miller, my roommate, also retired as an air commodore. Norwegian Vic Rynning became chief of the defence staff of the Norwegian air force. We had lots of talent in Course 5702.

On my final instrument ride with Paul Chevalier, "B" flight commander, I was required to complete the standard instrument takeoff, climb to altitude, executing turns to specific headings, as directed by the check pilot. The supervisor took control and proceeded to twist and turn, putting the aircraft into unusual positions. He said, "Recover," which I did using the instruments only—no peeking. I was also required to recover from a spin using the instruments only. Did I mention I was pretty good on spin recovery? This was followed by finding my position using the radio range, dit, and dah, (i.e., "A" and "N") to find what quadrant I was in. Then I tracked to the station (Lethbridge) and completed an approach to minimums, overshot and followed the missed approach procedure.

The supervisor asked me to take us back to Claresholm using the "aural null" technique. I had read about aural null but was nev-

End of Harvard course. Instructors seated —5702 clustered around the Harvard.
RCAF

er taught the procedure. The technique was to use the automatic direction finder without using the automatic feature. It was necessary to identify the station, place it at 90 degrees to you and time it while flying through 10 degrees. This would give you a distance to the station. Then you would turn towards the station and track inbound using the "null" feature—no dahs or dits. In any event, I somehow arrived back in the vicinity of Claresholm. The supervisor later stated that my "aural null" was rather unorthodox and asked who my instructor was. He smiled, obviously knowing about the Lethbridge girlfriend. He said I passed the instrument ride but if I didn't mind doing another flight with him he would show me the proper way to do an "aural null procedure." I accepted gladly. It was amazing how much easier his "proper" technique was, compared to my effort. We did a few exercises and he passed me as qualified in aural null procedures.

Another aspect of the training I thoroughly enjoyed was formation flying. Two aircraft would take turns flying close to each other. Eventually we did four-plane formations, line astern; i.e., one behind the other, flying the box. The lead aircraft had a Harvard tucked in on each wing and the "box aircraft" would fly on the tail of the lead. This was all great fun and gave everyone tremendous confidence in their own abilities.

Our training on the Harvard was now complete. Next would be

advanced training on the T-33, Silver Star aircraft. We had a graduation party and it was pretty wild. One of the lads, John Feil, had all his hair cut off as a joke. Our CO was not happy and he advised the CO at our next station that the individual concerned should be confined to base until his hair grew back in. The new CO concurred. John Feil was not a happy camper when we arrived in Portage la Prairie, Manitoba.

We were all glad to leave Claresholm and hopefully not see Group Captain Joe McCarthy again.

Our NATO coursemates were sent to Station MacDonald.

Chapter Seven

Portage and the T-33

The Canadians arrived at Station Portage la Prairie. The town of Portage was about five miles from the base, roughly a one-hour drive to Winnipeg. As usual, we had to attend ground school and learn all about the T-33 before we were allowed to fly the aircraft.

We were equipped with hard hats and parachutes. The chutes were worn on our back and fit into the ejection seat. Bimbo would have been disappointed as we could adjust our own chutes quite easily. The hard hats were very necessary on jet aircraft. The cockpits were narrow and, in turbulence, if you hit your head against the canopy without a hard hat, you could knock yourself out and lose control of the aircraft. Not a good scenario. In addition, the hard hats had a built-in microphone for radio communications and an oxygen connection. Both were plugged into onboard aircraft outlets.

Station Portage had a forty-five foot tower with an ejection seat attached to rails. We were all required to strap ourselves into the ejection seat, with help from the ground crew. On command, we would pull the ejection handles and ride the rails for forty-five feet.

I thought this was a great exercise. We now knew what the "kick in the pants" would feel like in an actual ejection, and it gave confidence in the seat itself. The aircraft seat charge was stronger, so you could actually penetrate the canopy with the top of the ejection seat on ejection.

Station Portage had the front end of a T-33 set up as a simulator. The aircraft had been in an accident but the cockpit area had survived. It had a similar set-up as the old Link trainer, in that all our procedures were traced out on a plastic sheet, easily erased after debriefing. I was working away on an approach when the instructor said, "McKay, you are on the bottom of Lake Winnipeg; get the fuck out of there." I had misread my altimeter by 10,000 feet. It was easily done when using the old altimeters. Another lesson learned. I never misread an altimeter again.

I had my first flight in the T-33 on February 24, 1958. Flying Officer Brian Smith was the instructor. My first impression was how quiet the jet was in comparison to the Harvard piston engine. We flew around the area so I could become familiar with the different landmarks. We climbed to over 30,000 feet, testing out the controls as we climbed into the thinner air. In addition, we did a few stalls, which were very easy to recover from, as well as a spin. The spin was considerably faster than in the Harvard, but the recovery action was the same and, besides, I had had lots of spin practice. We entered the circuit and completed three to four touch-and-go landings (land, select flaps to the take-off setting, apply power, and get airborne again).

One major difference between jet and piston engines is the engine response time. In a piston aircraft, if you needed power it was instantaneous, while in jet aircraft there was a lag. If you had the throttle full back on a jet aircraft it would take several seconds before you actually received the power you were asking for. The jet engine had to wind itself up to the requested power. One learned this lesson very quickly; you never pulled the power completely off until after landing. It could prove very unhealthy. Even then, idle power was never really enough for you to manoeuvre on the ground, so you had to add power to taxi the aircraft.

Initially I had great difficulty in taxiing the T-33. The aircraft required that you use differential braking to turn the aircraft. At first, I was not aggressive enough on the brakes and I would end up cocking the nose wheel. My instructor would take over control, add lots of power, kick the nose wheel straight with harsh braking, and away we would go.

I had a grand total of eleven hours and fifty-five minutes when Brian said, "Don, I don't worry about you in the air, but do you think you can get to the end of the runway without cocking the nose wheel?" I assured him I could. All strapped in, I started the engine and received a thumbs-up from the ground crew. I received taxi clearance from the control tower, released the brakes, and applied power for the taxi. After moving ahead about ten feet I started

T-33 over the Manitoba countryside.
RCAF

my turn; you guessed it. I cocked the nose wheel. My poor suffering instructor just shook his head, "What next." He came out and put his back under the fuselage, near the nose wheel and started pushing up and down. As the aircraft bounced up it took some weight off the nose wheel and I was able to straighten it out. Poor Brian shook his head again, gave me a thumbs-up, and away I went.

I had two more turns before I could line up on the runway. I managed the first one okay, but on the second I cocked the nose wheel again. I added lots of power and was able to get myself sorted out. Finally, I received take-off clearance, but as I turned onto the runway I cocked the nose wheel again. At this point I was really teed off. I opened the throttle and remembered saying to myself that it was make or break time. I was either going to get the nose wheel straight or end up in the grass. I had lots of power on and I kicked the sucker straight and found myself on the center line of the runway. I accelerated and was airborne. My aggressive action worked. I never had any more problems taxiing the T-33.

My first solo in the T-33 was great fun. I did all the required air work, including stalls, spins, rolls, and loops. I had burnt off enough fuel to return to the circuit. We burnt the fuel off so that the aircraft would become lighter and we would be able to land at safe landing weights. Now I joined the circuit for a few "touch and goes." Brian met me after the flight and we both had a chuckle after I told him of my initial "cocked-up flight," at least the ground portion.

The rest of the training was to increase proficiency in all phases of flight. Although I thoroughly enjoyed aerobatics, I enjoyed instrument flying much more; it was very satisfying. Instrument approaches were very different when compared to the Harvard. We flew higher and faster. The Harvard flew at 250 knots while the T-33 would cruise at 500 knots.

On an instrument approach, we would arrive over a beacon at 20,000 feet, close the throttle, and select the speed brakes. When extended, the speed brakes helped keep the airspeed from increasing. We would descend to 10,000 feet at 250 knots, and then turn back towards the beacon and track inbound, continuing to descend to outer marker crossing altitude. We would decrease airspeed to a gear-lowering speed. Approaching the beacon, we would select initial flap, usually five degrees, lower the gear down, and, once past the beacon, we would select landing flap and set a rate of descent of about 700 feet per minute, until we reached our minimums. At minimums we would look up and, low and behold, there would be the runway.

On one flight, Brian asked me to outline the symptoms of a flame-out—engine quits. I listed all the obvious—low jet pipe temperature, low oil pressure, no response from the throttle. It was at this point Brian said, "You forgot the most important item." I racked my brain for what I missed, when Brian stated, "It gets goddamn quiet." He was right.

In the Harvard, we always did straight-in approaches. In the T-33, we arrived over the button of the runway at 2,000 feet, then selected the speed brakes to lose speed and turned left 180 degrees for the downwind leg. Initial flap, 15 degrees, was then selected. We would judge our distance from the runway, turn left for the base leg and select the undercarriage down, then continue the turn to line up with the runway and select landing flap.

RCAF Station MacDonald was about thirty miles from Portage and both stations had runways aligned in the same direction. Students from Portage thought they were doing touch and goes at Portage. It wasn't until the student asked for clearance for a full-stop landing and the tower, with a chuckle, advised him to take up a certain heading for Portage that he would realize he was at the wrong field. MacDonald students made the same mistake at Portage. The tower knew where we were from by our call sign.

We did some formation flying in the Harvard, but a jet had a few wrinkles that we had to learn. Everyone initially pushed and pulled back the power, depending on if we were closing too fast or too slowly. My instructor would say, "McKay, the only time you are in position is passing through." We soon got the knack. Instead of wild throttle fluctuations, we would tuck in tight on someone's wing and use very small throttle movements to stay in position. Formation flying was also very satisfying. We had to have total confidence in the leader. All our concentration was devoted to maintaining our position. The "lead" looked for other aircraft, received clearance for the entire flight, etc. When flying in close formation we acted as one, even though we were four aircraft. Usually the lead would give instructions via the radio. We were required to know several different hand signals in the event of loss of radio or for a mission where radio silence was required.

One student on the senior course got into trouble and was unable to regain control of the aircraft. He elected to bail out. Unfortunately, he was travelling very fast and the bailout caused severe injuries. He died a few days after the incident. We learned never to take anything for granted in an airplane; keep alert or the airplane may bite you back.

There was a lovely park in the town of Portage la Prairie and we, as well as the town folk, took advantage to get away from it all. One of the instructors, while visiting relatives in Vancouver decided, as a joke, to bring back a small shark. The shark was about four feet long. It was placed in the luggage carrier beneath the fuselage, arriving in Portage frozen solid. Late Sunday night, the instructor and a buddy took the shark into the park and placed it in one of the ponds. The next day the shark was spotted. Police were called finally, and someone called the university in Winnipeg. Experts arrived and headlines were made in the *Winnipeg Free Press*: "*How Did a Shark Get into Manitoba Waterway?*" After much investigation, someone mentioned the air force base and the light went on. The culprit was duly found as he was the only one with a T-33 returning from Vancouver. He confessed and apologized, tongue-in-cheek, for all the problems he had created. All was forgiven and life returned to normal.

My friend from Saint John had difficulty passing the Harvard portion of our training, mainly in his instrument flying. On the T-33, things happened a lot faster than in the Harvard and Dave just could not master the technique. Unfortunately, he was CTd. I was sad to see Dave leave. He left the air force and eventually became an air traffic controller, based in Moncton, New Brunswick. Several times on my overseas trips I would recognize his voice and we would chat for a minute or two. Dave retired from the Ministry of Transport and is still living in Moncton. We have always exchanged Christmas cards and see each other on occasion.

The chief of the air staff, Air Marshall Roy Slemon, arrived for a base inspection and parade. This officer was a poster picture of what an officer should look like, from his well-trimmed moustache to his uniform, which fit like a glove. His visit coincided with our midterm leave. He advised that any cadet going east for midterm was welcome to accompany him to Trenton on his Comet. I leaped at the opportunity, along with two other cadets. Mr. Slemon was most gracious to us and treated us well. There are not very many air force personnel who can say they had a ride on the Comet. The RCAF had two Comets in service. A BOAC Comet broke up in mid-air in 1954, followed by another Comet two months later. The Comet remained grounded for four years until the problem was rectified. The investigation determined that pressurization fluctuations, combined with the skin on the fuselage being too thin, had weakened the fuselage to a dangerous degree. By that time the Americans had caught up to the British and the British lost their initial advantage in jet passenger aircraft. The RCAF Comets were grounded in the late '50s.

Years later, I was captain of a DC-9 leaving New York for Montreal. The flight attendant made the usual announcements giving my name as captain of the flight. A passenger thought he recognized the name and asked to visit the cockpit; I naturally said okay. In walked Mr. Slemon, now long retired, but looking as sharp as ever. He said he remembered my name from the trip in the Comet from Portage to Trenton. I invited him to join us on the jump seat and we had a great chat. He wanted to know where various people were. The first officer was fascinated by the man. We landed in Montreal and continued to chat after we landed. We chatted so long that the cockpit door opened and a customs officer said that they were closing shop for the night and we had better clear customs ASAP. Mr. Slemon accompanied us to the customs hall, thanked us for our hospitality and we went our separate ways.

One story that has prevailed over the years is when Air Marshall Slemon was deputy commander of NORAD under U.S. Air Force General Curtis Lemay, who, to say the least, was a taskmaster. He made his name in the Pacific in WW II and was responsible for the firebombing of Tokyo as well as other Japanese cities. One night, on Mr. Slemon's watch, radar from Alaska reported many blips that looked like aircraft heading south towards mainland America. The reports were duly reported to the deputy commander, Mr. Slemon, with the recommendation that SAC, Strategic Air Command, be launched immediately. It looked like the Russians had a pre-emptive strike on the way. Mr. Slemon calmed everyone down by stating that this was migration season and the blips were thousands of geese heading south. Further investigation proved him right.

The course at Portage seemed to pass very quickly. We had our final written exams as well as having to display proficiency in clear-hood, aerobatics, and instrument flying. We now eagerly awaited graduation and our future posting. Naturally, all the Canadians wanted to go on the F-86, the Sabre, and have a European posting.

Our course actually finished about a week before the graduation exercises. All of our coursemates received their post-graduation postings except for Elmer Dow, Carl Sandelin, Keith McConnell, and—you guessed it—yours truly. The rest of the course were assigned to CF-100s. The four of us were convinced we would be going on Sabres.

Keith Olsen, one of the instructors, approached me and asked if I wanted to accompany him to North Bay, Ontario. He had some time off and wanted to visit with family for an afternoon. I jumped at the chance. We landed in North Bay midmorning, just as it started to snow. I headed to the mess for lunch while Keith was picked up by family, after agreeing to see me about five in the afternoon for our flight back to Portage. The snow really started to come down and by midafternoon the airfield was closed and I advised Keith by phone. He said, "See you tomorrow morning around ten." However, as this was a day trip, I had no kit with me. The mess provided a room for the night so I was at least able to shower.

By the time Keith arrived the next morning, I had completed the flight planning and the external on the aircraft. The field was open and we were cleared to go. On arrival back at Portage, I was advised to report to the wing commander, training. I was convinced I was about to hear that I was to be posted on Sabres. I approached the office and the wing commander's secretary advised me to go right in; the wing commander was expecting me. I approached his desk, came to attention, saluted, and said, "Flight Cadet McKay reporting as directed." The W/C looked me over and in a rather direct and threatening manner stated, "What is wrong with your face, cadet?" At first I did not have a clue as to what he was referring, and then the light came on. I explained to him that I had been unable to shave that morning (heck I only had fuzz), because I was unable to return to base yesterday due to the airport being closed in North Bay. The trip was only to be a one day affair; consequently I had not brought any kit with me.

The wing commander asked me to sit. I had no clue why he was asking me to sit, after chewing me out about my face. He said that during the war he flew Wellington bombers out of the UK. One evening, he was scheduled to fly with other aircraft on a mission over France. His aircraft was the only one to return. The others were either shot down or landed at some other base. The W/C said that he felt that it was his duty to report to the base commander immediately on landing and explain the evening events. He entered the commander's office, saluted. The first words out of the base commander's mouth were, "What's wrong with your face, pilot officer?" The W/C smiled at me and said, "I have been waiting fifteen years to say that to a junior officer." I stopped sweating and there were smiles all around. Then he said, "About your posting." I just knew it was Sabres. "You will be reporting to Flying Instructor School for training as a T-33 instructor," and he shook my hand and wished me well.

I learned the other three, who also expected Sabres, were also to train as instructors. Initially, I was disappointed, but in actual fact it was probably the best thing that ever happened to me in my flying career. The military training forced you to fly the aircraft to its limits. In doing so you not only acquired confidence in the aircraft but you learned what your own limits were. I cannot stress how important that lesson was. In the future I would have to instil that philosophy on my own students.

I had acquired a total of ninety-two hours and forty-five minutes on the T-33. The course syllabus now completed, we were required to return our parachute and hard hat to the flight safety section. All parachutes had to be repacked every ninety days. The parachute given to me on the start of course had just been packed, so I wore it the whole course. On arrival at flight safety, I asked the duty corporal if I could pull the "D" handle of the chute. He said, "No problem." Well, there was a problem. I pulled the "D" ring but it would not budge and appeared jammed. The corporal said, "You must be doing it wrong," but there was only one way to pull it. Anyway, he had a go. He was unable to pull the handle. A warrant officer arrived and the problem was explained to him. Then he had a go; no luck. The back of the chute was then opened. The chute itself is held in its pack by six pins. To everyone's surprise, two of the pins were slightly bent; just enough to make it impossible for anyone trying to pull the "D" ring. I made my feelings known. I told one and all that I was not impressed and that I had worn the chute the whole course. If I had needed to eject, I would have been a statistic.

Throughout the rest of my RCAF career, each time I returned a chute for re-packing I pulled the "D" ring. Most of the people in the flight safety group were not happy when I did. I made it clear on more than one occasion that the packers were dealing with people's lives and that as far as I was concerned, if my chute did not open on return for re-packing, whoever had packed the chute should be charged. Flight Safety hated to see me coming back for a new chute every ninety days.

Our course was presented with our wings on May 16, 1958, by the base commander, Group Captain Hiltz. Needless to say, we were one happy bunch. Looking back to initial selection at London, Ontario, fifteen months earlier, there were roughly 150 of us hoping to be selected for pilot/navigator training. Now there were twelve

Aircraft flown to Wings Parade.
Top to bottom: T-33 Silver Star, Harvard, Chipmunk.
RCAF

pilots who had achieved the coveted wings. I later learned that sixteen navigators from our initial selection had received their wings. The attrition rate was rather high but was in line with other courses.

Naturally, we had a bit of a party. Our former NATO friends graduated from Station MacDonald the same day. We would not see them again for several years.

The Chipmunk and Harvard gave us a lot of solo time to improve our flying skills. On the T-33 we had lots of dual time, mostly under the "bag" in the back seat improving our instrument flying. On graduation we were given a "white" instrument rating, clearing us to land in weather with a ceiling of 400 feet and visibility of one mile.

Chapter Eight

JIRC, Survival, and SHIT Courses

June 10, 1958, we were sent to Saskatoon for the JIRC course (Jet Instrument Rating Course). The course was designed to bring everyone up to the "green" instrument rating; landing limits of 200 feet and one-half mile visibility. We flew with instructors and with each other—mutual flying. We all passed, and during the course I flew twenty-two hours and forty-five minutes, with only three hours solo.

In mid-July, we boarded a train for Edmonton, Alberta, for a summer survival course. The course was held at Jarvis Lake, about 150 miles northwest of Edmonton. We were only allowed to bring what we would havc on board an aircraft in the case of an ejection, which was not a lot. The kit included a knife, small hatchet, and a mirror with a hole in it to signal aircraft. The food was all concentrated and made up in bar form. If you wanted cereal, you shaved off what you needed, added hot water and enjoyed.

The guides showed us where to find dry wood to build a fire, how to construct a lean-to, as well as the proper way to use the knife, emphasizing not to put a piece of wood on your leg as you shaved it in case the knife slipped and you ended up stabbing yourself. Briefing complete, we paired off to build a lean-to. Shortly after we started, a loud voice called "Help!" We rushed over and there was one of the students with a knife sticking out of his leg; so much for listening at the briefing. He was shipped out to hospital and did not return.

My lean-to buddy was Jim Garr, a very nice guy. We got along well. After we built our lean-to, we started preparing some snares.

I had one completed and attached to a branch when a partridge landed on the end of the lean-to. I reached up with my snare—we now had supper. We made a nice fire, covered the bird in mud, and put it in the hot coals. The idea was that the mud would dry and cook the bird. We would break off the mud and the feathers were supposed to stay in the mud. Some did, some did not. In any event, we had a hot, but not large supper.

The staff allowed us to bring a fishing pole if we had one. I did not. I followed a stream leading into the lake and found a beautiful pool of water. Growing up in Sackville, New Brunswick, I had done a lot of fishing and just knew there were fish in the pool. I met two course members heading back to camp with fishing poles. They had had no luck catching anything, so I borrowed a pole. In about an hour I had caught four trout. I gave two to the lads who lent me the pole, and Jim and I had another hot meal. Heck, I was enjoying the course.

The second morning we woke up to find ourselves covered with snow. In mid-July in the mountains, anything can happen. The camp had a parachute harness rigged up in the trees. We would strap ourselves in and swing through the trees. An instructor would pull a rope, the harness would open, and we were to roll as we hit the ground so as not to hurt ourselves. No one did.

Camp over after a week, we headed for Edmonton, and everyone was hungry. The bus stopped at the first restaurant we saw. Everyone ordered double of everything for breakfast, but none of us was able to eat very much; our stomachs had shrunk.

My lean-to partner, Jim Garr, later joined Air Canada. He developed a drinking problem and eventually committed suicide by closing and sealing the garage door and starting his car. What a waste.

We were headed, by rail, to Trenton, Ontario, for the SHIT course (School of Higher Instructional Technique). We had finished our survival course, got through the jerk course, and now we moved on to the "shit" course. Many from the survival course departed at stations along the route from Edmonton to Trenton. The train conductors were excellent. At every stop they told us exactly where the beer could be bought and how much time we had to get there and back. No one missed the train.

On arrival in Trenton we were introduced to our instructors. We were back in the classroom learning the techniques of instruction. We would practice the patter with each other and then we would brief our instructor. He would critique our approach and give pointers. We would go flying and I would demonstrate a manoeuvre and talk our "student" through an exercise. The instructor at times acted as though he had two left feet and nothing between the ears. We were expected to identify his problem and help him do the exercise the right way. There were plenty of laughs.

The first thing air force training taught you about flying were "needle, ball, and airspeed." On the SHIT course the credo was "aim, motivation, outline, and link." This tied everything together and helped make sense of what we were doing.

Elmer Dow and I had been told that upon completion of the course we were to be stationed at Gimli, Manitoba. The new commanding officer of station Gimli was G/C Bert Studer. He elected to complete the FIS (Flying Instructors Course) with us. He was a gentleman of the first order. He proved to be the best station commander I had the privilege to serve with. He had pictures sent to him from Gimli of all the officers and other ranks. On the back of each picture were pertinent facts about the individual; married, wife's name, hobbies, etc. We would quiz him at night in his room. He provided the soft drinks and beer. We had the opportunity to fly with our new CO and got to know him very well. In turn, he got to know two of his new staff members very well. He had been a wartime instructor but had never seen overseas service.

On arrival at Gimli, he immediately started to greet his staff by their rank and last name. The airmen were surprised to hear themselves being spoken to by the new CO. Initial reaction was: "He knows who I am." At one point, the CO asked one chap if his daughter's broken arm was mending. Needless to say, G/C Studer had the base eating out of his hand within twenty-four hours. I spent four years at Gimli with him as CO. He was always respected. (More about Gimli later.)

Judy arrived by train from the Maritimes for a visit. It was great seeing her. I had made arrangements that she would be staying with a young married couple. Judy's stay was far too short. She had to return to continue her nursing course and I had to complete the FIS course.

One highlight of the course at Trenton was that they had a Harvard on the base. I talked to one of the Harvard pilots and made arrangements for a trip. What a difference after flying the T-33 for the past few months. It was great fun being back in the Harvard. We did aerobatics, stalls, and—yes—spins. The flight was to be my last in a Harvard.

The following few weeks passed quickly. We flew lots of mutual trips, practicing our "instructing" on each other. All remaining aspects of the course were completed and we finished in early November 1958.

We were given nearly a month off before having to report to Gimli. I packed the car and headed for the Maritimes.

Chapter Nine

Home – Then to Gimli

I was on cloud nine. I had earned the coveted pilot's wings and I now was a fully qualified T-33 instructor.

It was the first time I had been home since receiving my wings. Dad was particularly proud. He had a picture of me receiving my wings in his office for all to see. Judy and I spent a lot of time together and I saw many of my high school chums. The time at home passed much too quickly, but it was now time to head for Gimli, Manitoba.

I left Saint John on December 10, 1958, and planned on a week to drive to Gimli. I was nearly flat broke but too proud to ask Dad for a few dollars. Mum gave me a fruitcake. In addition, I had twelve soft drinks to see me through to Gimli. I had a coupon book to pay for gas, but no credit cards. The coupon booklet was issued by ESSO. I would fill the card out, tear off a copy for the gas station and keep a copy for myself. The bill was eventually sent to Gimli.

The drive was uneventful; I was able to get a good breakfast every day and lived on fruitcake and soft drinks the rest of the time. I slept in motels along the route; it was too cold to sleep in the car.

My route took me through the States towards Chicago and then north to Manitoba. In the vicinity of Chicago, I somehow took a wrong turn and found myself in the suburbs of the big city. Dusk was settling in and it would be dark soon. There were literally hundreds of neon lights that made finding my way back to the highway difficult. I noticed a motorcycle policeman motioning me to pull over, which I did.

A rather large African American in a police uniform approached me and stated that I had driven through three stoplights. I apologized and told him that with all the neon lights, I did not see the red lights; I was just trying to get back to the highway. He said that the fine would be $200. I had about twenty dollars left, so I explained I would have to wire for money. The officer started looking into the back seat. He noticed my RCAF hat on the back shelf and asked if I was RAF. I explained I was in the Canadian air force. I thought to myself, perhaps this officer served in World War II. I asked him if he were ever in the services. He said with a smile, "Army, World War II." I asked him if he ever went on leave. He said he had some wild times on leave. Then I asked him if he ever came back broke. He looked at me, smiled, and said, "I'll get you back to the highway; follow me," which I did. After about twenty minutes he pulled over, pointed to the highway, and waved good bye. I never had to pay a fine after all. Thank God for my RCAF hat!

The further north I went the more snow was on the ground. After I drove through Winnipeg, there were sixty-five miles to Gimli. I misread a sign and, instead of going straight ahead, I ended up in Selkirk, still driving north. The road was getting narrower and narrower with high banks of snow. I spotted a man walking and asked him where Gimli was. He pointed west saying, "About twenty miles on the other side of Lake Winnipeg." I was on the wrong side of the lake! I turned around, drove back to Selkirk, and finally arrived at Gimli, tired and hungry. I waited at the main gate until the duty officer arrived. He arranged a room for me and said I could get toast and juice at the officers' mess. Food never tasted so good!

Chapter Ten

Gimli

I awoke the next day and ventured to the officers' mess. I never knew the west could have so much snow. Everywhere you looked there were tunnels dug into the snow leading into buildings. I never really knew what the base looked like until the snow melted in the spring.

Living in the barracks was easy for a new officer. I shared a batman with other pilots. The batman would clean your room, make the bed, and he would even shine your shoes or press a uniform when asked. Naturally, we paid him extra for his extra duties. The batman was a carryover from World War II; sadly this extra help was cancelled due to financial cutbacks in the service. It was great while it lasted.

I was busy the following couple of days signing onto the station. I needed the full flying kit, parachute, and hard hat. I stopped by headquarters and gave my regards to G/C Studer. He expressed his delight at my being on his staff of instructors. Wing Commander Ken Lett was in charge of the flying school; Squadron Leader Mel Sherwood was in charge of the "standards flight." I was advised I was assigned to B flight. Flight Lieutenant Willy Arthurs was in charge of B. My call sign was "Biscuit 10."

It was necessary to do a few trips with the standards flight. This gave them a chance to evaluate my instruction technique as well as my flying ability. I was considered qualified and I proceeded to B Flight. A new course had just arrived and I sat in on the briefing to the new students as they were introduced to the instructors. I was the junior instructor and was assigned only one student. This gave me a chance to get my feet wet. John Howe was my first student. He was a pleasant individual and we got along well. I briefed John on our first flight—a familiarization flight—to see the area and to get the feel of a jet aircraft.

It is not very often as an instructor that you get a student who is a natural pilot. Most of us had to work hard to attain the desired standard. John was a natural, so I had my work cut out for me. I would demonstrate a manoeuvre and he would repeat it. His flying was smooth and accurate. I would sign myself out on a solo flight and practice aerobatics, steep turns, and whatever else I could think of. I would then take John on another flight, demonstrate, and he would still do it better than I could. John was the best thing that could have happened to me. I had to work hard to keep ahead of him. He thought I was teaching him but the reverse was closer to the truth.

John's instrument flying was very good as well. I would try to screw him up by rubbing on the radio antenna embedded in the canopy roof. This caused static and made things a bit more interesting. John made my instructing debut an easy one. He went on to fly the Sabre, where he excelled. He left the RCAF and joined United Airlines in the United States. He is now retired and living in New Jersey. At the graduation party, John approached and thanked me for teaching him to fly the T-33 and helping him achieve the coveted wings. If he only knew. I was grateful for his remarks and I was more than ready to get another student.

My first Christmas at Gimli was a bit lonely. I had just arrived in early December and did not know that many people. The officers' mess was shared by both the cadets and the officers. Christmas dinner was prepared for us, and I noticed that there were several foreign students in the lounge; most of them looked lost. I was feeling that way after only three weeks, while they had been away from home for over a year.

I promised myself that when Judy and I were married no cadet would ever spend Christmas alone in the mess. I kept that promise. Dinner would be cooking and I would drive to the base and tell every cadet sitting around the mess that they were coming home with me for Christmas dinner. To a person they were really happy. Some would rush off to their rooms for a few beer or wine to bring along. Musical instruments were also brought along. Cadets with cars carried the overflow of passengers.

We would sit around singing carols in about four different languages. Our neighbours, whom we barely knew, knocked on the door and asked if they could join in the party. We invited them in, and every year after that they joined us for dinner and the singing. Memorable times. It always seemed to Judy and me that after everyone had left, we always had more beer and wine than when we started.

The T-33 course took about three months to complete. We had four to five courses at different stages of flying. A graduation was held about every six weeks.

Our days started with a weather briefing at 0730. Tom Giolotti was the senior "Met. man." His briefings were always well presented and his weather predictions turned out to be accurate. Nick Turko was the other Met. man. In order to get to the base there were times we fought through the snow to get to the briefing; Nick would report the weather as sunny and turning warmer. He had to walk through the storm to get to the briefing room, but never saw the storm. We learned to take everything Nick said with a grain of salt.

John Balsar was a senior instructor. Once we got to know each other we learned that both of our girlfriends were on the same nursing course in Saint John, New Brunswick.

John and I would take turns applying for an aircraft on the weekends, classified as a training flight. We would fly to Chatham, New Brunswick, normally landing at North Bay for fuel. Several times my mum would meet us in Chatham and we would drive to Saint John. On other visits, if Mum could not make the trip, we had to take the bus to Moncton and then to Saint John.

On some occasions we landed at Greenwood, Nova Scotia. The Fundy Flying Club had a small school at Greenwood. They required that one of the aircraft be returned to Saint John for training students from the Saint John area on the weekend. I knew everyone in the club so I arranged, on different occasions, to fly the aircraft to Saint John. We would leave our T-33 in Greenwood. Late Sunday, we would fly the club aircraft back to Greenwood, pick up our T-33 and head back to Gimli. On many of our trips the girls were on duty, so we would sneak up the stairs to see them.

On one of our trips to Chatham we had very strong tailwinds.

We were confident we could do the trip non-stop. All was well until we passed Ottawa and I had to pee. I held it and held it, then I tried to go and couldn't. John was aware of my problem. I finally told him we would have to land in Saint-Hubert, near Montreal, or I would bust something. We landed. I required two airmen to help me out of the back seat. I leaned against the wing and unzipped. All the while the ground crew kept saying, "Think waterfall." Finally I started to go, first a trickle, then a flood. I smiled in relief. We filled up with gas and were on our way within thirty minutes.

On one occasion Judy had the Saturday off. We spent the day together and decided to go to the drive-in that night. Mum always let me have the car on these trips; Dad never did learn to drive. I had had a busy week with students and then had flown east and bused to Saint John. Judy had also had a busy week, so we were both tired. I remember getting us drinks before the main movie started. We both fell asleep and awoke to find that we were the only car in the drive-in. I never did understand why the management did not come and bang on our windows. Perhaps they did, but we were dead to the world.

Judy was now well past her curfew at the teaching hospital. The instructors were very strict with the girls and would often confine them to their rooms, on so-called days off. We were lucky; Judy managed to get to her room without being seen. No one, but no one, would have ever believed we fell asleep at the drive-in, but that is what happened.

John was transferred to Sabres, and then overseas. He and his girlfriend, Frieda, were married. Frieda and her family were immigrants, from Holland. But that was not the last we were to see of them.

I spent four-and-a-half years at Gimli. I arrived single, and Judy and I were married after my first year at Gimli. We left three-and-a-half years later with two young boys. During my first year at Gimli there were about seventy instructors and sixty of us were single. The second year, sixty were married and only ten still single. I remember many days at Gimli at minus 35 to 40 Fahrenheit. No wonder sixty of us got married after our first year at Gimli!

Weekends, when we were not flying east, were long. The base

started a flying club for ground crew wanting to learn to fly, as well as any local who was interested. I had lots of light aircraft experience, so I was welcomed into the club as one of the instructors. We were not required to fly a trip with an MOT inspector. We were all qualified air force instructors so the MOT requirement was lifted. The flying club was considered a secondary duty. All of us on what was called a short service commission (five years) worked at several different secondary duties in order to be noticed and hopefully earn a permanent commission.

The flying club had three Aeronca Champ and one Piper-22 aircraft; tandem seating, one behind the other. I had flown the Piper aircraft before. The Aeronca had been around for years and was very easy to fly. I had acquired many hours on light aircraft and often served as chief instructor. It was great fun. We flew with students in the T-33 all week at 500-plus knots and on the weekends with new students doing 90 knots.

Early in my days with the club, the CFI (chief flying instructor) asked me to give a solo check on a civilian student. It was a beautiful, but cold, winter day in Gimli; lots of snow piled up around the field. I was advised the student was having some problems and I was to help him along and send him solo if I thought he was okay. We departed and climbed up to about 3,000 feet. I had the student do turns, stalls, etc. He did okay and I asked him to take me back to the field for touch-and-go landings.

All was well until we were on final approach. He was very high and seemed reluctant to set up a good rate of descent in order to land within the confines of the runway. It was obvious he was too high to make a successful landing so I had him overshoot and place himself on final again. He was too high; I took control and sideslipped the aircraft to lose altitude quickly, cross control aileron and rudder to aid in a quick descent. I put him in a position where all he had to do was keep the controls where they were and land. It looked like he was doing okay when, suddenly, as we approached the button end of the runway, he pushed the control forward. I immediately grasped the control column and pulled back, but I was too late

We hit the top of a snow bank and the aircraft proceeded to turn end-over-end. I managed to turn all the switches off and exit the aircraft before it came to a rather abrupt halt. I raced to the aircraft and pulled the student out; neither of us was injured. We walked back to the flying club, and I called the control tower to advise that there had been an accident on the field. The tower was to monitor aircraft as they took off and landed, but the duty controller had seen nothing, probably asleep on the job. I was not impressed and I told him exactly what I thought of him. We could have been injured and in the need of assistance while he slept. Prior to flying, we always informed the tower that there would be flying club aircraft in the circuit. This duty flying control officer did not do a satisfactory job, to say the least.

One weekend, a resident of Riverton, Manitoba, arrived at the club. He had an expired pilot's licence and was anxious to get the necessary flying required to renew his licence. I was asked to give him a "check ride."

None of the club aircraft had battery starters. It was necessary to turn the propeller by hand three or four times. I had the man from Riverton sit in the forward seat and set the parking brake. I reviewed the starting procedure with him and advised I would now pull the propeller through. I called out to him, "Brakes set, throttle closed, switches off." He acknowledged my commands. I pulled the propeller through and the engine started immediately, slicing through the light jacket I was wearing. The pilot did the exact opposite of my commands. He had actually set the throttle and selected the ignition switches on! I was ready to kill him. I reached into the cockpit, turned the switches off, and literally pulled him from the cockpit, shook him, and told him to get the hell out of here and never come back. Never in my experience with the propeller had the engine ever started after the first turn. When I arrived home, Judy noticed I was white and shaking. Shock had finally settled in. The man from Riverton never did come back.

I also volunteered to do the morning weather check. I thoroughly enjoyed these trips. The weather check meant that I was up early and usually airborne about seven in the morning. I was the only one in the sky; it was peaceful and very enjoyable. I would fly 200–300 miles around Gimli just to make certain that when the students went solo the weather was good. I would relay my observations to the tower, who, in turn, passed the information onto the weatherman for his daily briefing. It was always surprising to me that, as I taxied out to do the weather checks, Wing Commander Bubbles Peters, chief maintenance officer, was usually sitting on a snow bank waving at me. There was never any vehicle around; he walked the taxiways and runways making certain they were clear of obstructions.

After one snow and freezing rain storm the field was a mess. The parallel runways were covered with ice and unusable. W/C Peters came up with the idea of spreading fuel on the runway to burn the ice off. Fuel was applied, lit with a flare. We all watched from across the field. The initial white smoke soon turned into billowing black clouds. It was evident that the asphalt that had been used to repair the runway the previous summer was now burning. After the fire had been extinguished all the cracks reappeared, only bigger.

The runway was declared unusable. The other runway was finally cleared of ice after two days of intensive, around-the-clock plowing. We were now down to one runway for operations the rest of the winter. The other runway was repaired in the spring. The W/C laughed the incident off, stating it worked during the war. Later, he admitted the field during the war was a grass strip.

I soon noticed that the ex-Sabre pilots were all wearing G-suits (anti-gravity suits). Naturally, I wanted one. The G-suit was form-fitting and had inflatable air sacs around the legs and stomach to prevent blood from pooling in the lower part of the body. Prior to the G-suits, pooling of the blood in the lower part of the body led to blackouts during high level of acceleration and the G-forces encountered in aerobatics or dogfighting. The bladders would fill with air, pushing against your body so you could prolong the G-forces without blacking out. Prior to wearing a G-suit during aerobatics you would tighten your stomach muscles, which helped you remain conscious when pulling "G."

One day, I was flying with a student who was under the bag, doing instrument flying. In the aircraft ahead of us were two instructors, Len Fine and Stu Graham. They were on a proficiency flight so that Stu could upgrade his instructor's licence. I heard them report outbound from the beacon and I never gave them much more thought. I was busy with my student. We started our descent, completed our procedure turn, and descended to minimums. It was snowing pretty hard. We were cleared to tower frequency for final landing instructions. I was asked if I had heard from Len or Stu. I advised I had heard them report outbound, but nothing else. We landed. By the time we entered the flight room the word was out that they had crashed south of the airport and both were killed.

Another time, I was flying with a student who had had very little time in the T-33. I had briefed him on our exercise, which would entail lots of aerobatics. All was going well. We had just finished doing a loop and I asked the student to do some rolls but heard nothing in response. I asked if he was okay; no response. I could see that he had lowered his head and to the right. I declared an emergency and asked for the ambulance to meet us on arrival. I made it back to Gimli in record time, talking to him all the while. I landed and came to a halt. I raised the canopy and shimmied to the front cockpit. I shook the student and he just moaned. I removed his mask and it was full of vomit. He was choking on his own vomit. I loosened his harness and hit him on the back once or twice. He coughed, then he spit up more vomit. By this time help had arrived and the student was taken to hospital. I visited him and he said he was going to quit, which he did. I learned later that he became a policeman in Winnipeg.

Sam Petersen, a Danish student, had spent time in the Danish army, reaching the rank of sergeant. Sam had had enough of army life and re-mustered to the air force to become an "officer and gentleman." Sam married a Canadian girl, Phyllis. She took nurses' training at the Saint John General Hospital and was in the same class as Judy. Small world.

Judy and Phyllis were happy to see each other and spent time catching up on old friends. Sam and I got along well, and the four of us spent some time together in Gimli. I was Sam's instructor for night and instrument flying. One night when we were flying, a group of the Danish students visited with Phyllis, with the intention of teaching her the Danish language. They asked her not to tell Sam but to keep her language skills secret. The lads were teaching her how to greet Sam's mother when they met for the first time. The lessons went on for a couple of weeks and Phyllis was anxious to show Sam her progress. Sam arrived at their motel, after a night flying session. Phyllis started speaking in Danish. When she had finished,

Sam quietly said, "Do you know what you just said?"

Phyllis said, "It is a greeting to your mother when we first meet."

Sam smiled. "What you said was, 'It is a fucking pleasure to meet you, you stupid, fat, Danish mother-in-law.'"

The lads had been teaching her every curse word they could think of and made her practice the speech to her new mother-in-law. Thankfully, she tried the speech out on Sam before arriving in Denmark and meeting her mother-in-law.

Years later, during our European tour, we visited with Sam and Phyllis at their home in Aalborg and their family summer home near Blokuus, on the North Sea. The area had several German bunkers in very good condition. The Germans thought at one time that the Allies might land in Denmark for the invasion and built fortifications accordingly. It was interesting to examine them.

One afternoon, Sam and I went to a fishery and bought lobster for our supper. Before we cooked the lobster we set up beer bottles with lit candles, made a runway, and raced the lobsters. The more beer we drank the longer the runway became. Finally, the moment arrived to boil the lobsters. North Sea lobsters are bigger and their shell rougher than the east coast lobsters. The big buggers did not want to be put into the pot, and even though their claws were wired, they clung to the sides of the pot. Eventually we succeeded and the meal was great. It proved to be a memorable evening, as both Judy and Phyllis conceived that night.

Sadly, Sam and Phyllis divorced. Phyllis stayed in Denmark with her three boys. Sam died in his mid-forties of a massive heart attack.

We had three Expeditor C-45 aircraft at Gimli. These aircraft were mainly used to ferry folks back and forth to Winnipeg, where training command headquarters was located. The aircraft were also used for trips to The Pas, in northern Manitoba. The Pas had an air cadet squadron that certain Gimli officers were responsible for, and they would visit the squadron twice a year for inspections.

The base was looking for another couple of pilots to become proficient on this particular aircraft. I applied and was accepted. I needed a break from instructing after the fatal at Gimli.

Our transition course was to take about two weeks. We proceeded to RCAF Saskatoon for the training. Thankfully, we did not have to build the aircraft before we could fly it. We were amply supplied with reading material and the EOs (engineering orders). All military aircraft had EOs, containing all pertinent information on that particular aircraft, such as weights, single engine procedures, etc.

The C-45 had two engines. The aircraft was used during the war as a light bomber trainer and for transport duties. The RCAF had a fleet of them. The course itself was quite straightforward. Two of us would go flying with an instructor, one student flying while the other observed. We would then switch seats. After a few landings, we were considered qualified to fly together. Neither my partner nor I had any difficulty with the aircraft. We spent many enjoyable hours setting each other up for one emergency after the other. We got to know the dos and don'ts very quickly.

One evening we were night flying, which included a short cross-country flight in order to burn off excess fuel before doing touch-and-go landings. When we returned to the city of Saskatoon, we thought we would circle the city a few times. We decided it best to turn our navigation lights off so that, although we could be heard, folks down below would not know in what direction we were going on leaving the city. We had a jolly old time circling the city and observing the lights outlining the city limits. The area around the city remained pretty black with few lights. After a while, we decided to do our landings. After landing, we talked to another mutual crew about their trip. They mentioned they circled the city with their navigation lights off. We compared notes. We were in the same sky passing each other, with no lights, over the city. The city was not that large at that time. How we missed hitting each other is a bloody miracle.

I now added another aircraft to my list of planes flown. Saskatoon was also home of the B-25, Mitchell course. The aircraft had a wonderful reputation during World War II. The Mitchell aircraft was selected to take off from a U.S. aircraft carrier for the Jimmie Doolittle raid on Japan. The RCAF used this aircraft to train navigators out of Winnipeg, Manitoba. While we were on course, a B-25 instructor was giving a checkout to another pilot. The tower called him and advised him that his student had a problem at home and was asked to land ASAP, which he did. The student was obviously preoccupied and instead of walking to the rear of the aircraft to avoid the spinning propellers he walked forward into the propellers, and was killed instantly. Lesson: never, never state the reason for a recall of a mission until the individual concerned is safely on the ground and clear of the aircraft.

One of my first trips as captain in the C-45 was to The Pas. The officers in charge of the inspection of the air cadets headed for town and hotel. The first officer and I called a local fishing lodge. They picked us up, fitted us with the fishing gear we required, and checked us out on an outboard motorboat. We spent the weekend fishing Lake The Pas, eating the fish, laying on the dock, and swimming; rough duty. Soon other instructors got wind of this goodie trip and wanted to check out on the C-45. I managed to get two other trips in before others took my place.

In the summer months, we were authorized to train air cadets. An old abandoned World War II field south of Gimli was used for the duration of training. We flew with our regular service students during the week and with the cadets on the weekend. It was a very busy three-week period. None of the cadets had ever flown before so we were back to basics. I was right at home in the light aircraft.

We had many NATO students at Gimli; Danes, Norwegians, Brits, and Turks. The Turks were different, to say the least. They all came from wealthy families and were expected to do well. On arrival at Gimli, they put on a precision drill demonstration, and they were very skilled. In addition, many of the Turks had Canadian girlfriends, who followed them from base to base. Some eventually married. They experienced great difficulty on arrival in Turkey; most ended up divorced and were very grateful to be back in Canada.

Unfortunately, there were two kinds of Turks, the very good and the very bad; there was no in between. If a Turk failed the course, he was sent home, disowned by family, forced into the army, and sent to their frontier, bordering Iraq. The Kurds/Armenian people in this area hated the Turks, even to this day, because of the ethnic cleansing of their people in 1918. The new army recruits were not expected to live very long. Somehow we managed to get the so-called "bad" students to an acceptable level. We did not want to see any of them arrive home in disgrace.

However, there was one exception. A red-headed Turk named

Galishaloo had two left feet, did not have a clue what to do with his hands, and was oblivious to where he was at any time in an airplane. He went flying with Weldy Feedman one cold morning. They climbed to twenty-some thousand feet, and Weldy asked him to do a spin. He entered the spin okay but when Weldy asked him to recover, he had frozen onto the controls. Weldy hollered at him to let go, let go, but he was a big strong man and held onto the controls. The T-33 was spinning down and losing altitude rapidly. Weldy was ready to eject and let the Turk meet Allah when he felt a loosening of the controls. He managed to pull out of the spin at about 1,500 feet above Lake Winnipeg. He asked the student, "What were you trying to do, kill me?" Answer, "If Allah wills it, sir." That was Galishaloo. Weldy was a bit greyer after that trip.

Our Turkish student was in a four-plane formation, again on a cold winter day. He was in the number four position. If you look at your right hand, with your thumb under the fingers you can understand the formation. Left to right on the fingers: number two position, lead, number three position, and far right number four position. Fred Allport was the instructor with Galishaloo. Fred was a very experienced pilot, who had flown the F-86 in Europe and had been a T-33 instructor for three years. The aircraft lined up in the finger four formation, power was applied, and the aircraft became airborne. Almost immediately, the aircraft with our Turkish friend broke right and was headed straight for the control tower. Those inside the tower were certain the tower was about to be hit and headed for the stairs to exit the building. Fred managed to recover control of the aircraft and missed the tower, but not by much. He asked the student what had happened. Galishaloo stated, and I quote, "Sir, my hands were cold, I was rubbing them together to get them warm." Galishaloo had no clue where he was or what he was supposed to do.

Galishaloo had one saving grace; he was a very nice person. We did not want to see him return to Turkey in disgrace. Normally, the full pilot course to wings took about fifteen months. We had Galishaloo in Canada for over two years, making up all kinds of excuses as to why he had not completed the course. Finally, the Turkish air attaché arrived at Gimli from Washington to review his status. We learned that the attaché was a good friend of the Galishaloo family, and he had a solution to our problem. Galishaloo was thought to have a rare medical problem, which allowed him to cease training and return to Turkey and family; in effect, saving face. We were all glad to see him go. He certainly was a unique challenge and those of us who flew with him will never forget him. I have often wondered if he is still alive.

The Turkish military attaché often came to Gimli for proficiency flying. He was a gentleman and we all enjoyed his company. The tower would always advise pilots flying that day that "Turk 1" was in the air. He was not a very good pilot, so that was a heads-up to watch out for him. Years later, the RCAF delivered several surplus T-33 aircraft to the Turkish air force. Our pilots asked about the former military attaché and were told his name was not mentioned anymore. Apparently, he was involved in a political situation and possible coup, and ended up in front of a firing squad.

In the spring of 1959, several officers of the new German air force arrived for a jet conversion course on the T-33. These gentlemen were ex-Luftwaffe pilots who survived the Second World War.

The German air force had been reinstated in the fall of 1956 and acquired old equipment from the United States and Canada, such as Dakotas, Harvards, and some old F-84 jets. The F-84 was known as a "runway creeper," because it needed all the runway it could get, in order to get into the air. It was also known as a "widow maker." I saw one take off from Cagliari, Sardinia, on a hot summer day. It was returning to Germany, heavy with fuel and required JATO to get airborne. JATO bottles were attached near the back of the fuselage. They were like a small rocket and gave tremendous power for a very short time. The aircraft was just airborne when one of the JATO bottles failed. The aircraft quickly rolled and the pilot had no time to recover. There was a rather large fireball when the aircraft hit the ground.

The pilots who arrived at Gimli were part of an expansion of the new Luftwaffe. I flew with several of them and they were all excellent pilots. Most had ME-262 as well as ME-109 experience. I was probably the age they were when they were on active duty during the war. I really could not teach them very much, but I was able to give them pointers on the T-33, which the German air force was acquiring.

Friday night was beer call night. Pilots got together and got into their cups; stories started to be told. One of our Canadian instructors, Ray Goeres, was a re-tread who had served during the war, tried "civilian" life and did not like it, so rejoined the RCAF. Ray was talking to several of the Germans about his wartime experiences, specifically when he was shot down over France in 1944. One of the Germans inquired about the date Ray was shot down and in what area of France. Ray gave him the information and the German said that he had shot a spitfire down that day in France. Both individuals left the mess to get their log books. After comparing dates and times, it became almost certain that it was this German who had shot down Ray. There were hugs all around, and the beer flowed rather freely that night. It was quite an experience to have been in the mess that night and hear the stories.

Later, during my tour on 104s in Europe, I met some of these individuals again. By this time, they had all been promoted to senior positions and were active in the German air force 104 program. German aircraft landed at our bases quite often, as we did at German fields.

The German air force at this time was having great difficulty keeping their best people. Mechanics and technicians would literally be met, after they completed their courses, by civilian airline, auto, and heavy industry in general. Their skills were in great demand, and the recruiters were quite willing to pay for their release. The service could not hold them.

Consequently, the quality of maintenance in the German air force deteriorated. Often on arrival at a Canadian base, the tires on their 104 aircraft would be peeling rubber. Our maintenance crew brought the aircraft up to our standard and they happily flew away. Naturally, we sent a bill to the German government, which was readily paid.

In July 1959, I was scheduled to take a CF-100 course at Cold Lake, Alberta. Students were not asking for a CF-100 transition course upon graduation. The military sent a few of us to Cold Lake on the theory that we would be able to talk to our students about the "clunk," as it was affectionately known. We had a great time on course. Once again we were able to fly the aircraft without having to build it first. We flew the Marks III, IV, and V. The Mark III had two

T-33 formation over Lake Winnipeg.

pilot seats, front and back, and was used basically for transition. In the back seat, if you wanted to see the compass, you had to make a 30-degree bank turn, in order to see the compass. It made you wonder who designed such an arrangement. I do not think anyone ever figured out the fuel system. Once I was cleared for solo, my instructor pulled out a black marker and put marks on the eight different fuel gauges, and said, "When the fuel reaches the marks, turn around and land ASAP."

The Mark IV and V five aircraft were leap years ahead of Mark III. The rear seat on the Mark IV and V was reserved for the AI (airborne interceptor). He was the radar "geek" who would spot another aircraft and direct the pilot for the intercept. The Mark V was very easy to fly. It was the most stable military aircraft I ever flew. I used to remark that on a GCA (a ground-assisted radar approach) you could read a book it was so stable.

One of my coursemates on 5702 was Ted Buckman. He was the only person I ever knew who could do 100 push-ups at the drop of a hat. After he graduated, Ted trained on the CF-100. He completed the course and was on squadron in North Bay, Ontario. He and his AI were on alert one evening when they were "scrambled." I have no idea what happened in the cockpit, but Ted somehow lost control. The navigator bailed out and survived. Ted was found the next day, still strapped in his seat. The seat was a Martin Baker, the best available. Something went wrong and the auto seat separation

The CF-100 I flew out of Cold Lake, Alberta.

never occurred. Either Ted strapped in incorrectly or there was a malfunction of the auto system. I never did learn the cause of the accident. Ted was the first Canadian killed from course 5702 in an aircraft accident.

When I arrived at Gimli, there were three stations that gave advanced flying instruction on the T-33; Gimli, Portage la Prairie, and Station MacDonald. MacDonald was the envy of the other two stations because their CO, by hook or by crook, was able to acquire three F-86 Sabre aircraft for his instructors to fly. As luck would have it, an announcement that Station MacDonald would soon be closing was confirmed. Our CO was successful in acquiring the F-86 for the Gimli pilots. Initially, pilots with Sabre experience flew the aircraft. Our group was classified as "pipeline," meaning no squadron experience. The senior pilots wanted the Sabre for themselves. We junior pilots balked and we soon had our chance to fly the Sabre.

I recall my first flight vividly. One must remember the Sabre was a single-seat fighter; no instructor to fly with you. All we did was strap in and go flying. I was scheduled to fly the Sabre 323, on July 21, 1959. I was given a copy of the EOs to read that night. I thought there was too much to absorb in one evening so I concentrated on the re-light procedure in the event of a flame-out and the ejection procedure. I also decided I would just use the T-33 speeds in the circuit.

Next morning, Bill Mitchell, an experienced Sabre pilot, helped me do the proper walk around, pointing out what I should look for.

I climbed into the cockpit and Bill helped strap me in; there was a proper sequence. Bill said, “Okay, start the engine.” I said I hadn’t read that chapter. Bill shook his head and showed me the start procedure. Once the engine was going he tapped me on my helmet, with a thumbs-up, “Have fun.” I had always heard how easy it was to taxi the Sabre. I did not find it that easy. I was pushing the proper button on the control column but was still having to use differential braking to steer the beast. I then noticed a round bar sticking out from below the instrument panel. It looked out of place. I put my hand on it, felt for a retract switch, found it and the bar disappeared. I immediately had hydraulics available for the nose wheel steering. The bar was also a rudder lock used on the ground in windy conditions to keep the rudder in place and not thrash around. Luckily I found it before I got airborne; otherwise I would have had to bail out. At least I had read that chapter.

I lined up on the runway and ran up the engine with the brakes on. The instruments looked fine. I released the brakes and was airborne in about 3,000 feet. I selected the gear and flaps up and accelerated to about 450 knots and climbed to 41,000 feet. It was an old airplane and would not go any higher. I rolled it into a steep dive and accelerated, exceeding the speed of sound, at about 700 mph, no doubt scaring those on the ground with my sonic boom. I gently pulled the aircraft into a climb. I then proceeded to do rolls, loops—generally just flying the aircraft all over the sky. By this time, my fuel was getting low so I returned to Gimli for a few touch-and-go landings. During my first overshoot my seat fell to the bottom position. Instead of my being high in the seat and enjoying the scenery, I now could hardly see over the cockpit sill. I flew on instruments up to 3,000–4,000 feet and tried to get my seat back up. In the back of my mind I remembered a bar that stuck out from behind the seat. I pulled it down, no luck. I then remembered I had to take my weight off the seat in order for the handle to work. I had to loosen all my harness and lift my butt, then, feet on the floor, pushed myself up while jiggling the handle. Eventually, my seat came up to its proper position. I locked it, fastened my harness, and headed back to the circuit. The next time I flew the Sabre, I made certain my seat was locked on the ground. I mentioned the rudder lock to Bill after I landed. He said he had never seen it and that it must be used by maintenance to isolate hydraulics. On subsequent Sabre flights, I never saw the bar out again.

That first flight in a Sabre was memorable, particularly in view of the fact that there was no one to show you what to do; you were on your own. It was a good feeling to know that I could handle the aircraft.

Chapter Eleven

Air Shows – RCAF Formation

The years 1959 and 1960 proved to be busy. I flew with lots of students and built up my flying time on the T-33. I was also considered proficient on the C-45, CF-100, and the F-86 Sabre. I was earning my pay.

Brian Frank was another of my students who had a hard time passing the course. I wanted to cease his training but I was overruled. Brian was married to a squadron leader's daughter. The squadron leader was CFI (chief flying instructor) at Moose Jaw. He pulled a few strings and assured command that if we let Brian graduate he would have him transferred to Moose Jaw. He would personally fly with him and bring him to a standard before he reported to multi-engine school.

By the time I joined Air Canada, Brian had been with the airline for about two years and flying the DC-9. Initially, I flew the Viscount and was a flight engineer on the DC-8 followed by first officer on the DC-9. Brian was promoted to captain on the DC-9 and, as luck would have it, I was his first officer on his first flight as captain. We flew from Montreal to Moncton. All went well until we descended towards Moncton airport, which we could see miles away. Brian ended up too high to make a safe landing so he was forced to overshoot. I knew he was embarrassed. He asked me if I thought he was high on the approach. I said, yes, I knew he was too high. Well, why did I not tell him? I told him that the only way to learn was by making mistakes and that he did the right thing by overshooting and not trying to salvage a bad approach. Once an instructor, always an instructor. He was quiet on the return trip to Montreal. Thankfully, I never had to fly with him again.

One of my students appeared preoccupied and was not up to his normal flying standard. When I asked him what was bothering him, he spoke of both family and girlfriend problems. He told me he was from Saskatoon and was hoping to return as soon as he could to get his head straightened out. The base was planning a long weekend, so I advised the student I would fly him to Saskatoon early Saturday morning but he was to make certain he was back on base by Tuesday. The trip to Saskatoon was uneventful. After we landed, the student secured the back seat ensuring his parachute and hard hat were secure as well. I checked my fuel and decided I had plenty for my return to Gimli. I wished the student well and took off for Gimli. I was cruising at 20,000 feet when I had the sudden realization that my fuel was going to be very tight for my return to Gimli.

I climbed to 35,000 feet and my fuel consumption decreased. I felt a bit better. I planned to stay at high altitude until I arrived over Gimli. On arrival over the station, my low-level fuel light was blinking, indicating I had 79 gallons left, good for twelve to fifteen minutes of flight. I throttled off, selected speed brakes and rapidly descended to 2,000 feet. I was descending from very cold air to relatively warm air in the lower altitudes when the inside of my canopy frosted over. I had my instruments but I could not see out even though the sky was clear. The low-level light continued to blink while I cleared some of the frost from the canopy. I managed to clear about two to three inches—enough to see out. I continued my approach and landed okay, looking through my peep hole. Lesson learned; do not skimp on fuel when it is readily available. I would never put myself in such a position again. The student arrived back on time in a much better frame of mind and went on to graduate. I never told him of my experience. I was probably too embarrassed.

The highlight of the week for the instructors was Friday afternoon. The students had to report to ground school for a review of current events. Then the instructors could play. Each of the four flights would gather as many instructors and aircraft as were available. The flights would take off in formation. Once airborne, everyone flew towards Hecla Island, on the east side of Lake Winnipeg. We all flew about 20,000 feet and, when the time was right, we pounced on each other. Everyone tried to get on the tail of another aircraft and stay there as long as possible. You also had to look behind to ensure your tail was clear. Once locked onto the other aircraft, the other pilot would try his best to lose you by throwing the aircraft into every manoeuvre imaginable. At times, there were thirty aircraft all twisting and turning and having a great time. This dogfighting certainly improved our flying and gave us a lot of respect for the T-33. It is probably a small miracle that we never had a mid-air collision or incident of any kind.

During my first year of instructing, it seemed every time I got into the air I had something go wrong. I landed with the fire trucks on more than one occasion. It was getting to the point that I was being considered accident prone. I wrote up every incident. The CFI reviewed all emergencies and in each case maintenance was at fault. I had such things as fire warning lights coming on more than once. On one occasion, my student said the controls felt very heavy. I took control and he was right, something was wrong with the elevator. I could hardly move the stick fore and aft. I flew back to the field and made a long straight-in approach using a secondary trim function that just moved the elevator tab. I advised my student that if things were okay at 2,000 feet and I felt I had some control I would continue with the approach. If not, he would bail out first, and I would follow. The landing was not the best, but we were on the ground. Maintenance had failed to apply a graphite lubricant to the rudder control; it was, in effect, frozen.

At the completion of my first year at Gimli, I had had just about every imaginable emergency happen to me. I followed my training and all went well. Further incidents I had seen before—repeats of old experiences.

We normally did a cross-country flight during night flying in order to burn off fuel so we would be light enough for touch-and-go landings. I was with a student one evening over Kenora, Ontario. At 33,000 feet, we were chatting and he said that he had never used the alternate trim switch before. I told him that it was okay but first I wanted to make certain he had his flashlight on the proper switch because the next switch was the main fuel cut off. I could see him using his flashlight and he assured me he had the alternate trim switch and not the fuel cut-off switch. I said, "Okay, select." It got very dark. He had turned the main fuel switch to the off position and the engine had quit. All I could think of saying was, "Put it back on." He did; I pulled the throttle back, and there was a rather loud bang as the engine re-lit and the jet pipe temperature began to climb rapidly. I managed to keep the temperature within limits. The incident gave us both quite a surprise. Then we both started laughing. All was well, and we headed back to Gimli knowing the system "as labelled," worked.

Different student—another cross-country. We were cruising at 35,000 feet and I asked the student to descend to 20,000 feet. The first action was to close the throttle. The student advised me he could not move the throttle. I tried as well but it was stuck at 90 percent thrust. I selected the speed brakes to lose some speed. When we reached 250 knots, I selected the undercarriage down creating more drag. We descended slowly, and I gradually decreased the speed so I could lower some flap to help in the descent. I had to keep the nose quite high to achieve the descent. I advised the tower of our problem. I knew that as we approached the field, I would have to lower the nose and the airspeed would start to build. It was a Catch-22. I continued the approach and, when I was certain we could make the field, I pulled the fuel high pressure cock off, which shut the engine down. We glided the rest of the way to the field and completed a dead-stick landing; no engine.

After this incident, word filtered down from training command that if any other pilot found himself in the same situation, engine thrust could be reduced by slowly bringing back the high pressure cock. It was emphasized not to bring the high pressure cock back too fast or too far as a flame-out would probably occur. Naturally, all the pilots tested the new method. It worked. I never heard of anyone having to use this method in an actual emergency. If I had known of the procedure before the incident, it would have made things easier, but no one else knew about it until it was released by training command.

Klaus Dassel was another of my students. He was very good. During a two-plane formation flight, he advised me that he had a fire-engine light come on and he could hear popping from the engine. I could tell from his voice that he was quite concerned. I had had a similar experience and I knew that 90 percent of engine problems could be solved by throttling back. I instructed him to pull his throttle back to about 75 percent, which he did. He advised that the light was out but some of the popping remained. I had broken from my lead position and looked his aircraft over for signs of smoke, etc. Everything looked okay. I advised the tower that we were returning to base with a possible engine fire in my number two's aircraft. I told Klaus to do just as I told him, and all would be okay. I talked him through a visual approach and when he was just about to touch down, I had him close the high pressure fuel cock, shutting down the engine. He landed safely with the fire trucks waiting for him.

Klaus did very well on squadron but his one vice was for the ladies. He was well built and good looking with blond curly hair. He attracted the ladies like bees to nectar. During his squadron tour he actually went AWOL, taking the squadron fund with him. Klaus was found living with an Italian princess in Italy. He was released from the RCAF and disappeared.

All students, when they went solo, experimented with different aspects of flight. I know I did and scared myself on more than one occasion. It was all part of the RCAF teaching you to fly the aircraft to its limits. In doing so, you soon learned your own limits as well as capability.

One of our Danish students completed his assigned solo exercise and wondered what would happen to the aircraft if at 450 knots he applied full rudder. He found out very quickly. He nearly lost control of the aircraft. He reported control problems and headed back to base. The landing was uneventful. Inspection of the tail plane showed the riveted aluminum covering the protected portion of the rudder had popped out. The aluminum itself was actually ripping. No wonder he had control problems.

All students were instructed that in the event that they encountered a thunderstorm they were to make a 180-degree turn to get out of the storm. One of our fearless students took off and, rather than turn to avoid a thunderstorm north of the field, flew right into the storm. The aircraft was tossed and turned, buffeted and encountered heavy rain and hail. The student did the 180-degree turn and proceeded to descend back through the storm. He could easily have turned left or right to evacuate the storm but he took his direction literally. When it landed, the aircraft looked like it had been hit by ball peen hammers. There were thousands of indentations from the hail he encountered. Maintenance was unable to repair the damage and the aircraft was robbed for spare parts and scrapped.

Another summer activity was flying air shows—mainly Toronto and Ottawa. Gimli and Portage together formed a formation, spelling "RCAF." It was an impressive sight from the ground. Portage aircraft formed the "RC" and Gimli the "AF." The Gimli aircraft would form up and stay straight and level while the Portage aircraft would close and join our formation. A spotter aircraft flew overhead and called out a call sign to either move up, slide back, etc., to ensure proper positioning. I was always the lead in the bottom half of the "F"; the join-up manoeuvre could be tricky. If the aircraft closed too fast, they would fly over us, slightly decrease airspeed, fall back and attempt another rejoin. You have to remember that all the aircraft took their positions in relation to the lead. Everyone concentrated on the aircraft he was flying formation on. The lead had to use all his experience and skill to ensure a safe join-up. On one beautiful sunny day, we in the "AF" were in position and waiting for the Portage "RC" to join up with our formation. The lead was closing too fast, but rather than going over us, he put on bank and, in effect, flew through our formation. I distinctly remember seeing a tip tank from a Portage aircraft pass over my canopy. I throttled back, popped the speed brakes, and pointed the aircraft straight down. I recovered at about 1,000 feet and headed for home. Upon landing, the Gimli pilots were more than just angry. We would probably have lynched the Portage lead if we had caught him. He made a stupid blunder and almost caused a very serious accident. He was removed from the lead position and Ron Beehler, a pilot from Gimli, replaced him. We all had confidence in Ron and we never had a problem with him as lead.

Although we did our practice north of Gimli, we would fly to Trenton, Ontario, and use it as the central field for the shows at Toronto and Ottawa. All the aircraft would taxi out in their assigned position. My section was the last four-plane in position. The jetwash from all the aircraft ahead of us really stirred up the air. On takeoff, we would extend our take-off roll to increase our speed; once airborne we cleaned up, gear and flaps up, as soon as we safely could. Depending on the wind direction, we would turn into the wind, the theory being the wind helped dissipate the jet wash away from us. In calm wind conditions, some takeoffs were rather hairy. I recall Dick O'Bryan was on my right wing and as he closed on my aircraft to join the formation, his aircraft started to fall away. I hollered to Dick, "Gang load." There was a puff of smoke indicating his engine had re-lit. Normally, we would "gang load" (put all the fuel switches to the "on" position) so we did not have to worry about changing tanks. Dick forgot and ran the number I tank dry, flaming out as he tried to get into position. Many times, returning from the shows, you would be low on fuel and rather anxious to land. The tower would advise that you were number two or whatever in the flame-out pattern. This was more of a joke than anything else. Everyone always landed safely.

Between air shows at Trenton, we would play golf on the station course. Most of us were duffers, but we had a good time. We were playing one day on a hole that paralleled another with a pond common to both holes. When we approached the pond, a player on the other hole threw his clubs and bag into the water. We all got a great kick out of his action. We were now on the parallel hole and approaching the pond, when the lad who threw his clubs arrived. He removed his shoes and socks, rolled up his pant legs, entered the pond, and began to feel for his clubs. He advised us that he had forgotten his car keys were in his golf bag. Eventually, he was successful in finding his bag. He took out his car keys and threw the bag and clubs back into the pond. It was the highlight of the day, as we finished our game laughing the whole time.

One afternoon, aircraft from both Portage and Gimli flew to Saskatoon for an air show. Altogether we were about thirty-five aircraft. At the time, one runway at Saskatoon was closed for resurfacing, leaving just one serviceable runway. Half the runway had been paved and could be used in an emergency. We landed at Saskatoon with staggered times. Once we were all on the ground, the aircraft were serviced and refuelled. The show was again featuring the "RCAF" formation. The pilots all attended a briefing. Due to the closed runway, we were briefed that on landing, the lead would land on the left side of the runway, while number two would take the right side, the aircraft behind him the left, etc; always staying on the side you were assigned. If you were too close to the aircraft in front, you were to overshoot, but not change your assigned side. This was a standard briefing given before each air show.

The show was well received and the "gaggle" of aircraft approached for landing. All was going well, until one Gimli pilot thought he was too close to the aircraft ahead and elected to land on the opposite side of the runway, rather than overshoot. He did not broadcast his intentions. The aircraft behind was in his turn and could not see the aircraft changing his position. As luck would have it, the third aircraft in this string could see an accident in the making, but he was unable to broadcast because his radios were unserviceable.

Number one landed on his wrong assigned position. Number two was still in his turn and belly-up to number one and therefore could not see him. Number two landed smack on top of number one. The nose wheel of number two went through one of the Plenum doors, which were on either side of the fuselage and would flutter open and closed at low speed to provide air to the engine and heat to escape.

The aircraft were now locked together at about 120 knots. Both aircraft went off the side of the runway creating a large dust cloud. The following aircraft were forced to overshoot due to the lack of visibility. Those of us still airborne did not have enough fuel to divert to another airport. There was a mad scramble in the tower to clear the closed runway of paving equipment so we could land. Once the runway was clear, we fitted ourselves into the circuit and everyone landed safely. The two aircraft in the field were badly damaged but both pilots managed to evacuate their aircraft. Neither had any injury other than pride. Another miracle.

One of the pilots involved in the accident was Leon. He had a student who had a tendency to raise the undercarriage too soon after takeoff. Leon was not happy; he was afraid they would sink back into the ground. Visualize the cockpit: the undercarriage handle is bottom left, the hp fuel cock is right above and forward of the undercarriage lever. The throttle is to the immediate left at about waist level when sitting in the cockpit.

Leon was going to teach his student a lesson. On takeoff the student tried to raise the undercarriage, but he couldn't because Leon had his hand on the handle. The student thought there was something wrong so he closed the throttle. Leon let go of the gear handle and pushed the throttle back up. The student was now really confused. He reached down and closed the hp cock. Leon saw the hp fuel cock closing, but it was too late, the engine flamed out. The student, now totally confused, selected the undercarriage up. The aircraft slid on its belly to a stop, off the end of the runway. Poor Leon was one step behind his student. No one was hurt but we all learned a lesson from the incident. If you plan to do something unorthodox, brief the student so he is not surprised.

Leon was one of the nicest men you would ever want to meet. There were times he reminded me of the comic strip and the lad with a cloud over his head. Things were always happening to him. When we were stationed in Europe, one of our T-33s landed at Ramstein Air Force Base, near Frankfurt. Leon was flown to Ramstein to retrieve the aircraft after it had been repaired. Ramstein was a large U.S. Air Force base and Leon thought he would show the U.S. pilots just how superior our T-33 was to their T-33. The runway was about 10,000 feet long. Leon accelerated, became airborne, and selected gear up. He was planning to keep the aircraft low for the full length of the runway, building up speed for a spectacular pull up. It did not happen. Leon had selected the gear a little early and mushed back onto the runway. Memories of Gimli, but in reverse.

On another occasion, Leon was taking off from Zweibruken, Germany, when he was forced to reject the takeoff. He used hard braking and popped his drag chute to stop the aircraft and he ended up on the side of the runway in a cloud of dust. Unknown to Leon, there was a camera crew taking movies of landing aircraft. The film showed the aircraft leaving the runway and the cloud of dust, which settled about two feet above the ground. In the film, you can see two legs running. Leon had evacuated the aircraft and was getting clear ASAP.

Another group of Gimli pilots were selected to be in a new display formation called "the smokers." It was a group of nine pilots and their T-33 aircraft who would visit small towns, as well as the Toronto and Ottawa air shows, putting on a formation demonstration. Each aircraft was capable of making smoke, which added to the display. Burt Studer, our CO, made it a habit to meet the group after they returned from their weekend show. On one occasion after landing, he put out his hand to shake the lead's hand. Larry Moser answered, "I can't shake your hand, sir; I just shit my pants."

On another occasion, the flight landed in Thunder Bay for fuel, and one of the pilots forgot to unfasten his automatic chute connection. He stood up to leave the aircraft and heard, "pop." His chute opened and he was surrounded in silk. There was no one around to repack the chute so he and a couple of others stuffed the chute back into its container. He flew back to Gimli praying he did not have to use the chute.

Due to the large body of water making up Lake Winnipeg, we had a search-and-rescue boat. Once the ice left the lake, the boat went into the water. Any time flying was in progress, the boat had to patrol the lake. It was also a requirement that an instructor be on board to assist any aircraft in an emergency situation. I spent many enjoyable hours going up and down Lake Winnipeg as an "officer and gentleman." I just sat back and enjoyed myself. There was a barbecue on board and we were always well supplied with steak, potatoes, and all the trimmings. The airman on board did the cooking, I helped in the eating.

I often asked Jesse Wang to come along. Jesse was a nursing sister at the base hospital. We became great friends. Jesse married a Dutch exchange officer. During our tour in Europe we saw a lot of them while visiting back and forth. Jeff, her husband, became the Dutch military attaché in Ottawa, so we saw them quite often during his tour in Ottawa, attending functions with them.

The officers' mess decided that it was time to have a lobster dinner. Calls were made to Station Chatham. Arrangements were made for Chatham to fly the lobsters to Trenton. Gimli was to pick up this delicate delivery by C-45. I was volunteered as captain of the C-45, along with Chuck Harris as my co-pilot. Chuck knew next to nothing about the C-45, but no matter; he was a well-qualified pilot. We landed in Trenton early Thursday evening. The aircraft from Chatham was delayed and did not land until 10 p.m. We had a snack at the officers' mess and left for Gimli at 11 p.m.

It was a beautiful clear night, and we were cruising about 11,000 feet, over the middle of Lake Superior. We were drowsy from a rather long day, when both engines quit. We obviously ran out of fuel. It was customary to burn off the fuel in the nose tank before selecting another tank. We did what was customary, but in our drowsy state we let the nose tank run dry. We quickly switched to the wing tanks. It was necessary to activate a "wobble pump" to build up pressure back in the fuel lines to feed the engines. The pump had to be manually pushed fore and aft several times for this to happen. Finally both engines started up. We were now wide awake and laughing away. The mess enjoyed their lobster supper Friday night.

One other favourite time for a party was the Grey Cup. Winnipeg at that time had a good team. Kenny Ploen was the quarterback and he was very good. The officers' mess was arranged so that two TVs were placed back to back. Those favouring the east would sit on one side while the west sat on the opposite side. Naturally, if your side got a goal there were loud cheers. Beer flowed rather freely and as the game went on, the cheers got louder. All great fun.

Another mess game was "night landings." Most of the officers would be three sheets to the wind and well into their cups. Beer bottles were lined up, simulating a runway. Candles were placed into the empty beer bottles and then a quantity of beer was splashed onto the runway. The vinyl cushions from the chairs were removed and were to be used like a sled. Each would take turns, running, and sliding down the runway, cheered on by all those present. The aim was to go straight and not hit any of the beer bottles. Not many succeeded.

While we were living in barracks, one of our instructors knocked on his friend's door and knowing he was in his room, he opened the door. He found his friend dead from a self-inflicted shotgun blast. This individual was always the life of any party and he relished being the maître d' at mess functions. No note was ever found or reason given as to why he took his own life. I often thought how much easier it would have been for him to sign out a T-33, climb to altitude, put the aircraft in a steep dive and cross his arms as he crashed into Lake Winnipeg. No one would have ever known it was suicide.

One problem that became apparent in the early days of the T-33 was that the aircraft had a tendency to "tumble." It was caused by gross mishandling of the controls. We had some students who claimed that they were in a tumble. We, as instructors would take the same aircraft up and attempt to get into a tumble; we never succeeded.

It was determined that with a certain fuel load, low speed and nose high attitude, combined with gross mishandling of the controls was probably the reason the tumble occurred. All you had to do for recovery is to take your feet off the rudders, fold your arms, and let the aircraft do its thing. Altitude permitting, the aircraft would soon settle into a recognizable position from which you could recover.

Each flight had a "rumble book." Students were fined a dollar or two for any infraction that incurred either on the ground or in the air. When they graduated, the monies in the pot would go towards beer for the grad party. Willy, our flight commander, entered the flight after having flown with a student. He was white as a sheet and he grabbed the rumble book and wrote, "Did a spin instead of a stall—$20." It was the highest fine ever paid by a student during my time at Gimli. Willy was caught unprepared when the student entered a spin rather than the stall.

I had a similar incident when I was adjutant. I was asked to do a check ride on one of the Danish students. We proceeded to the aerobatic area and I asked the student to perform his aerobatic sequence. I bent forward to turn the ADF (automatic direction finder) to the "off" position. This was standard procedure. The moment I bent over the student pulled about 5 G and I could not move. He completed his sequence and asked me how it was. I actually did not see any part of his aerobatic display; I was bent over. I told him it was just fine.

All officers had to take their turn as orderly officer. You were on duty for twenty-four hours. During the quiet hours you would have a room in the barracks; the phone always seemed to ring just as you were getting to sleep.

One of our duties was ensuring that the different messes closed the bar at the assigned hour. I entered the airwomen's mess to close the bar when a voice said, "You're having a drink with me." It was Bimbo, the Harvard parachute fitter. I said, "Yes, Ma'am!" I was not going to start an argument with Bimbo. I would be the loser in more ways than one. I had a beer with her and then closed the mess, with no argument.

One of my students was Paul Irwine. He was not a very good pilot. I tried very hard to get him up to standard. I was about to go on leave to get married and another instructor took him over. When

I arrived back from our honeymoon, a month later, our flight commander smiled at me and said, "He's yours again." Apparently, Paul went through every instructor in the flight. Now he was back with me. I really do not know how, but he actually graduated.

Years later, I arrived for my first day of ground school with Air Canada. Paul was sitting in the front row. He smiled at me, and I told him I could not believe that he was still alive. He chuckled. Paul passed the course and retired as an Air Canada captain. Miracles do happen.

Chapter Twelve

A New Beginning – Marriage

Judy and I were married on October 3, 1959, in Saint John, New Brunswick. The weather in Saint John had been foggy for many days prior to our wedding and our wedding day was no different. The fog was thick as soup. When the ceremony was completed, Judy and I walked down the aisle smiling like two very happy people. The church door opened and the sun shone in. We looked up and saw the clouds rapidly disappearing. No day ever felt so good.

Our relatives and friends did a number on our car, which was decorated from front to end with little plastic airplanes and many references to "amateur night."

The reception was at the Royal Hotel, followed by a party at Judy's home. Judy changed into travelling clothes; we climbed into our vehicle, waved good-bye, and headed towards Calais, Maine. We had a few cars follow us beyond the city limits, honking horns and generally giving us a rousing send-off. We stopped along the way and removed the small aircraft from the car and stopped at two service stations to get the car washed. Each station looked at the car, smiled, and made up an excuse as to why they could not wash it. Eventually, a service station in St. Stephen took pity on us and washed the car. There were no automatic car washes in those days.

We found our motel and proceeded to look over the town of Calais for a place to have dinner. Imagine our surprise to find Ivan and Betty Hashey in the same restaurant. Ivan and I had been great friends growing up. We were unable to attend each other's wedding because they both took place on the same day and at the same time. Naturally we were all smiles and nervous, to say the least.

Dinner over, Judy and I proceeded to our motel where we had an enjoyable evening. I woke up shortly after midnight with an unbelievable thirst. Water did not do the trick. I recalled seeing a service station on our drive around town that had a Coke machine outside the door. I snuck out of the motel and headed for the station to purchase a Coke. Approaching the station, a car passed me going in the opposite direction. There was a sound of breaking glass. I thought nothing of it at the time. I put my money into the machine and retrieved my Coke. I could see a police car with its flashing lights reflecting in the window. I turned around and a police officer wanted to know why I threw a bottle out the window. I told him that I had not, but the car passing me in the opposite direction had thrown something out the window, which could have been a bottle. The officer was skeptical. Here I am in front of a Coke machine in the middle of the night, explaining that I had been married that morning and I had awoken with a terrible thirst. In the meantime, Judy had woken up and found me gone. She figured I was a hit and run. The officer obviously had never heard a story like mine and gave me the benefit of the doubt and let me go, but he followed me back to the motel. I had no key, so I knocked on the door. Initially, Judy was reluctant to let me in. I had a policeman at my back and a locked door in my face. Judy finally let me in, but I had some explaining to do. We later had a good laugh. The next morning we went for breakfast. Ivan and Betty were there as well. Everyone had sheepish grins on their faces. Quite a twenty-four hours.

That day we drove towards Washington, DC. In Washington we visited the Mint, the Smithsonian Museum, and had a tour of the White House. General Eisenhower was president at that time. Our trip from Washington took us north towards Winnipeg and finally, Gimli. I even managed to avoid driving through Chicago.

We lived in a "winterized" summer cottage. Hah! The cottage was about twenty minutes from the base and right on the shore of Lake Winnipeg, in an area called Sandy Hook. All we had for heat was an oil stove, which only heated an area of about two feet around the heater itself. We had a kitten and if we fed it a small dish of milk and it was not consumed right away, the milk would crystallize. The electrical plugs were all covered in about a half inch of frost throughout the winter. I would come home from the base and Judy and I would have supper huddled around the oil heater. We would then heat water for the hot water bottle and jump into bed. Every blanket we owned plus sleeping bags covered the bed; it was the only way to get warm.

We had running water but we had to run for it. There was a well outside the front door. It had about a three-inch pipe into the well that was frozen for about four to five feet. Judy would heat water in the kettle and then pour it slowly into the pipe while I tried to break the ice with a long, steel pry bar. Eventually, I would break through the frozen ice and quickly shove a garden hose down the pipe. The hose itself was attached to a small electric pump. I would stay by the well and Judy would fill an old tea chest, which was our storage tank. Once full, I would quickly remove the hose and drain it; things were starting to freeze by this time. We followed this procedure about once a week. In order to preserve water, we would pour the water from our hot water bottle back into the kettle, heat it and jump right back into bed. We did have an indoor toilet, a "honey bucket" in a small closet. I was always chastised for not "going" at the base. Heck, how was I to know when Mother Nature would call? Judy, being a nurse, volunteered to dump the contents on a daily basis—he says with tongue in cheek. Heck, she was the nurse.

One morning, I walked into the "kitchen" and slid across the floor. The tea chest had sprung a leak. The water had frozen on the floor and all the way up to the spout of the tea chest.

Judy and I were snug in our bed early one Saturday morning when there was a rather loud knock on our front door. I quickly put on a pair of pants and noticed it was just starting to get daylight. I staggered to the door, opened it, and there were two old and rather grubby looking individuals wearing toques displaying the RCMP badges; one of them I recognized. Paul Hughes was a couple of years behind me in school but lived near to us, so I knew him very well. He and his fellow RCMP officer had spent the night investigating a fatal car crash involving an airman from Gimli. They had completed their investigation and since no restaurants were open in the town, they came to us for breakfast. We fed them, had a good chat, and sent them on their way.

On another occasion during the spring breakup, we were woken by what sounded like dynamite exploding. I got up and looked out the windows but could see nothing because of the darkness. In the morning when we looked out the window, there was ice piled up on our lawn, about fifteen feet from our door. The ice was at least ten to fifteen feet high. What we had heard was the ice on Lake Winnipeg breaking up. The afternoon and evening before was clear but cool and the ice on the lake was flat with some ice ridges.

Dr. Warner, a retired dentist, was the owner of our cottage. He would be nice as pie one day and the exact opposite the next day. The dentist kept several animals, mainly goats and one fawn. Naturally, Judy was attracted to the animals and she spent quite a bit of time with them. Judy was particularly fond of the fawn, which grew rapidly. She would go into the enclosure and hand-feed him, all the while with the small goats nipping at her legs. The deer sensed Judy was not a threat and she could hug him, or pat him.

It was great having the animals so close. Judy could visit on a daily basis and amuse herself while I was away at the base. By spring, Judy was looking rather pregnant and the deer had developed a great set of antlers. The deer would place his head on Judy's tummy and the antlers would surround her. I was afraid the deer might just decide to tear her open with his antlers, but he was as gentle as a lamb.

We thoroughly enjoyed our "winterized" cottage, but it was obvious we had to find accommodation with a few amenities, like heat and water, before Dave was born. Whenever a wife was pregnant, she was referred to as having "one in the hangar." Once the child was born he/she was now considered "on the ramp."

When we were first married, Judy felt she had to get up with me and cook me a big breakfast. I am a morning person and never had any trouble getting out of bed. Judy is not a morning person. Naturally, I enjoyed a good breakfast, not at 5:30, but around ten in the morning. I finally convinced Judy to stay in bed while I ate a light breakfast, and since there was no point in her getting up with me, she finally agreed. During my air force career we would snack four to five times a day at work, not really sitting down for a big lunch. Supper was the meal of the day. If we wanted to go to the mess for lunch, mess protocol required us to strip off our flying suits and put on a uniform. The protocol was eventually relaxed and we could have lunch in our flying gear. Each flight had a small canteen with hot dogs, soup, etc. It was more convenient to snack in the flight.

Our neighbours at Sandy Hook were Sandy, a technician from the base, and his wife. We enjoyed their company. One weekend in late July we decided to go fishing. Our destination was three lakes straight north from Gimli, where the road ended. Two of the lakes were St. George and St. David, the third lake name escapes me. Judy and I had purchased a tent when we bought the sleeping bags to help keep us warm. It was a package deal from Sears.

We had our Ford and Sandy had an older Mercedes. All the gear was loaded into the cars and away we went, arriving at Lake St. David in the early afternoon. After the tent was set up and the supplies were put away, the fishing poles came out. It did not take long to catch whitefish from the lake, which were six to eight pounds each. We hooked them onto a fish chain, tied it to a small dock, and placed them back in the lake. It was starting to get late so we decided to get supper ready and clean the fish the next day.

We knew that there were bear in the area so we put all the fresh food into the trunks of both cars. By now it was dark, so we decided to call it a day and settled into our tent for the night. Judy was pregnant at this time with David. Like all pregnant women, Judy had to pee a couple of times during the night. The wind was blowing quite hard so she did not venture too far from the tent. The next morning I woke to find that there was a hole in the tent over my head. I thought it was rather strange. By now everyone was waking up and I went outside to see how the hole got there. It did not take us long to figure it out. The side of the tent was covered with paw prints—bear paw prints. We thought the bear must have bitten into the seam of the canvas and ripped the hole in the tent. We also noticed that the trunks of the cars were covered with mud and scratched as well. The bear obviously smelled the food locked in the trunks. What we could not figure out was why the bear just stopped chewing on the tent and not had one of us for a snack. Our only conclusion was that he must have heard a strange sound that made him back off. The only strange sound we could think of, besides our snoring, was when Judy raised the zipper on the tent to go potty. That sound must have scared him off, but the bear did not leave empty handed. When we went to retrieve our fish there was nothing but the heads left; he had eaten them all. Discretion being the better part of valour, we packed up and left for home.

Gordie Keith and his wife, Laurette, also became great friends. Laurette was also a nurse so she and Judy hit it off from day one. At the time Laurette had one child and Judy would often babysit for them. When Dave was born, they often babysat for each other.

Gord had been at Gimli for about three years and was due for a posting. To his delight, he was given a CF-100 transition course, followed by a squadron posting to Saint-Hubert, just outside of Montreal. Judy and I were sad to see them go, but that was military life; every three years or so you moved on to a new station, often encountering old friends and renewing friendships.

Gord and his navigator took off from Saint-Hubert one rather dark and dreary evening. Radio contact with them was lost and it was assumed that their radios had failed. When they became overdue, the worst was suspected, but no wreckage was ever found. One of the first things I did when I was posted to Ottawa was ask for the accident report on Gord and his navigator. It stated that the probable cause was that the pilot had misread his altimeter by 10,000 feet. I have mentioned before that the old altimeters were easy to misread. It was assumed the aircraft flew into the St. Lawrence River; nothing was ever found. The investigation pointed out that the pilot on different occasions during simulator training did misread his altimeter. As I mentioned earlier, I did the same thing during a simulator trip at Portage. My instructor made me do extra time and continually asked me to give him my altitude. It worked because I never misread an altimeter again. The altimeters we used were the same as those used during the war. Technology increased the speed of the new aircraft; climbs and descents were so quick we could get to altitude or descend rapidly. The lag in the old altimeters was such that they could not keep up to the manoeuvres we were engaged in. Eventually, new altimeters were introduced, but not before many lives were lost. We wrote Laurette but never received any answer. The accident happened in 1963–64. Laurette had three children.

After I left the service, we moved to Dollard-des-Ormeaux, a suburb of Montreal. Judy had asked me to pick up a few things from the grocery store for her, and I was coming around a corner and hit another cart coming from the other direction. It was Laurette. We were both surprised to see each other. Gossip was exchanged. Laurette said all the boys were fine and that she was engaged to be married. Her new husband was Ron Doucette, a super nice guy. The three boys kept their dad's name. They had just bought a home in Dollard and it turned out it was just around the corner from our own home. The boys became re-acquainted. Judy and Laurette caught up on the past and they were back to kid sitting again. We often camped together and Ron and I would go on the odd fishing trip together. Ron and Laurette now live in Brookes, Alberta. Laurette is retired while Ron works for an oil well company. Judy and I visited with them when we did our trailer trip to Alaska. Small world.

Normally, just before my student was to graduate and receive the coveted wings, I would take him on a long cross-country trip. We would fly from Gimli to Calgary and fill the aircraft with fuel. Once airborne again, we would fly across the Rocky Mountains at a low level, weather permitting. It was great fun. We would descend into valleys with speeds in excess of 450 knots and soar up over the hills. The next stop was Vancouver where, again, we would refuel. After takeoff, we would stay at a low level and proceed along the coast to Victoria and fly to the north end of Vancouver Island, then south along the coast. The trip was planned to land at RCAF Comox, British Columbia, in time for beer call. Next morning we would fly directly to Gimli. I have met several of my students over the years and they all remembered our trip to Comox and back.

In the spring of 1960, I was given a job at ground school. I was told one of the subjects I would be teaching the cadets was geopolitics. I asked for a dictionary to find out what it meant. Actually, the subject was very interesting and the more I read the more I enjoyed geopolitics. I also gave lectures on escape and evasion. These lectures prepared pilots transferred to Europe on what to do in the event a pilot found himself behind the Iron Curtain, those countries under communist domination. There were several cases of the eastern bloc military trying to lure pilots to fly in a direction ending up in communist territory. The communist controllers spoke excellent English, but to my knowledge never succeeded in their actions, although there is one case where a Canadian Sabre took off and disappeared. The aircraft was never found and the pilot is still reported as missing.

Each new pilot arriving in Europe had to complete an E and

E (escape and evasion) exercise. The pilots would be driven to an area at night, given a map and a marked destination. Some pilots joined up for travel while others preferred to travel alone. French and American troops were assigned the task of capturing the pilots. If captured, the pilot was handcuffed, bag over the head and placed in a holding cell. The cells were well lit with music playing loudly.

After a few hours alone, the pilot would be led to a room for interrogation. Techniques used were tried and true, good cop, bad cop. Some pilots were stripped and a hose with cold water used on them. Some pilots could not take the interrogation and they would be taken back to their base. Several actually suffered both physical and mental abuse from some of the interrogators, who got a bit carried away. The exercises were very well run and many pilots learned a great deal about themselves. By the time I arrived in Europe on the 104, the escape and evasion was cancelled. We were told that too much money had been invested in our training to have us hurt on an escape and evasion exercise. Most of us were disappointed that we could not do the exercise.

I was also required to review current events with the students. I enjoyed my time in ground school. It gave me confidence to stand in front of a group of people and teach. While I missed not having a student to fly with, I knew that this secondary job, if I did it well, would look good on my record.

I finished my six months in ground school and fully expected to return to line flying. The officer in charge of the flying school on my arrival was W/C Ken Lett. He was replaced by W/C Lloyd Liggett, who asked me if I would like to become adjutant of the flying school.

W/C Liggett never had a full-time student, but he would go from flight to flight to fly with students and observe the instructors. He arrived at "B" flight to fly with a student in a four-plane formation that I was leading. He was not in a very good mood. As the lead of the flight, I was required to outline what we would be doing. I also reviewed the hand/head signals to be used in the event of a radio failure. If, as lead, someone did lose radios, I would advise the other aircraft in the formation that we were reverting to hand signals. The formation took off and flew to our practice area. I asked the formation to change from a finger formation to line astern. Nothing happened. I had lost my radios. During the next hour or so, I gave

F-86 Sabre I flew at Gimli while instructing on T-33.
RCAF

hand and head signals and we were able to complete our exercise. On our return to the field, I, again by hand signals, gave the lead to number three in the formation and I assumed the number four position. The tower was advised I was NORDO (no radio) and gave me the green Aldis light for landing clearance. The W/C was thrilled that the whole exercise was completed by hand and head signals. He patted me on the back and gave me a thumbs-up. This exercise was flown before I went to ground school. I must have left a good impression.

I would not have a regular student, but I would do the final tests on clear-hood, formation, and instrument flying, for students nearing the end of their training and approaching graduation. I accepted the position. I was given an office next to the W/C; I was also in charge of the orderly room. There were six airmen/airwomen in the orderly room and two civilians.

There was a lot of paperwork to be completed for each student. I was the go-between for the W/C and the different flights of the school, as well as training command headquarters. I would remind them when reports were due and they, in turn, would ask me for direction on perhaps a weak student or a transfer, etc. In addition, I was in charge of the graduation parades, which were held every six weeks. I would drill the students and we would review the protocol required when they received their wings.

Another aspect of being adjutant was that on many occasions

the PADO (station personnel administrative officer) would be away on leave or taking a course. I would replace him while he was away. The PADO position was interesting. Anyone who wanted to see the CO had to go through me for permission. The orderly room was five times larger than the flight-line orderly room because they were dealing with all of the station personnel while on the flight line I had only students to look after.

Ken Peck was the station PADO and would give me a good briefing before he would leave. I was told there were situations outlined in a book in the safe that might come in handy when dealing with the station personnel. I reviewed the book contents and the information soon came in handy. An airwoman knocked on my door and asked if she could speak to me privately. Naturally, I said okay. I closed the CO's and orderly room doors while she closed the door to the hallway. When I asked her what I could do for her, she started to cry and said, "I'm pregnant." Luckily the "book" covered this situation. I called the base hospital and a station nurse arrived to take care of the young lady. I was twenty-three years old but learning quickly. On another day, shortly after payday, a senior sergeant asked to see me. He entered my office, and as he had been instructed by the regular PADO, he had to advise where his money went (i.e., how much he paid on his bills, groceries, etc). I felt bad having to listen to him. He was twice my age and had served during the war. He had trouble handling money and the PADO had set up a protocol to help him out.

Normally, over the weekends, many airmen got drunk and into fights. Charges would be laid and the individual involved had to report to the CO to hear his/her punishment. The CO and I would put our caps on. I would march the offender into the CO's office. I would read the charge and the CO would ask a few questions and render the punishment. Usually the punishment was a fine or confinement to base for a few weekends, with no bar privileges.

The CO, Bert Studer, would usually get us both a cup of coffee after the proceedings and talk things over. He was a fine CO and a gentleman. I learned a lot from him.

One incident that shows the leadership of Bert Studer was when the AOC (Air Officer Training Command) issued a letter to all commanding officers. The letter was in response to a series of accidents and incidents that happened at the three T-33 stations. The letter (in effect, the Riot Act), stated that all COs would gather their instructors together and read the letter to them. The letter stated that any instructor having an accident or incident would be court marshalled. We were all gathered in a hangar and the CO read the letter as directed. He then said he had full confidence in every instructor and that everyone was doing an excellent job. Then Group Commander Studer crumpled the AOC's letter and threw it on the floor. He cancelled flying for the day and opened the bar. Stations Portage and MacDonald continued to have a series of incidents. Gimli did not. Leadership by our CO proved the difference.

On many occasions I had to attend social functions as part of the job, and Judy was expected to attend. We were always the youngest and I the most junior officer. It was all good experience, and I knew I was being observed and groomed for more responsibilities. I wanted the permanent commission and was happy to accept extra duties.

One afternoon the W/C received a phone call. I could hear him say, "Are you sure? Okay." My office was next to his and the door was open, so I heard his side of the conversation. I just knew something was wrong. I entered his office and he had his head in his hands. He looked up, and said, "Close the door." The call had been from Deer Lodge Hospital in Winnipeg. He was told that he had leukemia and had three months to live. He was in shock; heck, so was I. He could not believe that the doctor had called him and told him over the phone, which was rather insensitive on the doctor's part. We chatted for about ten minutes, when the phone rang. He listened for a moment or two, and then proceeded to give the caller a piece of his mind. He did not hold back. Slamming the receiver down he said, "That was the doc, from Deer Lodge; he said there was a mix up on the tests and mine was okay but another Liggett had leukemia." Needless to say, he was upset with mixed emotions; happy for himself but saddened for the other individual. We closed up shop early and went to the officers' mess where I bought him a beer.

I was busy in my office on the flight line late one Friday afternoon, when headquarters called. I was advised that two seats were available on the new CL-44 Yukon, for a trip to 1-Wing Marville, France, Saturday night for five days. Headquarters said they needed two names

ASAP. I gave them mine and went to the mess where I knew everyone was gathering for Friday night beer call. I explained the proposal to the W/C and he agreed I could go. Cy Leadbeater heard the conversation and "volunteered." I called headquarters with Cy's name, and we both headed for home to give the news to our wives and pack.

The next morning we flew a T-Bird to Trenton, Ontario. We parked the aircraft and proceeded to the transport lounge. The flight left early in the evening and we landed in France around six in the morning. We were given a bedroom, had a rest, and proceeded to the mess for a beer and supper. Both Cy and I were anxious to go to Paris. We picked the brains of everyone about train schedules, where to stay, etc. We were told loud and clear to bring our own booze; Paris was expensive. We purchased two bottles of rye for about $3 each at the PX.

Next morning we were driven to the rail station. Neither of us had ever been to Paris and we did not know what to expect, but we were excited. We rode along to the clickety-clack of the train, enjoying the scenery. We thought it would be a good idea to have a short drink. The car was occupied by an older gentleman, tam and all. He had just pulled a loaf of French bread and some cold cuts out of a bag for his lunch. We chuckled away making remarks about his sandwich and nipping on our rye. Suddenly, in perfect English, the gentleman asked us if we were enjoying our drink. Naturally, we offered him one, which he accepted. He told us that after Paris was liberated, because of his fluency in English, he had a job with the Allies as an interpreter. The gentleman said he was now a professor at a university and was on his way to Paris for a conference. We enjoyed his company and he gave us hints on what to see in the big city.

We arrived in Paris and found our hotel. We dropped our bags off and proceeded to make the best of our three days in Paris. We walked for miles and had our dinner. By this time we were thirsty and, going on the advice of the lads at Marville, we went back to our hotel. In order to reach the hotel there was a long alleyway that opened onto the hotel grounds. The entrance was locked so we rang the bell. Eventually an older man arrived and let us in. We nipped up to our room, had another drink or two, and left for more sightseeing. We returned to the hotel a couple of times before we called it a night.

Next morning we awoke fresh and ready to hit the pavement. We had our breakfast in the hotel and went back to our rooms to wash up. We arrived to find our bags packed and outside our room. Even the lock had been changed. We took the hint. I guess the old lad complained and wanted us out. He did not like our comings and goings, which tired him out.

The desk staff was very nice. They even made a reservation for us in Place Pigalle. The room was nicer at our new digs. That evening, we went to the Crazy Horse Café. It was packed. The waiter would come through with a tray of drinks in one hand and a stool in another. He would push people aside, drop the stool and point his finger to someone standing; room for one more. We eventually ended up next to an American couple, with whom we chatted. It was so crowded the man's wife looked at us and said, "You know I could be raped and I wouldn't even know who did it." We did our hotel return trip throughout the evening with no complications.

On our last day in Paris we walked for miles. That evening we went to the world famous Lido, on the Champs-Elysees, the main drag of Paris. The cover charge was a bottle of champagne. We agreed to split the cost and went in to see the show. (To get some idea of the show, Google Paris nightclubs, click on Lido, the English version, sit back, and enjoy.) The show was beautiful. Full of gorgeous girls on swings, bare breasted and with little else for clothing. Songs were sung; a one-act play took place, and there was even a comedian whom we did not understand but laughed at anyway. It was a most enjoyable and eye-opening experience for both of us. We slept well that night. The train back to Marville left around one in the afternoon, so we were able to have a leisurely breakfast, pack, pay our bill, and walk to the train station. We flew back to Trenton the next day, where we picked up our T-33 and headed back to Gimli, weary but happy, after a truly wonderful experience.

My flight commander Willy A. had two houses, one on the lake and one in the town of Gimli. He was moving to the larger place and we were lucky enough to rent the house on the lake. Move-in date was late August 1960. Judy and I did not have much to pack so we were able to enjoy the cottage and lake for another month before we moved into the town of Gimli. Our new house had a garage and a lovely backyard that backed on a breakwater on the shores of Lake Winnipeg. We now had running water and a furnace—what a treat. The town itself was not large. Gimli was originally an Icelandic settlement. The civilians made their living by fishing in Lake Winnipeg and trading with local First Nations bands.

Judy was able to go back to nursing at the Johnson Memorial Hospital. Indians arrived by boat in the summer and snowmobile or dog team in the winter. It was not unusual to see a dog team in the middle of the lake in winter.

The grocery store contained a butcher, whom we got to know quite well. When he saw me coming he would say, "How many and how thick?" The steak was very good.

Somehow or other we acquired a dog, Mugsy, who was a Heinz 57. She was a very good pet but caused problems when she was in heat. Dogs came from everywhere to get at her. I would climb onto the garage roof and when the dogs started to assemble, I would let fly with the hose, scattering them in all directions. It was great fun. The house had black-speckled tile floors which were a bugger to keep clean. Mugsy solved the problem nicely. Anything that hit the floor was licked up. Our furniture was mostly orange crates.

Judy kept busy with her hospital duties while we waited for David's birth. One evening, we were in bed and I sensed movement under the blankets. I woke Judy and told her, "I think you are having the baby." She looked at the blankets as well, lifted them up, and there was the dog trying to get into a comfortable position. I will never live that down.

Judy was finally admitted and was treated like royalty by the nuns whom she had worked with and who ran the hospital. During her stay in hospital all she wanted was chocolate cake, chips, and anything sweet. David was born October 28, 1960. He was blond and blue-eyed and cute as a button. Judy asked me what I thought of him; I said, "He has a great nose for an oxygen mask." Wrong thing to say.

Dave was three months old when, with Chuck as my co-pilot, I was asked to operate an Expeditor to Winnipeg via Portage la Prairie, where we were to drop off a couple of passengers. After Portage la Prairie, we were to proceed to Winnipeg and leave the aircraft for maintenance. Station Winnipeg did the maintenance on all our Gimli Expeditor aircraft. Another Expeditor was tasked to pick up passengers in Winnipeg and wait for us to arrive from Portage. It was our ride back to Gimli.

We were running a bit late from Portage. After we landed in Winnipeg, I could see the other Expeditor waiting for us with the engines running. The aircraft was in the parking area, approximately 300 feet from Runway 36, the active runway. Harry was the captain of the other Expeditor. As I taxied into the parking area, Harry had his window open and was pointing at his watch. He was anxious to return to Gimli. I had to enter the maintenance hangar, sign over the aircraft to Station Winnipeg and write up a few minor snags. I then hustled to the waiting aircraft. Chuck was already on board. I climbed on board and, as I was closing the door, the aircraft started to taxi. Harry had obviously asked for taxi clearance as soon as he saw me approaching the aircraft.

All the seats were full and I was ushered to the co-pilot seat. By the time I sat down, Harry had take-off clearance and the power came on as I was strapping into the seat. I had completed putting my lap strap on as the aircraft became airborne. Harry asked for gear up, which I selected. I had my hand on my shoulder strap when the right engine fire warning light came on. I let the strap go and turned to observe the right engine telling Harry there was no sign of flame or smoke. But by this time Harry had reached up and feathered the engine. I saw the airspeed was fewer than 80 knots. Minimum speed for single engine on the Expeditor was 80 knots. I knew we were in trouble.

My first action was to advise the tower of our problem. Harry tried to make a turn back to the runway. The aircraft started making noises I had never heard before on an aircraft, and the airframe started to shake. We were approaching the stall. I hollered at Harry to stop the turn, which he was already in the process of doing. Throughout this time I kept the tower apprised of our problem and I also advised the passengers that we were going to land in a field and to tighten their belts and brace themselves. I was busy assisting the captain, talking to the tower, and forgot to fasten my own shoulder harness. The tower was able to dispatch rescue and fire vehicles to the site from the information I was giving to them.

C-45 Expeditor Accident, December 28, 1960.
RCAF

Everything happened rather fast. The engine was feathered at about 300 feet and we hit the frozen ground, wheels up, at about 78 knots, or 92 mph, ripping off the antennas and losing our radios. We slid for a few hundred feet. I looked up and saw Duff Roblin's bypass flood relief ditch. (Roblin was the premier of the province of Manitoba and was instrumental in having these large ditches build around Winnipeg to divert water during the spring floods.)

We slid up a slight rise. I had visions that we would crash into the face of the other side of the ditch. Luck was on our side, and we had enough momentum to fly over the ditch and land on the down slope of the ditch. By this time our speed was very low and we hit rather hard. During the time from when we first hit the ground and flew over the ditch then hitting the ground again, we were tossed around quite harshly.

When we finally came to a stop, we fired the engine fire extinguishers, shut the battery off, and exited the aircraft in a hurry. At this point I noticed my shoulder harness had never been fastened. I assume I had released the strap when I first looked at the engine. After that, things were happening rather fast and I forgot to attach the shoulder straps. During our ride along the ground, I recall the control column moving quite violently from side to side and hitting my knee.

Except for my knee being smacked, everyone was okay. Rescue and fire trucks arrived and we were taken to hospital, where we were asked if we were okay, but never examined. The only complaint was from me about my knee being hit as we rode along the ground. The date was December 28, 1960. It is hard to believe that the accident happened over fifty years ago.

Most accidents happen by inattention or not following regular procedures. Ours was no exception. The Expeditor manual stated that if the engines were at idle power for more than twenty minutes on the ground, the engine power should be increased for two to three minutes to clear carbon on the plugs. The times given are from memory and it has been a long time since I flew the Expeditor. It was surmised that the captain had neglected to run up the engines; consequently we had the fire warning light. In addition, if he had waited another few seconds before feathering the engine our airspeed would probably have been in excess of 80 knots and we could have made a successful turn and land with the single engine. Hindsight is a wonderful thing.

Time seemed to pass very quickly. Judy was busy with Dave and I had my duties at the base. I arrived home one night and Judy said to Dave, "Walk to Daddy." The little guy got up off his butt and walked to me. He was seven months old. I certainly was surprised. He was a going concern and just never stopped. Just following him around from one disaster after the other was exhausting. Eighteen months later Bryan arrived on the scene, April 8, 1962.

One afternoon, Judy and I were sitting outside on a beautiful summer day overlooking Lake Winnipeg. A sailboat passed by, arms waving, and we waved back. I knew it was Cy Leadbeater and Tex Johnson. Tex owned the boat and Cy wanted to buy it, so Tex was giving Cy lessons. Later in the afternoon we had a terrific thunderstorm. I was hoping Cy and Tex were back at the dock.

I arrived at the base early next morning and was advised that both Cy and Tex were missing and a search was being organized. I immediately asked for the C-45 to help in the search. I gathered up airmen to fill the seats to look for our missing friends. The aircraft had a full fuel load so we were able to stay airborne for about four hours. Nothing was spotted. On landing I was advised that the CFI wanted to see me ASAP. I went to his office and he advised me that my currency on the C-45 had lapsed and that I should not have taken the aircraft. I was ticked at his attitude. I told him I just completed four hours of searching over Lake Winnipeg and I now considered myself current. I got up and left before I said or did something that I would live to regret. End of conversation.

I was preparing to leave for another search pattern when I was advised that the sailboat had been found and two bodies recovered by the search-and-rescue boat. It was a sad few days.

Cy's wife, Mary Jane, had her sister, who was pregnant, living with them. At that time if a girl got pregnant out of wedlock, she was sent away to have her baby. The baby would normally be put up for adoption or a relative would raise the child. Mary Jane's sister had decided that the baby was to be put up for adoption. Judy and I discussed adopting the baby if it was a girl; we had Dave and Bryan and we both wanted a girl. We approached Cy and family and they concurred. If the baby was a boy, Cy and Mary Jane would adopt the baby. Mary Jane's sister's baby was a boy.

It was a real tragedy. Cy had drowned and his wife and sister-in-law were forced to put the baby up for adoption. Judy actually drove the sister to the adoption agency in Winnipeg. A few years later we heard that Mary Jane had remarried. We often wonder what became of the baby.

We had a priest from Ireland on the base. He was a small man and reminded everyone of a pixie. He would often come around and visit the parishioners. Everyone had a bottle of Irish whiskey. Father would be asked if he wanted a drink; he always politely declined. We would say, "Father, it's Irish whiskey." He would get a twinkle in his eye as he slowly opened his thumb and forefinger, "Well, then, just a little bit."

In the summer months when he would be on leave, he was replaced by a priest from Ottawa, Dillon Cahill. Dillon was a physics teacher at St. Patrick's School in Ottawa. He was a bit of a character but very likable. He thought nothing of knocking on your door at eleven in the evening with an armload of wine, French bread, and cheese. We always invited him in and we had many great cheese fondues.

During our tour in Ottawa, we tracked him down and visited back and forth. One evening, we were invited along with his many friends for a beef fondue in his laboratory. The room had egg cartons on the walls and ceiling to enhance the sound of his very good record player. He had a wide variety of good music. The small fondue pots were heated over Bunsen burners. The atmosphere and the very nice people made for a memorable evening.

In the spring of 1962, the CF-104 Starfighter was about to be introduced to the RCAF. The 104 was a Mach II aircraft and, although originally designed as a high level fighter aircraft, in typical Canadian mentality we were going to use the aircraft in the low level, strike role. The aircraft was destined for the European bases and would be equipped with nuclear weapons.

In my capacity as adjutant, I was well aware of the new aircraft and I wanted to get in on the ground floor of the introduction. I had spent nearly four years at Gimli and I was due for a transfer. I applied for the 104 course. Initially, command stated that only pilots with squadron experience need apply. I, as well as many others, thought this very unfair. We as a group, non squadron, proved our ability day after day in our instructor duties. The policy was soon changed to allow pipeline pilots to apply. My application was recommended and endorsed by both Group Commander Studer and Wing Commander Liggett.

Lloyd Liggett passed away in the fall of 2010 at the age of 93. I always regretted not having been able to sit down with him for a chat.

Chapter Thirteen

On the Move – Chatham and Cold Lake

It was July 1962, and I was to report to Station Chatham, New Brunswick, for low-level training on the F-86 Sabre in August 1962.

Judy and I had a busy few weeks to pack up and arrange for storage of our furniture and things. I was able to secure space on an RCAF aircraft for Judy and the boys to fly to Trenton, Ontario. In Trenton, Judy and the boys boarded a train for the Maritimes, where they would be living with Judy's parents until I was able to acquire accommodations in Chatham.

The officers' mess had a "mug party" for me and wished me well in all future endeavours. I loaded up our trusty Volkswagen, and Mugsy and I were off to the East. No motel would allow me to have the dog in the room along the route, so I slept in the car to keep Mugsy happy. I awoke early one morning near what was then known as the Lakehead (now Thunder Bay). I had breakfast and stopped for gas. I paid my bill but I was unable to open the driver's door. Before I gassed up, I had locked the door with keys in the ignition. The station attendant said, "Try the passenger door." I told him I had locked it last night. He was nice enough to get me a clothes hanger. We pushed and prodded, but still the door would not open. The dog was frantic to get out. The attendant suggested again, that I try the passenger door. I walked around to the passenger door, pulled on the handle and it opened; I had not locked it after all. Mugsy was happy to be free to have a pee. The attendant and I both had a good laugh and the dog and I went on our way. The rest of the trip was uneventful, and I arrived in Saint John safe and sound. It was good to see Judy and the boys and the rest of the family. I spent about a week in Saint John before heading for Chatham.

My course was scheduled for three months. I managed to find and rent a twenty-four-foot travel trailer, which was to be our new home for the duration of the course.

Once everyone had settled in, I started the F-86 conversion. The course was great fun. We flew low level all over northern New Brunswick and I mean low level; most of time the trees were higher than we were. In addition to scaring all the animals, we would fly over the Northumberland Strait and Prince Edward Island. The fishermen were not happy with us. We would fly below the height of their masts, which gave them a fright when we passed by. We would wave and they would give us the friendly finger.

We were given targets to find, which entailed studying maps to find the best approach to the target. The goal was to be on time, on target. One of the instructors would circle the target marking our times as we crossed the selected spot. It was not difficult, but it was noticed that in order to cross the target on time, some aircraft would be doing 500 knots while others would have flaps and gear down and doing 130 knots. This was unacceptable. Procedures were quickly changed so that we would be given a departure time. We were expected to make up or lose time, en route, to cross the target on time at 480 knots.

Initially, we did quite a bit of formation flying. This type of flying helped those not familiar with the F-86 to get proficient as quickly as possible. I thoroughly enjoyed myself.

On one flight, I was in the "box" position of a four-plane formation. The instructor asked us all to tighten up the formation. I was so close to the lead chap in front of me that I could see the flame in his tailpipe and feel his exhaust hitting my tail and rudder. Out of the corner of my eye I could see a river bank; it was above me. We were rather low. The lead flew up the river twisting and turning, expecting us to keep a very tight formation. We soared up over the trees and followed the lead into rolls. All great fun.

Bruce Sheasby was a very experienced F-86 and test pilot. He and I became good friends. I would pick his brain about the aircraft and flying in general. I always picked up a few good tips.

Another course member was Squadron Leader Gerry Theriault.

Gerry was an excellent pilot and fluent in both official languages. He used this fluency to further his own career on more than one occasion. Gerry was scheduled to be the deputy squadron commander of 421 Squadron. His biggest problem was his lack of people skills. Gerry played the language game and would be French or English depending on the circumstances. I often heard him say to other French Canadians, "We are in the mess now and we speak English only." He ticked off many fellow French Canadians. Gerry eventually became chief of the defence staff.

I often had conflicts with Gerry while on squadron in France and Germany. Many others did as well. He hated to be proven wrong in his decisions, which he was on several occasions. Years later, when Gerry was retired and I was with the airline, we both attended the 75th anniversary of the Canadian Air Force. The dinner was held in the aviation museum in Ottawa. Gerry singled me out and he had to show me several items in the museum that were related to his new job with a German aircraft company. Very few who attended the dinner actually talked to him. He had ruined more than a few careers in the RCAF. My friends asked me many questions as to why Gerry singled me out for conversation. I actually felt sorry for Gerry. He had few friends in spite of his high rank. Less than five years after retiring Gerry died of prostate cancer. I did learn that he had neglected having a medical after he retired. I found it hard to believe that someone so smart, who had had a medical every year during his service career, neglected a medical in retirement. I attended his funeral in Ottawa.

Our conversion course was coming to an end when the Cuban crisis happened in October 1962. There were several tense weeks leading up to a final confrontation. Russian transport ships carrying missiles, capable of carrying nuclear weapons, were headed to Cuba. U.S. ships were ordered to stop the ships. President Kennedy gave Chairman Nikita Khrushchev, in effect, a line in the sand; that he either turn his ships around or the U.S. navy would board the merchant vessels and take control. Khrushchev backed down and a nuclear confrontation did not happen, but it was a very close call.

While this was going on, as a family, we were told to find a family on the base that had a basement. This was to be our bomb shelter. All the base pilots were gathered into a hangar and briefed on the pending conflict. The rumour was that the pilots would be asked to confront Russian bombers approaching from the north. The F-86 had had their weapons removed a year or two before. We were to climb above the bombers, dive on them and, just before we thought we would hit a target, bail out. Hah, did they think we were kamikaze pilots? I often wondered what would have actually happened if the Russian ships had not turned back.

The 104 program slowed somewhat and, instead of staying on course number three, I was reassigned to course six. Unfortunately, this occurred after we gave up our trailer. Judy and the boys had moved back to Saint John in anticipation of my going to Cold Lake, Alberta, for the 104 transition course. We managed to find an apartment for Judy and the boys in Saint John. Judy's parents' apartment would have been a bit crowded for an extended period.

I had finished the F-86 conversion course and was in limbo waiting for my 104 course to begin. My instructor rating was still valid, so Station Chatham asked me to remain at Chatham to ensure all remaining pilots waiting at Chatham kept their instrument rating up to standard. In effect, I became the unit instrument check pilot. I could make my own schedule and come and go as I pleased, as long as the instrument rides were completed on the T-33.

I was very flexible. I would plan instrument rides on Wednesday and Thursday, arriving in Chatham late Tuesday and leaving Thursday. The rest of my time I spent in Saint John with Judy and the boys. I was also given permission to fly the F-86 any time I wanted, and I took full advantage.

On one particular Sabre flight, I flew to Saint John airport and asked the tower if they would like a low flypast. I knew the tower operator and most of the airport and Air Canada staff, from working on the ramp throughout high school. Leo, the tower operator, said, "The airfield is yours; no other conflicting traffic." I know he called the flying club and the rest of the airport staff to get out and watch my little show. Well, I beat the place up really well, high-speed passes, steep climbs, rolls, and tight turns. Leo thanked me for the show and I returned to Chatham. The following week I visited the Saint John airport and everyone was happy to see me and said they had enjoyed the show. I was also told that after my show, an

Pinocchio—Modified DC-3 used for radar training before flying the CF-104.

RCAF air commodore arrived at the terminal. He had been at a cottage on Loch Lomond. He wanted to know who the pilot was that did the low passes, because he was going to "court martial" him. The TCA and flying club staff came to my rescue by telling the AC, "You can't do that. That was Don McKay; he is one of ours." I thought for certain after my name was given that I was in for some trouble, but my luck held out; I never heard a word from anyone concerning my low passes.

The 104 program was finally back on track, and I started the conversion course in May 1963. Judy and the boys stayed in Saint John.

Our course gathered for breakfast shortly after our arrival in Cold Lake. Gerry Theriault joined us. He wanted to know if anyone heard the moose, which, to him sounded like a male in heat. The group all started to laugh. What Gerry heard was the run-up of a 104 engine by maintenance. Most of us had heard a moose before and, from a distance, the 104 engine did sound the same. The engine had a very distinctive sound, indicating the thrust and power of a jet engine. The moose analogy is a good one; the engine, like the moose, grunted, snorted, and howled but with a much higher decibel level. The Harvard was a piston engine, which also had a distinctive sound. It is a sound you never forget, and when you hear it, you automatically look up.

I have mentioned the 104 was a supersonic aircraft capable of speeds over 1,400 mph. The aircraft were built in Montreal and had an Orenda J-79 engine. The engine produced 10,000 pounds of thrust without afterburner, and 15,800 pounds of thrust with the afterburner. The afterburner was new to all of us. It was mainly used on takeoff to produce extra power or, in the air, if you needed extra power. In effect, raw fuel was introduced into the tail pipe producing the extra power. It was a good kick in the pants. The 104 weighed just over 28,000 pounds. In comparison, the venerable DC-3 weighed 25,000 pounds carrying twenty-eight passengers.

We spent time in ground school learning all aspects of the aircraft, both the good and the bad. The good was that the aircraft moved like a scared rabbit. Then, there were sections in the operating manual with a wide black border that referred to stalls and spins. "These areas have not been explored." A test pilot probably got himself in trouble and the restriction was added. Normally, on all other aircraft, we did spins and stalls as a regular part of training. This aircraft had to be flown by the numbers. We were told not to get ourselves into a position where the aircraft would bite back.

Another new feature on the 104 was inertial navigation. Similar equipment was used to take the Americans to the moon. Up to this point in our career we had used maps, both regular and nautical, as well as airways charts. Training taught us to keep a mental picture of our position at all times. The inertial system had a device about the size of a package of cigarettes, called an SSU (station storage unit). A cover, when removed, exposed twelve pairs of tiny screws. One screw was for latitude and the other for longitude. The device was placed into a machine and the desired latitude and longitude were entered. Base or home was always entered first so that the system knew where it was—similar to a GPS system. Using a small screwdriver we moved the little screws until an arrow on a gauge showed we had programmed correctly. The device only had space for twelve pre-programmed positions.

Most of us were skeptical of the new navigation system and we made certain we always had maps close at hand. Once airborne, you knew in about three to four minutes if the system would work or not. If it did fail it was back to basics, needle, ball, and airspeed. Some of our group believed in the new system totally. Once low-level cross-country flights were introduced, these same individuals got lost. More than a few had to swallow their pride, climb to altitude and request a radar heading back to Cold Lake. Gradually the reliability of the system increased, but one still had to be aware that it was not perfect.

Dick O'Bryan was a very good pilot, but he believed that the inertial system was never wrong. He was one who continually flew off his map and ended up climbing to altitude for a radar steer back to Cold Lake. We talked to him to try to convince him to rely more on his map to ensure the INS information was accurate and not blindly follow the inertial system. Dick just could not accept the fact that the inertial system could be wrong. Dick failed the course. I had instructed with him at Gimli where he was also flight safety officer.

Dick was transferred to transport command where he flew the C-130 Hercules aircraft. He reached captain status and had a very successful career in transport command.

Dick was approached by representatives of the Quebec government to become the chief instructor on the C-130 that the Quebec government was buying for the James Bay hydro project. Dick was a few years from retirement in the RCAF, but big dollars were waved in his face and many promises made. He elected to accept the offer. Once all the pilots had completed their training, he was unceremoniously shown the door. He spoke English only; all the other pilots he trained were French Canadians. I wish he had sued the government, but he didn't. Dick eventually found a flying job with a new airline, flying from downtown Montreal to Ottawa. I believe the name of the airline was Air Transit. Dick was happy, but the happiness was short-lived; the outfit folded after three years. De Havilland, the builder of the Twin Otter aircraft, offered Dick a job as a demonstration pilot. His job was to fly with prospective buyers and demonstrate the capabilities of the aircraft. He was demonstrating an aircraft's single-engine capability to a prospective buyer, when one engine was feathered. Things happened rather fast after that. It was speculated that when Dick went to unfeather the engine he inadvertently feathered the good engine. Dick made an attempt to land in a field but the aircraft flipped on landing. Both Dick and the prospective buyer were killed.

The inertial system on the CF-104 also controlled some flight instruments, which led to some problems. The system had a set of potentiometers and accelerometers mounted on the inertial platform. The platform then sensed the position of the earth in relation to the aircraft position. Sometimes, a condition called a "slow topple" occurred. The slow topple would give the pilot inaccurate information and, similar to vertigo, make him believe that he was in an attitude position when he was actually in a completely different position. I had a slow topple in France. I was doing a ground radar-controlled approach to Grostenquin Airfield. I broke out of the cloud at about 300 feet and found myself practically on my back, while my flight instruments told me I was right side up. I just rolled the aircraft into its proper position and landed. (More about the incident later.)

An air data computer supplied information for speed and altitude from sensors attached outside of the aircraft.

Yet another feature of the 104 was that we had ground-reading radar. We could see from our map what we should see ahead, and our radar would help confirm our position. Lakes, hills, towns, farms with metal roofs—all showed up well on the radar in the Cold Lake area. In Europe the radar readouts could be a bit confusing.

The radar also had a terrain avoidance feature. When activated, it was supposed to "contour fly" and avoid hitting the ground, but we had little confidence in the system. One test pilot out of Prestwick, Scotland, was completing a flight after a major inspection of a 104 by Scottish aviation. He was over water and selected the terrain avoidance feature and promptly flew into the water. He killed himself and wrecked a perfectly good airplane.

The number one bonus of the 104 was the autopilot. Having to fly the aircraft, observe the radar, and navigate at altitudes below 1,000 feet in all kinds of weather, at speeds of up to 600 knots, would have been next to impossible without the autopilot. The whole concept actually required a two-man crew—the pilot and a radar systems operator. In typical Canadian fashion, we sucked it up and did the job with one pilot. Everyone did a fantastic job.

There were three dual 104s at Cold Lake and we were all scheduled for one trip with an instructor for our check-out on the aircraft. As the course progressed, we all flew about twenty-five hours in the back seat of the dual, instructor in front. A hood was pulled over the

CF-104 in the vicinity of Cold Lake, Alberta, 1963.

canopy and we were required to complete the whole trip, using the INS and radar to reach the target. When reaching the PUP (push up point), speed was increased and, approaching the target point, the practice smoke bomb delivery was completed.

Our instructor would mark us on our accuracy in navigation, as well as accuracy in timing and target delivery. We all became proficient in all aspects of the aircraft.

Prior to our flight in the dual, we all had to have a ride aboard "Guppy." Guppy was a converted DC-3 with a long nose containing the 104 radar gear. We sat at a console, and an instructor would show us how the radar operated. Our radar checkout lasted less than one hour.

Like all aircraft, an external inspection was always required. My instructor pointed out what to look for. One item he mentioned was the leading edge of the wings. The wing (if you want to call twenty-one feet, eleven inches, wings) was very sharp. More than one person would get a cut above his eye doing an external. Because the wing was short, if you lost an engine in the air, the aircraft glided like a rock. If a pilot was lucky enough to be directly over an airfield at 15,000 feet and at a minimum of 250 knots, there would be enough time for one turn towards the field. It was best to bail out.

Once the external was completed, I strapped myself into the front seat while the instructor did the same in the back seat. I started the engine and received taxi clearance. Once take-off clearance was received, I lined up on the runway. The runway at Cold Lake was 12,000 feet long. I started the take-off roll and selected the afterburner by pushing the throttle outboard and into the slot. The extra power would push you back into your seat from the increased acceleration. The speed increased rapidly with the afterburner but it consumed fuel at a great rate. I had been well briefed on the take-off technique so the instructor was quiet on the take-off roll.

After we got airborne and cleaned the aircraft up (gear and flaps retracted), my instructor said, "Suck it back." We were going nearly straight up and, as we passed 35,000 feet, the instructor had me roll over and look down. I could see the button of the runway we had just taken off from. It was very impressive. We were still accelerating even after 35,000 feet. In order to get the wings level you had to be careful lowering the nose. In other aircraft I had flown, you just moved the aileron and brought the nose to level flight. The 104 had little wing surface; the technique of lowering the wing was the same but you had to be more careful. I have said before that the air force made you fly the aircraft to its limits and, in so doing you would learn your own limits.

My next trip in the 104 was a solo trip to get used to the aircraft. When I flew the F-86, on your first trip you broke the speed of sound. This aircraft was capable of twice the F-86 speed. I was level at 35,000 feet, selected the afterburner, the aircraft leaped forward, and I could feel the kick in the pants. The day was beautiful; not a cloud in the sky or telephone poles to give any sense of speed. The only indication of going Mach 2 was the speed indicator and a slight jump on the altimeter. I had covered about fifty miles from the time I lit the afterburner until I was at Mach 2. I now qualified for a Mach 2 pin.

Use of proper take-off technique was critical. It was necessary to hold the nose wheel on the runway until 170 knots. If you pulled the nose up too early you created a blanking effect and the aircraft would be slow to accelerate. This was not a problem on a 12,000-foot runway, but in Europe the military fields were all a standard length of 7,000 feet. Whenever a new pilot arrived on squadron, he was briefed again about the take-off technique. One of the established squadron pilots would go to the tower to observe his takeoff and critique him after landing. In addition, runway markers were installed with the runway distance. As an example, if you did not have 130 knots by the 3,000-foot marker, you were to abort the takeoff. The aircraft would not be able to accelerate to the take-off speed of 190 knots. We called the speeds, "Go; no go."

Hero picture after exceeding Mach 2 (1,400 mph+) in a CF-104.

One bad feature of the 104 was the cockpit-locking mechanism. Once you strapped yourself into the cockpit, you had to reach up to the canopy, compress a switch to unlock from the open position, and manually lower the canopy. The problem occurred when you were locking the canopy in the down position. Once you locked the canopy, you had to visually ensure that the locking lugs were in the proper position. It was awkward to see the rear lug with all your straps on. However, it was imperative that you made certain that the rear lug was in its proper position, because if that lug was not in position, once airborne, the airflow would force the canopy open. Once that happened, all lift was lost and the aircraft would no longer fly.

Prior to my arriving at Cold Lake this actually happened to a trainee. His canopy flew open right after takeoff and he was able to eject successfully. Unfortunately, the chute opened at the exact moment the aircraft hit the ground and exploded. He was engulfed in the fireball; his chute caught fire, and he ended up in the wreckage. He did not survive.

Another course member had the canopy open on him just before liftoff. He was able to come to a stop and returned to the ramp so maintenance could ensure the canopy was not bent. Initially, the American 104 had downward ejection; why, is beyond me. Thankfully, the Canadian 104 had upward ejection. The American test pilot and selected astronaut, Ivan C. Kincheloe, was killed when his engine quit after takeoff. He had the presence of mind to roll the aircraft and eject sideways but he was too low and went flying into tall trees that killed him instantly. Kincheloe Air Force Base was named in his honour. This base, near Kinross, Michigan, is now an industrial park.

The Canadian 104 had a Martin-Baker upward ejection seat; the best in the world. The seat was capable of getting you to 300 feet if you had 90 knots or better on the airspeed indicator, and assuming you were strapped in properly on the take-off roll. Once you pulled the ejection handle, the sequence all happened automatically, including chute deployment and seat separation. There were two ejection handles. The first handle was a ring that you reached up and behind and pulled, while the other ring was between your legs at the front of the seat.

Previous ejection seats had a cartridge that fired, and out you went. The ejection was instantaneous and anyone who used the seat usually ended up with back problems. The 104 had a rocket system, which activated in stages. This prevented most back problems.

The 104 was unique in that you had to wear "spurs." The spurs were strapped to your boots, and you placed the back of the spur into a round steel ball attached to a wire that was part of the seat. In the event of an ejection, your legs would be pulled into the proper ejection position to prevent them from flailing all over the place. In addition, canvas-covered restraints would go forward forcing your arms in, again to prevent flailing.

The ejection procedure was used many times and saved many lives in Europe. The German air force had a larger number of 104s than Canada, yet statistically, we lost the same number of aircraft. The big difference was, once things started to go "south," Canadians rode the parachute to earth. The Germans usually ended up crashing and killing themselves. It was all in the training.

I was in a four-plane formation and flying in the box position. I became conscious of a flashing light in the upper centre of the control panel. The light was flashing "slow" meaning "slow down." We were only doing about 450 knots so there was really no concern. The light was intended to come on at near maximum speeds indicating the engine was getting warm and could melt, so, slow down.

Two other new features of the 104 were the drag chute and the hook. The drag chute was deployed on every landing. Once on the ground, we selected the chute, which was stowed near the rear of the fuselage. The chute helped reduce the forward inertia and was particularly useful on the short runways in Europe. The hook, similar to those used on landing on an aircraft carrier, was used as a last resort to get the aircraft stopped, to prevent it from going off the end of the runway. A cable was placed the full runway width on both ends of the runway, approximately 1,500 feet from the end of the runway. It worked well.

As a matter of interest, while the speed on takeoff was 190 knots, the landing gear and flaps had to be selected up and retracted, prior to reaching 240 knots. Final approach speed was 190 knots, reducing to 160 knots as you approached the button, or end, of the runway. Touchdown was roughly 145 knots. Remember, the aircraft had a small wing surface, so speeds had to be high.

Once we all had a few trips and felt comfortable in the new aircraft, bombing was introduced. The 104 was to become a low-level bomber while stationed in Europe and would carry a nuclear weapon.

The aircraft was equipped with a practice bomb holder, which was attached to the bottom of the fuselage or centre line of the aircraft. The practice bombs would show smoke once they hit the ground, giving us a chance to see how close we were to the intended target. Normally, we would program all the necessary information into the bomb control panel on the ground. Once activated on our bomb run, the bombing sequence would be automatic.

The bombing range was located at Primrose Lake, north of Cold Lake. We would take off in a four-plane formation and, once we approached the range, separate, as briefed. We would complete a bomb run and initiate the delivery by increasing the speed and pulling into a 15-degree climb. The bomb would drop from about 3,000 feet, the altitude you would reach when delivering a nuclear weapon. After the bomb was released, you would roll over on your back and head for the tops of the trees, accelerating all the time, with speeds in excess of 600 knots.

One type of delivery was called a "lay down." We would fly at 90 to 100 feet at a speed of about 540 knots. This exercise was always visual. The 104 had a long pointed extension to the nose, which contained the pitot tube for flight instruments and was painted candy cane—alternate red and white. We soon learned that at low level, if you had the right speed and height, you could drop the practice bomb when the second red stripe appeared in relation to the target—a very scientific method. This type of delivery would normally be used against communication centres. One particular nuclear weapon was actually designed with a very large spike in the front. The weapon would penetrate a hard target a certain distance before exploding.

On one trip, the target was an old abandoned shack. I actually saw the orange-coloured bomb go right through the front door entrance. I averaged about fifty-foot accuracy in this manoeuvre.

Low-level navigation was then introduced. We would be given a target and need to prepare a map of the route. The map was about six inches wide, which represented three miles either side of track. The map was fastened to a map holder that was attached to your upper thigh. The map unfolded manually, accordion style, as your trip progressed. The map was used as a check on the inertial navigation to ensure you were where you should be. Everyone was given a time to be over the target. Trips were normally flown at 480 knots. If, at a checkpoint, it was determined you were either running late or early, the airspeed would be either increased or decreased to make up time or to lose time. Speed changes were made in increments of 60 knots. A change of 60 knots would either gain or lose a minute.

Everything was done in multiples of 60 for easy mental calculations.

On the final approach to the target, when we reached the PUP (push-up point), the bomb selection would be activated and the aircraft accelerated to 540 knots. Once over the pull-up point, the aircraft was pulled into a 15-degree climb angle and held until the bomb was dropped. The aircraft was then rolled over, accelerating away from the bomb as fast as possible, in excess of 600 knots, descending to tree-top level. The theory was that when you dropped your nuclear weapon you put the tail of the aircraft towards the blast. This action would absorb most of the blast effect and some radiation. This delivery was known as the "lob" technique. My average was somewhere between 200–300 feet using this type of delivery. Anywhere close with a nuclear weapon is considered okay. No one ever mentioned that, in the event of a conflict, there would be bombs going off all over the place and the chance of survival was nil.

The commanding officer of Cold Lake was a weird individual. When we arrived, all those starting the transition course were gathered in the officers' mess, given a lecture, and told to leave the base nurses alone. They were for the base personnel only, not transients. The majority of the course were married and were at Cold Lake to complete the course and get back to their families. We certainly scratched our heads on his briefing. I wondered what the nurses must have felt; they probably were not aware.

Just before we started night flying, we were again gathered as a group and again briefed by the CO. He stated that he had a yellow line, twenty-feet wide, painted on the 3,000-foot mark of the 12,000-foot runway. He said that any pilot landing short of the yellow line would be court marshalled. Needless to say, we all looked at each other and wondered if he was off his rocker.

One thing a pilot hates to see is unused runway behind him. During our night exercises, the CO would often park his car opposite the yellow line and clear of the runway. On final landing clearance the tower would add, "Check the obstruction at 3,000 feet." We knew then the CO was in position and we would land on his precious yellow line.

On one Friday night beer call, most of the pilots gathered for a "cool one." This particular night the CO was in attendance. The bar was quite crowded. Apparently, some junior officer with his back to the CO somehow nudged him and spilt a few drops of the CO's beer. The CO went absolutely ballistic; he ranted and raved, swore at the officer, threatened court marshal, and raised his fist to strike the poor guy. About this time several people grabbed him and tried to calm him down with no luck. The base hospital was called and they arrived, assessed the situation, and took him away in restraints.

We did learn he was taken to Edmonton for assessment. He was later released from the RCAF on medical grounds. Years later, I learned that he was appointed Quebec's representative in Paris by René Lévesque's PQ government. Certainly makes me wonder how he ever received the appointment.

One aspect of our training was completely different. We were required to spend one to two sessions with a psychiatrist. Visits were scheduled in an office or perhaps in the officers' mess. The idea was to see if we were stable enough to handle the nuclear responsibilities we would be exposed to in the European environment. We also knew that we were being observed in the mess and the bar area. I never heard of anyone not being allowed to continue training due to a psychiatrist report.

On our low-level flights out of Cold Lake we often flew over farms. Complaints were many, particularly from the mink farmers. Once we knew where all the different farms were, we marked them on our maps and tried to avoid these locations.

Our course was rapidly coming to a close. I had flown a total of fifty-eight hours solo and twenty-five hours in the dual aircraft. It was now time to head for home and prepare our families for the trip overseas. Prior to leaving Gimli, all our furniture had been put into long-term storage in Winnipeg. We were flown to Trenton, Ontario, where I took a train to the Maritimes. It was so very nice to see Judy and the boys after nearly six months at Cold Lake.

We had about two weeks to visit family and friends before our departure.

All the McKay clan met in Moncton for lunch. I thought at least my older brother would want to contribute towards the bill, but I was wrong. I ended up paying for our going-away lunch. We were to return to Trenton by train and then service air to Europe. Somewhere near the New Brunswick–Quebec border, we woke because it was damn cold. The train had broken down in a snowstorm and could not provide heat for the passengers. We were stuck for about four hours. In Trenton, we were billeted in transient quarters to await our flight overseas. It was the first time many of the wives had ever met. Everyone had kids running around and all were excited about our overseas trip.

On the day of departure we gathered to board the aircraft. Once all were on board, we were advised there was a mechanical problem and we all had to disembark. During our wait in the terminal, Harry Stroud, a pilot on our squadron, advised me that he had just heard that Bruce Sheasby had been killed in a 104 at 3 Wing, Zweibrucken. Harry knew that Bruce and I were good friends. Harry, in his wisdom, also had a bottle of scotch. We drank to Bruce; actually, we finished the bottle. Consequently, neither of us was much help to our wives with the kids on the flight to Marville, France.

I must admit I thought that if Bruce, with his experience, was killed in what became known as the "widow maker," I probably would not stand a chance of surviving the tour. I still wonder why I survived and others did not. Years later, when I was stationed in Ottawa, I was able to read the report on Bruce's accident. It was determined that he probably misread his altimeter by 10,000 feet. He realized at the last second he was going to hit the trees. Bruce selected afterburner, but he was too low to recover. The afterburner on the 104 was what we called a "slow light," since it took about seven to nine seconds for it to light. The voodoo, or 101, had an instantaneous light.

Chapter Fourteen

Marville, France, and 421 Squadron

On arrival in Marville, we were scheduled to take a bus to 2 (fighter) Wing, Grostenquin, France. To our surprise and delight, we were met by Wing Commander Hal Knight, who was 2 Wing base operations officer. He managed to "borrow" the DC-3 belonging to the Air Officer Commanding the Air Division. We certainly were happy not to have to face the bus ride after the Atlantic crossing.

We got to 2 Wing and were bused to Saint-Avold where the married quarters were situated. The town was about forty-five minutes from the base.

It was standard procedure that when a new pilot arrived with his family, another pilot, already on station, would ensure that basic food items were on hand for their arrival. Milk, bread, and more were all in the refrigerator. I do believe there was a bottle or two of wine as well. Our benefactor was Leo O'Donovan and his wife, Jane. Naturally we reimbursed our benefactor. The date we arrived in France was November 8, 1963. Judy and I were "benefactors" to many other arriving families during our European tour.

The PMQs (permanent married quarters) were on a hill overlooking the town of Saint-Avold, near Metz. Some mornings during the winter, the hoar frost clung to everything, and the valley below would be full of fog—a beautiful sight.

I was not required to go to the base for a couple of days. However, I was anxious to see our new station, so I drove in with Leo and he introduced me to Wing Commander Arnie Bauer, the chief of flight operations. We toured the base, so I received a good picture of the layout. We arrived back in Saint-Avold in time for supper. Judy and the boys were unpacking and settling into our furnished apartment.

Suddenly, there was a frantic knock on the door. I opened the door and it was Leo. He said he had just heard on the radio that John F. Kennedy, the U.S. president, had just been assassinated. Everyone was in shock. We did not know what to do. We had just arrived in Europe and there were a grand total of four new 104s on the base and no weapons. The general opinion was that the Russians must have killed President Kennedy.

We fully expected that the Russian army was on its way to occupy Europe. The air was ripe with rumours. It was well known that if the Russian army did attack the West at that time, there were not enough NATO forces to stop them. It was estimated they would have overrun Europe and be sitting on the English Channel in two weeks. The Russians had an overwhelming number of tanks. The deterrent to stop such an attack was our 104 aircraft and other Western air forces equipped with nuclear weapons. We were not fully equipped with aircraft or weapons. It was a tense period in history. It soon became apparent that the Russians were not involved, and life returned to normal.

Charles de Gaulle, the president of France, had a running feud with the United States over control of nuclear weapons on French soil. He insisted that France have full control of all nuclear weapons. The United States was not going to allow this to happen. The French nuclear deterrent was called, "force de frappe." We called it "force de crap." Charlie put some pressure on both the United States and Canada by insisting that wives of U.S. and Canadian personnel be issued with a "*carte de sojourn*." The only other people in France forced to have such a card were French prostitutes. Discussion continued and we proceeded with our phase training. I did recall that during World War II, Churchill had his problems with de Gaulle and the Free French forces. He is known to have said, "Everyone has their cross to bear; mine is the cross of Lorraine," de Gaulle's birth place. There had been many attempts on de Gaulle's life. His estate was situated in the Vosges Mountains, hills really. The area was surrounded by 57mm anti-aircraft guns, and any aircraft flying through the area would be fired on. We kept a wide birth.

Algeria was a problem for France at the time. I recall an incident in Paris with Cy Leadbeater. We were about to cross a street when a car stopped at the traffic light. Out of nowhere, French police pounced on the vehicle and the driver was thrown roughly to the ground. He and his vehicle were thoroughly searched. His colouring was swarthy and the police thought he was Algerian; he wasn't and he was released. This often happened in Paris as well as other cities throughout France.

Our quarters at Saint-Avold were fully furnished and quite comfortable. Each day, a French army truck would arrive and all the Canadian kids would be put into the back of the truck. The kids were off to school, similar to day care, with French children. Dave was close to four and he went as well. He loved it. The trucks had canvas sides and benches for the kids to sit on, but no seat belts. Judy asked Dave if he thought the kids talked differently, he said, "They are not different; they speak French."

Prior to leaving Saint John, I had purchased a Volkswagen bug for delivery in Germany. The boys stayed with friends while Judy and I boarded a train for Stuttgart, Germany, to pick up our vehicle. When we arrived at the Stuttgart station, we were both anxious to use the railway facilities. We determined the "*herren*" sign was for the boys while the "*damen*" was for the ladies. I did my business and went to meet Judy. She was literally dancing up and down and explained that in order to get toilet paper she had to pay an attendant and she did not have any German marks. Judy grabbed the money out of my hand and scurried off. When she returned I asked if she had any change. She did not and the visit cost $5.

We took a cab to the designated address to pick up our new car. When we arrived we were escorted into a room, with much bowing and smiling from our guide. We waited a few minutes, and then a tall, aristocratic-looking individual approached us. He bowed and clicked his heels, a habit he probably acquired during the war, and introduced himself. All the necessary papers were in order and we were presented with our Volkswagen. The "clicker" explained all that we needed to know about the vehicle and then we were on our way back to Saint-Avold. The new car cost us $1,250 Canadian.

The drive back took us onto the Autobahn, the equivalent of the superhighways built in the United States after General Eisenhower became president. The Germans built their super highways in the mid-thirties after Hitler came to power. He knew that ease of transport would be critical to his plans.

I arrived at the squadron and was ready for work. There were a total of six pilots on our squadron and another six pilots on 430 Squadron. We had four airplanes, three ready to fly and one still in its transport livery, just off-loaded from an RCAF Hercules aircraft.

Everyone was jockeying for a flight to maintain our qualification and to fly in the European environment. A roster was set up with all the names; when your name showed, you went flying. It was difficult to acquire many hours until aircraft started arriving at a much faster rate, bringing smiles to everyone's faces. When an aircraft arrived, the different parts were installed and a test flight was completed. The aircraft was then released to the squadron. It was like buying a new car; everything smelled new and there was not a scratch anywhere.

I had been smoking a pipe for a few years and heard many complaints about my smelly pipe. Ken MacCrimmon and Neil Gillespie opened my locker, took my pipe tobacco and added pencil shavings to it. Over a period of time my tobacco became mostly pencil shavings. It took a while, but I finally caught on. Naturally, the group had a good laugh at my expense.

The weather in Europe in the winter is normally overcast for days on end. The top of the cloud would be about 3,000 feet and very flat. During trips over Germany, we could see many old castles sticking out of the cloud, a truly beautiful sight.

I mentioned earlier that at times the inertial navigation system could develop a slow topple and give the pilot inaccurate information. I was on a flight on a particularly cloudy day with tops well over 20,000 feet. I had completed several approaches at different bases, mostly in cloud, and returned to 2 Wing. I completed my approach phase and was handed over to the GCA, (ground-controlled approach) operator. The GCA operator would advise you on the weather, the alignment on the centre line, and advise you to correct your rate of descent as required. They were worth their weight in gold and helped many to a safe landing.

I was advised that I was on centre line and on the glide path. I completed the before-landing check, gear down and appropriate flap selected. I broke out of the cloud about 300 feet above the ground. To my surprise I was practically upside down, although my instruments told me I was right side up. I rolled the aircraft to correct its attitude and landed. My inertial system's slow topple was so insidious that I had not noticed the change, probably because I was busy doing approaches in cloud with no ground reference. Live and learn.

During November and December 1963, and January 1964, as aircraft became more available, we did a lot of formation flying as well as low-level navigation flights. If you recall, I mentioned that radar returns were different in Europe than in Canada. As a classic example, rivers in Canada are easy to identify. The banks are natural, but in Europe most rivers, over generations, have been built up and smoothed out, so, very seldom would you get a good radar return. We soon learned that the best radar altitude was 700 feet above ground. Our radar would show us the contour of the land and we could check our maps against the inertial navigation system to confirm our position.

In addition to the 104 flying, we did many hours in the T-33; mostly instrument flying, doing approaches into Canadian, American, and French airports. These flights made us more familiar with the European environment.

Another twist in navigation was the application of variation when we programmed our SSUs. The prime meridian went through Greenwich, England. West of the prime meridian the variation was added to true heading to get a magnetic heading. In Europe you were east of the prime, so you subtracted variation from true to get a magnetic heading. If you added variation east of the prime, each degree gave you an error of nautical miles; not a good thing to screw up on a low-level navigation trip close to the East German border.

We had a very pleasant surprise at 2 Wing, by being re-acquainted with John and Frieda Balsar. John was working in the operations room. One evening, we planned to go to their favourite local restaurant. We found a babysitter and away we went. The restaurant was located in the town of Montmédy, infamous for the first use of machine guns by the Germans in World War I. As we approached the restaurant it looked closed. We ventured to the front door and we were greeted by a waiter, who had to be in his nineties.

The owner, who was also the cook, took us to a table. We were the only ones in the restaurant. The elderly waiter kept running to the kitchen asking the cook, "Good linen or regular?" "Good silver or regular?" The cook answered, "Good" to both questions. Frieda was fluent in French so she translated what was transpiring. The waiter took our order and brought us wine and French bread and all the goodies. He did not walk but ran from place to place. The meal was excellent. I asked to see the cook and we all thanked him for a wonderful meal; I gave him a cigar, which he accepted. He left the table and came back two minutes later with a bottle of cognac. He smoked the cigar and gave us the cognac, as a thank you. A memorable evening.

On February 3, 1964, we departed Grostenquin for the island of Sardinia in the Mediterranean. Our destination on the island was an Italian air base named Decimomannu. The base was to be our home for two weeks while we did practice bombing at the Capo Fresca bombing range.

Our route to Deci took us over Nice and Corsica. We passed a position report to French Air Traffic Control. Shortly after our transmission, an RAF Canberra gave his position, neglecting to give his altitude. The controller requested the altitude once or twice. The RAF pilot said, "Sorry, old chap, classified." I visualized a Brit with a great handlebar moustache sticking out from his oxygen mask and a big grin on his face.

Any time you fly out of gliding distance of land in a single-engine airplane, you start to hear strange noises coming from the engine. The engine instruments indicated that all was normal, and this trip was no exception. Although I experienced strange sounds before, the aircraft engine did not sound right to me. After landing at Deci, I mentioned to our maintenance staff that I could not put my finger on any specific problem other than the engine did not sound right. The following day, maintenance asked me to do an air test on the aircraft. I completed the test flight but I still thought there was something wrong with the engine. Maintenance asked the detachment commander, Squadron Leader Bill Bliss, to do a test flight. They probably thought I was not qualified to make a determination. In any event, Bill completed the air test and all seemed okay. He landed and, as he was taxiing in, the engine seized solid. He had to be towed to the parking area. I did mention to maintenance, "I told you that the engine didn't sound right."

The Germans also did bombing at Deci, flying 104s and F-84s, which, in their minds, were both widow makers. We would have four aircraft on detachment at any given time while the Germans would have twenty-five or more. Seldom were the Germans able to get more than two or three aircraft on the range. Their maintenance was the pits. We normally had all four of our aircraft on the range at the same time. Once we finished our bombing runs for the day, our maintenance staff would go to the German side of the airfield to work on their aircraft.

Normally we would start our flying early and complete two trips to the range before noon. The temperatures in the afternoon were so hot one could literally fry an egg on the aircraft wing. All the squadron pilots from the four wings paid $100 towards the purchase of a Volkswagen van, which we used after flying. Our favourite destination was Lido Beach with its beautiful white sand.

We would arrive at the beach around one in the afternoon, with a couple of cases of beer and a bottle or two of Asti Spumanti, an Italian white wine. The empty wine bottles we always kept; we refilled them at many different locations as we drove around the countryside.

When we arrived the beaches were normally empty. The locals were having a siesta. I now know where the term "Only mad dogs and Englishmen go out in the noonday sun," comes from.

Many areas on the island were off limits; particularly at night. The Italian police would erect barriers to keep people from entering the hills. The bandits ruled the hills at night. Rumours started that all pilots were to be given a letter, in the event we had to eject and were found by the bandits. The letter was to explain that we were Canadian pilots and a reward was guaranteed if we were returned safely to the authorities. Personally, I never saw such a letter; perhaps others did.

Halfway through our deployment we were advised that, on our return trip to Europe, we would be landing in 4 Wing Baden Soellingen. Grostenquin was now closed. The Americans had finally told Charlie to "fuddle-duddle." Charlie reacted by shutting down U.S. and Canadian bases.

Our main concern, on learning of the base closing, was for our families. We had just settled into a routine in Saint-Avold and now we would have to find new housing. Our German was nil; thankfully the Germans we spoke to wanted to learn English more than we wanted to learn German. Use of our English–German dictionary became a daily way of life.

Chapter Fifteen

4 Wing, Baden-Soellingen

On our return to 4 Wing we were advised that our families had been made aware of the impending move and that they were already packing. Transportation was arranged for us to return to 2 Wing to lend a hand. We had about ten days to pack, find new quarters near 4 Wing, and move lock, stock, and barrel over to our new base.

We had been told that there were no accommodations available on the base and that we would have to look in the small towns surrounding 4 Wing. Living off base was called "living on the economy."

The pilots headed back to 4 Wing to look for a place to live. I eventually found a two-bedroom, street-level apartment, in the town of Rastatte. The town was about twenty minutes from the base. I arranged for a military vehicle to move our trunks and boxes.

Judy had not seen her new home but when she did she was happy with the apartment. The landlady spoke very good English. The family ran a shop out of two outbuildings. Our back entrance opened onto a bricked passageway. It was great for the boys and their bikes. In addition the front yard, while small, was fenced in and was a great place for the boys to play.

We really enjoyed living in Rastatte. Close to our apartment was a park. In the centre there was a small café; the bread and jam was to die for. The café was surrounded by small gardens that the locals rented from the town and grew fresh vegetables and flowers in. Some of the lots were quite lavish with one-room huts brightly painted. We spent many hours walking the paths with the boys.

We thoroughly enjoyed German food; it was very similar to our diet. One farm had a restaurant in the main house and the food was great. Usually the service started with a large tureen of soup, followed by the main course, all of which were very good. One of the staff would always take the boys, Dave and Bryan, for a walk to the barn, leaving Judy and I a chance to have coffee and dessert in peace and quiet. We really appreciated this gesture; the Germans really loved and took care of their children.

Kitty-corner to our apartment on Rosenstrasse was a small grocery store, and every morning a delivery of fresh rolls arrived. We kept a close eye on the truck's arrival, as the locals loved the rolls as well. The store sold beer and wine as well. One red wine we would buy was called "rotgut." Naturally we called it, "rotgut," in English; it was pretty good. We still have an empty bottle with an outline of a monkey etched in the glass.

Judy mentioned that she had seen the same man watching the house for the past few days. I told her he was probably working for the Russians and was studying my routine for some weakness he could exploit. He soon stopped watching the house and never returned.

In the town of Rastatte there was a small chapel. It had an ebony Madonna, very beautiful and different than what we normally saw in the Catholic Church.

On the weekends when I was not working, we visited the local gliding club. The boys loved to watch the gliders; it amused them. I could not help but think of the Versailles Treaty, which had forbidden Germany to have powered aircraft. Hitler, initially, trained all his pilots on gliders. He then tore up the treaty, and powered flight was once again available for training.

I can truthfully say that moving from France to Germany was like going from darkness into the light. In France as we drove around we noticed that in the villages there were large manure piles in front of the farms. The animals lived under the raised houses and helped provide heat in cold weather. The larger the manure pile, the more well-off the farmer. De Gaulle tried to get the villagers to move the manure piles to the back of the houses and install indoor plumbing. Pierre Mendès France became president, after de Gaulle. He tried to have the children drink milk instead of watered-down wine. Louis Pasteur started the process of pasteurization, but it never caught on in France. All our milk and dairy products on the base grocery store came from either Denmark or Holland. We would visit the French

PXs and grocery store for wine, French bread, and escargot (snails).

The French military would also visit our PX and store. I caught one French officer opening jars of jam, putting his finger in and tasting the contents. If he did not like it he put the lid back on and placed the jar back on the shelf. We now knew why we had indentations in our jams. I put the item he had placed back on the shelf into his cart, indicating that he would have to pay for the item. He was not a happy camper.

Gas cost us ten cents a gallon on the base. The PX sold a bottle of Bacardi for $1.90. Other liquor was just as cheap.

We had a few records but we had no record player. I purchased a *telefungen* player through the PX. It was a beautiful piece of furniture. One end held a tape recorder while the other end was the record player. In the middle was a beautiful radio. We used the same machine for many years after we returned to Canada.

The town closest to the base at 4 Wing was Hügelsheim, famous for its "spargel," or white asparagus. We were told that even Hitler visited the area in the spring for his fill of spargel. True or not, it is a good story.

The base itself was situated with the Rhine River on one side and the Black Forest on the other. The base was called Baden-Soellingen while the main town was Baden-Baden. The town was lovely, nestled in the foothills of the Black Forest. It was famous for its Roman baths and its Kurhaus gambling casino.

We were right in the middle of the Rhine valley; beautiful but dangerous, due to the pollutants from the Ruhr industrial area. The pollutants were carried down the Rhine valley on the local prevailing wind. These pollutants would later pose a problem for our boys.

Judy would daily visit local markets and pick up fresh vegetables and fruit. There were no superstores at that time.

Another favourite weekend activity was travelling in the Black Forest and looking for old castles. We found many; most were in rather bad shape. The kids loved these trips; they could climb all over the ruins. The castles usually had a small eating kiosk that provided sandwiches, sausage, cold beer, and great German white wine.

The move to Germany was now completed and, with everyone settled, it was time to get back to work. My squadron was 421; our motto was *bellicum cecinere* (They have sounded the war trumpet). Our crest was unique in that our aircraft carried the then-familiar emblem of the McColl-Frontenac Oil Company. One of the company's products was Red Indian aviation motor oil. The Indian head had two tomahawks on either side.

The 421 fighter squadron was formed at Digby, Lincolnshire, England, on April 9, 1942, and was equipped with Spitfire aircraft. The squadron participated in brief periods of combat followed by many months of tedious convoy patrol. In January 1943, the squadron moved to Kesley, an active station, in the front line of the air offensive over northern France. In 1944, they were assigned a new role; dive bombing, in preparation for the D-Day landings. After D Day, the squadron moved to Normandy and began intense activity against enemy aircraft and ground targets. The squadron was disbanded in July 1945, but was reactivated in September 1949, initially flying the British Vampire jet and re-equipped with Sabres in 1951. At the end of the Sabre era, the squadron was equipped in November 1963 with CF-104 Starfighter aircraft, entering the all-weather, low-level, nuclear strike role.

One of our last duties at Grostenquin was to dismantle the 421 Squadron totem pole. The totem pole was made from forty-five-gallon oil drums with two sheets of metal for wings. Our first duty on arrival in Baden-Soellingen was to assemble our totem pole and place it in a hole we dug in front of our squadron operations room.

Wing Commander "Bud" Lawrence arrived to become our new squadron commander, replacing Gerry Theriault, who now became deputy squadron commander. I knew Bud from Gimli, where he was base standards officer. He immediately made me squadron adjutant—more paperwork. I was also a squadron pilot, weapons officer, and sometimes test pilot. Bud had been a wartime Spitfire pilot near the end of World War II. He asked me if I wanted to accompany him to London, England, for a weekend. Naturally, I was keen to do the trip. This would be my first trip to London.

We landed at Wethersfield, a U.S. Air Force base. We were transported to the train station in Braintree and headed for the big city. Bud had made arrangements for accommodations at the army-navy club and now proceeded to show me the town. He was reliving some of his own experiences while a young pilot during the war. We were walking along and Bud suddenly stopped and looked at the entranceway into a local shop. He started to laugh, telling me that this was the spot where he had been beaten up by two Australians. Apparently they were out for a pint or two and Bud had made some remark about the Aussies, which they took offence to. They went outside to settle the matter, and he lost.

I thoroughly enjoyed the visit to the city, but it was now time to take the train back to Braintree and pick up our T-33 and head back to 4 Wing. In order to start the T-33, a battery cart was required. All Canadian battery carts were modified to give a gradual increase in power to 24 volts. The American carts gave an instant 24 volts. We were aware that we might have a problem on start because the instant 24 volts could break the starter motor "quill shaft." We always carried a spare quill shaft in a compartment in the wing tip tank. Our engine started okay, but a rather large African American airman came running towards us and climbed up the ladder, shouting, "She's gonna blow, get outta there!" When we started there must have been a pool of fuel in the tail pipe and it ignited, sending a large flame out of the tail pipe. The flame soon burnt off and we advised the airman all was okay. Bud and I both got a kick out of the airman's alarm. He was just doing his job, but at the time we chuckled over it.

We were now in full training for our base and squadron tactical evaluation. The "tac-eval," would be completed by a group of RCAF and USAF senior officers. They looked into every aspect of base and squadron operation to ensure we could complete the mission before we were given nuclear weapons.

The pilots flew many low-level navigation missions in all kinds of weather, both at night and during the day. We were all rapidly becoming proficient in all aspects of the aircraft and the mission profile.

Practice tac-evals were scheduled to give us some idea of what was expected of the base and squadron personnel. When the weapons were delivered, they would be guarded by one Canadian and one American, both armed. Visualize a 104 aircraft with a yellow line, one foot wide, all around the aircraft. Standing on the line it was physically impossible to touch the aircraft, The only time an armed aircraft could be approached was when the assigned pilot to that aircraft wanted to complete the walk-around, set the target settings on the weapon, and complete his cockpit checks, including placing his parachute in the position he was comfortable with and placing his hard hat in an easily accessible spot. This was all completed so that no time was wasted in the event of a launch.

We were expected to be airborne within four minutes, from a dead sleep, once the launch horn went off. The assigned pilot and the two guards would stand on the yellow line, and when the pilot walked towards the aircraft, the two guards were allowed to assist him, mainly in the cockpit. The rule was that if at any time anyone walked across the yellow line towards an armed aircraft and it was not the assigned pilot, the guards had authority to shoot the intruder; no ifs, ands, or buts. This was serious business.

During one practice tac-eval at 3 Wing, Zweibruken, there were not enough personnel to have two guards on each aircraft; some only had one guard. A Canadian wing commander approached an American sergeant, the lone guard around a 104. Our W/C asked the guard, "Sergeant, what would you do if I walked across the yellow line?" The sergeant answered, "Sir, I would call my top sergeant." The W/C thought this to be a strange answer and asked the sergeant, "Why call your top sergeant?" The guard replied, "So he could help me drag your dead ass outta there."

There were three active squadrons at 4 Wing—421, 422, and 444. We were given a practice bomb that weighed about 2,500 pounds and was the same shape and weight of the nuclear weapon we would soon have on our aircraft. Each pilot was to deliver the bomb on a Vleiland Island range off the coast of Holland. I was assigned the task of selecting the route for all to follow. I was required to brief all 4 Wing pilots, not only on the route but diversion fields in the event of emergency, and other pertinent information.

I was one of the first airborne. I approached the push-up point and increased my speed, entering the delivery mode, which was to pull the aircraft into a 15-degree climb and the weapon would release, about 3,000 feet. Then you would roll over an escape at high speed feet. The weapon was released from the aircraft by two charges; the forward charge had 40,000 pounds of thrust and the rear 20,000 pounds of thrust. In effect, the aircraft was thrown or pushed away from the aircraft. After rolling my aircraft over to initiate my escape manoeuvre, the bomb was right there; it was following my trajectory—I could almost reach out and touch it.

The weapon was supposed to release a tail cone and a parachute would deploy, decreasing the bomb speed and putting the bomb into its attitude for delivery. The parachute on my bomb did not deploy. I visualized the newspapers the next day saying "*Pilot Missed Target, Sank Ship.*" The coast off Holland was a busy shipping lane to the North Sea and the English Channel. Once I landed, I was advised that several chutes had failed to deploy. The mission was cancelled before we lost more practice weapons. The practice bombs were American and had been in storage for quite some time. American maintenance was supposed to check the tail cones. They did not. The tail cones were rusted and would never release without proper lubrication. It was an expensive lesson. I had to write the report on the exercise.

One beautiful day, I was flying a low-level navigation trip south of Munich. I checked my position as I approached a turning point and, as I started to turn towards my next heading, I heard a very loud noise. I checked my engine instruments and they indicated everything was normal. I looked around but I did not see anyone else in my vicinity. I had no clue what the noise was. After landing I proceeded to our lunch area. Ron Beehler, a 422 squadron pilot was telling another squadron pilot about the strange noise he heard as he made a turn on his navigation flight. My ears perked up. I asked Ron where he heard the noise. We compared turning points and enroute times. We determined that what we heard was each other as we made our turns. We must have been belly-up to each other at the same time, hearing each other's engine noise but seeing nothing. We had to have been very close.

A short time later on another low level flight, Ron had an engine fire and was forced to bail out. The ejection worked beautifully but as he looked up he saw that his ejection seat was hooked onto one parachute rib. The seat fell away after a few seconds, but not before tearing one rib section of his chute. Ron noticed his rate of descent increased quite a bit when he heard another rib tear. His rate of descent increased even more. Luckily, he was approaching a newly plowed field and he landed without any injury. The farmer was still working his field and came to assist Ron.

Another squadron pilot was also forced to eject over the Vosges Mountains, in France. He ejected over a forested area and was unable to steer towards any open area. His chute caught onto a large tree. He thought of hitting the quick release on his parachute harness but he realized he was too high up and on a slope overlooking a path through the woods. He decided to "hang" tough. Eventually, he noticed a couple walking towards him on the path. In his best French he called, "*Aidez moi, aidez moi.*" The couple looked around trying to see who was calling. They eventually looked up and saw his situation. The girl went for help while the man conversed and generally kept company. Help soon arrived and the locals helped him down, none the worse for wear.

Don Caldwell was also forced to eject when he had a compressor stall right after takeoff.

A pilot from 3 Wing ejected at about Mach 8, which was too fast for a safe ejection. After he landed, he was bleeding from his ears, eyes, nose, and mouth. He gathered up his parachute and started to walk down a path where he encountered a young French soldier. Our trusty pilot said, "*Aidez moi, aidez moi.*" The soldier took one look at the bleeding man in front of him and promptly ran away. A few minutes later he returned with his sergeant and medics, who rendered the pilot assistance. Apparently, a French army unit was on an exercise in the Voges Mountains.

Another 3 Wing pilot was on a low-level trip northwest of Frankfurt. It was a beautiful, clear day and he was contour flying and enjoying the scenery when he went over a hill, and there was an RAF Canberra, contour flying as well, coming straight for him. Before either aircraft could react they struck each other's wing tip. The Canberra landed at Ramstein, a U.S. base, with wing damage. The Canadian 104 was able to return to Zweibrucken with restricted aileron control. Lucky lads.

One of our low-level navigation trips was over the Mohne Dam, of "Dambusters" fame during the Second World War. Our trip took us on a meandering route to arrive over the dam. We used the same turning point, church on a hill, as 617 squadron used on their bombing run. We would go very low over the reservoir and cross over the dam. Villagers below the dam complained that we were scaring them and we were ordered to avoid the Mohne. I guess the locals thought the dam might collapse one more time. I can only imagine their feelings when a 104 crossed over the dam at zero feet with all the accompanying noise from the aircraft.

Arrangements were made for some 104 pilots to visit an American "Hawk" missile site. The hawk was designed to locate and fire on low-flying aircraft. Several of our pilots had already visited the site, so we knew where it was. The routine on arrival was pretty standard; lunch, briefing, and a visit to the trailer site around one in the afternoon. We thought it would be interesting to see if they could pick up two 104s at low level. Arrangements were made to have the two aircraft arrive over the site around one. We proceeded to the missile site with a young U.S. army lieutenant. He was expounding about how good his missiles and radar were at detecting low-flying aircraft. We entered the control room and showed us the radar, which he said was not detecting any aircraft. He hardly had the words out when two Canadian 104s came screaming overhead. The look on his face was worth a million dollars. Our plan worked beautifully.

I was on a low-level flight north of Frankfurt when my INS packed it in and became useless. I was flying now at about 500 feet to maintain visual with the ground. I knew where I was when the INS quit so I took up a southerly heading, knowing I would eventually cross the Rhine. All I had to do then was follow the river south to 4 Wing. Suddenly, I passed over a rather large airport, which I recognized immediately as Frankfurt International. Now I knew my exact position. I mentioned that we would normally have our radios dialled into 121.5, the emergency frequency. A voice with a distinct German accent speaking English asked, "104 vicinity of Frankfurt, identify." I ignored his call. When he repeated for me to identify, I answered, "Do you think I'm nuts?" and left it at that. I descended to about 200–300 feet to keep above any wires and below Frankfurt radar. Helicopters were very prevalent in the Frankfurt area, so I had to keep a good lookout. As expected, I started to notice familiar landmarks and landed back at 4 Wing. I never heard anything about my crossing over Frankfurt at 500 feet.

In our free time we had lots of activities, from castle hunting to car rallies. The car rallies, held most Saturdays, were great fun. We would be given a sheet of paper with clues to places that we were to find. One would drive while the other navigated. Once we found our spot there would be a referee there to sign our sheet. On arrival at the different spots, which were conveniently located next to a beer hall or wine stube, we would wait for our departure time. Naturally, we would have beer or wine. By the time the race ended at the officers' mess, we were all a bit giddy, to say the least. We had another beer or two before we headed for home.

As a squadron, we arranged to have a squadron dinner in the Black Forest—guys only. There were about ten of us with our deputy squadron commander, Gerry Theriault, at the head of the table. The food and wine were great. The waiter arrived with the bill and we all pointed to Gerry. The waiter placed the bill before Gerry, who immediately put his hands to his head and elbows on the table. He was calculating what each of us owed. He was so engrossed with the bill that he did not notice that we had all quietly left. When he looked up we were gone. We knew what we each owed and reimbursed him the next day. Some may call it a dirty trick but we thought it was okay.

We had a mixed-costume party in the officers' mess one Saturday night. Everyone was having a great time. Wing Commander Bill Bliss, the skipper of 422 squadron, came along while Judy and I were talking to a few friends. He picked Judy up and deposited her into one of the fountains in the mess. She was thoroughly soaked. She dried off as best she could, with Bill apologizing to one and all. He had had one drink too many. We stayed for the rest of the party.

We, as a family, spent many wonderful hours sitting and having a picnic along the Rhine River. We watched each riverboat as it chugged its way to, perhaps, Amsterdam or Basel, in Switzerland. Most of the boats were colourfully painted. On many weekends during the summer months, beer tents were erected and the "oom-pah-pah" bands would play away and the locals would sing. The boys loved it all. On many occasions when we first arrived near the Rhine, Bryan would be almost immediately bitten by a hornet. They would leave him alone for a while and then attack again. Bryan was the only one the hornets attacked. We often had to move to another location. Something attracted the hornets to him and not the rest of us.

Our trusty Volkswagen took us all over western Germany, France, Belgium, Luxembourg, the Netherlands, as well as Denmark. We put a piece of plywood in the back seat with a mattress on top. The boys played and slept as we drove. There were no such things as seat belts or turn signals at that time. The boys could say, "Put a tiger in your tank," in the language of the country we were in.

Jeff and Jesse Boudens and family lived in Holland. We would visit with them and they would drive to Germany to visit with us. In Holland we toured the Madurodam, a miniature village. It contained everything a town or village would have: windmills, trains, cars, busses, and people—all in miniature. The boys loved the place. We also visited the Keukenhof Gardens, with their vast tulip fields, as well as many towns and villages.

On one trip to northern Holland we had difficulty finding a room for the night. I stopped at a local restaurant to get information about where we could find a room. The owner made a phone call. He advised me that a boy on a bike would be arriving soon and we were to follow him. It turned out our destination was a family home. The boy showed us in. His mother and father were in the process of moving out of their room and into the attic. We said we would take the attic, but they would not hear of it. The family told us to go for supper and they would look after the boys. We slept well and breakfast was provided. Initially, they would not accept any money, but we managed to leave some as we left. Canadians helped liberate Holland from the Germans and to this very day, Canadians are always greeted with open arms.

I mentioned earlier that one of Judy's classmates in nursing married a Dane, Sam Petersen. They lived in Aalborg and had a family cottage on the North Sea. (During one visit, Bryan was bitten by a zebra at a local zoo. The skin was not broken but he certainly made it known to all what bit him.) In order to reach the cottage, we had to drive down the beach; all the cottages were behind the sand dunes. The road in was made of planked wood similar to railroad ties. The North Sea water reminded Judy and me of the Bay of Fundy. It was cold and the wind never stopped blowing. One evening, we were driving back from dinner when I spotted someone walking along the beach. I asked Sam to stop because I knew the walker. It was Ken Kensick. We both were instructors at Gimli. He told us he was at a party and had gone for a walk but could not find his way back to the party. We put him into the car and returned to the pub where we had dinner. Ken bought us a beer and we chatted but it was not long before he spotted a local girl, and we lost Ken. As we left, we waved good-bye. I have not seen him since that night. He went on to fly for United Airlines and is living in California.

Judy's Aunt Helen and Helen's long-time friend, Percy Harrison, visited us from Saint John. Helen did nothing but complain about the food and that no one even served a half-decent hamburger. I tried to tell her that she was now in Germany, not Canada, and to enjoy the food; it was great. Percy complained that he was having trouble sleeping and wanted to know if he could have a drink of rum when he could not sleep. I said, "Help yourself." He did, usually drinking the bottle dry. I would buy him another for the next night. Bacardi was $1.90 for a forty-ounce bottle. I, for one, was looking forward to their departure.

We had planned a trip to an American recreation area in Berchtesgaden, Bavaria. This is the same area that was rumoured to be the last stronghold of Hitler's Reich. It is also the area where Hitler's Eagle's Nest retreat was located. When we made the reservation we did not know Helen would be with us so we had to take her along. Percy, being a World War I vet left on his own to visit the different battlefields of the World War I era. I had contacted the U.S. reservation folks and advised them we were now a party of five not four. On arrival we were told that as the "elderly lady" was not a family member she could not stay at the retreat. I told them we had had a long drive to arrive at the rest area and asked if they could make an exception. They came up with the idea that Helen would be called our maid; that way she could stay. Helen was not happy with the title but at least we got to stay. The hotel was called the General Walker and was directly below the Eagle's Nest, which was closed to the public at that time. The hotel once housed Hitler's SS guards. The town itself is situated in a valley and is very picturesque. We visited a great deal of the area, dragging Helen along. We promised ourselves we would come back for a visit, but without her. On our return to Baden we put Helen on a train. She was to meet up with Percy in Paris. Good riddance.

A few months later, we stayed in the recreation area again, but without Helen. We visited a salt mine where we had to dress in coveralls, little hats, and leather aprons. In order to go from one level of the mine to the next we would turn the apron around and slide down a wooden ramp. It was great fun and the boys loved it. We also visited Lake Chiemsee, where we boarded a boat to visit King Ludwig's castle, on an island in the lake. The castle was a miniature of the castle in Versailles, France. Ludwig was also known as the mad king, and history tells us he was not popular. He was found drowned, near his castle. His death was suspicious but no one was ever charged. The castle was never completely finished and remains a tourist area to this day.

I was scheduled for another deployment to Sardinia. We departed as a four-plane formation. One of the pilots was Al Seitz. Al was one of the very first Canadians to use an ejection seat. He had engine failure while flying an F-86 Sabre over the English Channel. He entered the water, which is always very cold, and when he bobbed to the surface, there was an RAF rescue boat heading his way. He was a very lucky man, having spent less than two minutes in the water.

Al's previous flight to Sardinia proved also very interesting for him; he had engine failure. Once again, he had to eject, joining the "Caterpillar" Club a second time. The "club" issued a caterpillar pin to all those who had safely parachuted from an aircraft. Al landed on a small peninsula, on the island of Corsica. The peninsula was actually a penal colony for French prisoners. The guards soon had him in their control and he was flown back to Germany.

Approaching Sardinia, we were advised that all the landing aids, beacon, etc., were not operating. This did not pose a problem for us because we could see the island very well with our radar. We followed the exact method the pilots of World War II used. We descended out over the Mediterranean and, when we were below the overcast, we just turned towards the island and used our radar and INS system to locate the field and land.

We had good weather for our bombing trips to the Capo Frasca range. On my first run, a very Italian voice speaking English said, "Number onea, thatsa bull's eye." After my second run, the voice said, "Number onea, thatsa nother bull's eye." It really sounded funny.

One of our formation spotted a car on a nearby road, and the driver appeared to have a camera. We assumed it was probably someone spying on us. We made a slight correction in our formation and headed directly for the car. We were all very low and probably cleared the top of the car by ten feet. That was enough; the driver jumped in his car and drove away. The sound of four 104s at that speed and height was enough to scare anyone.

One afternoon, we were watching a flight of German F-84s taxiing out for their return to Germany. The F-84 was not a powerful aircraft, the one referred to as a "widow maker." The combination of full fuel for the trip and the hot temperatures required that the F-84 had to use JATO, or jet-assisted take-off bottles to get into the air. JATO bottles were like small rockets, producing tremendous power for short periods of time. Two bottles were used and placed near the aft bottom fuselage, and, once airborne, the bottles were jettisoned. The first two aircraft took off with no problem. The next pair rolled and accelerated, the JATO bottles were lit and away they went. Unfortunately, just as they were airborne, one bottle failed on one of the aircraft. The thrust of the other bottle forced the aircraft into a sharp roll and it crashed at the end of the runway, blowing up and killing the pilot instantly. The poor devil had no time to react.

On our second day, a flight of Americans landed for the night. They were off an aircraft carrier sailing in the Mediterranean. They heard that there were Canadians on the base so they joined us for a beer. Everyone was anxious to do something, and it was suggested that we challenge the Americans to a go-cart race. We piled into our Volkswagen bus. There must have been ten guys; some even sat on the floor. We knew where the track was because we had seen it on our travels to Lido Beach. Well, what a race. We all went flat out; the beer helped. Cars were going off the track, and guys were hitting each other and generally having a good time. No one really won, but the next night we went back to the track with replacement Americans. We were met by the owner of the track and a group of local police. We understood that we were no longer welcome as we had wrecked half his fleet of go-carts. Reluctantly, we went back to the base and a few more beer.

On this particular deployment there was an Australian doctor under contract to take care of us. The three of us, the doc, Leo

O'Donovan, and I, proceeded to drive all over the island in the doc's convertible. We would stop to refill our Asti Spumanti every now and then. As the day wore on, I started to feel ill and knew I had a fever. I asked the good doc to check me out. He said, "Can't you see I am driving? Shut up and die like a man." Leo and the doc got a great kick out of my misery. I just curled up in the back seat and dozed off. The next day I was better. It was probably too much sun.

Friday arrived and we were due to fly back to Germany. We received word that French Air Traffic Control was on strike and we would not be allowed to take off. We were anxious to leave. As section lead I approached the Italian station commander, a colonel. I explained to him that we had been "ordered to return immediately." I was lying through my teeth, but we wanted to get out of Deci and go home. He mulled this over for a minute or so and said, "Okay, you go, but call Roma control when you are airborne." We got airborne and ignored the calls from Roma. We flew back to Germany with no problem. My first transmission was to 4 Wing Tower asking for landing instructions. No one ever inquired about our flight.

I had just landed from a flight when Bud Lawrence advised me that the SMO (base medical officer) wanted to see me ASAP. I had no clue why I was being summoned. I entered the SMO's office and he gave me a sheet of paper to read. It stated that "Mrs. McKay's urine test indicated that she is partially pregnant." When I finished reading the paper the SMO said, "Now for Christ's sake go home and finish the job!" He got a great kick out of the literal translation from German to English. Judy was scheduled to have a little repair work completed after having had two babies. The operation would have to wait—Chris was on the way.

Judy had a rough time carrying Chris. She spent the last three months before he was born in bed, on doctor's orders. They thought she might miscarry and did not want to take any chance on losing Chris. We were fortunate to have friends who took care of the boys when I had to be at the base. It seemed every time we went for a drive Judy would start to have labour pains. We were at the Heidelberg Castle illumination, a re-enactment of the burning of the castle. The roads were packed with cars and the streets with people when

Judy advised me she was having labour pains. We found our car and fought our way south towards Baden-Soellingen. I knew where there were several U.S. bases, including Heidelberg, along the route home, where we could have stopped. Each time I mentioned that we could pull off the Autobahn, Judy would say, "I'm okay, press on," which we did. Judy was admitted to the base hospital, only to have the contractions stop. Home we'd go and back to bed for Judy. This exercise happened three or four times before Chris was finally born.

One evening, with friends, we had dinner near Zweibrucken 3 Wing. The food and wine flowed and it came time for dessert. Judy asked for chocolate but was advised they had no chocolate dessert of any kind. Judy, obviously very pregnant, was not going to have her chocolate fix. I noticed our waitress put her coat on and leave the restaurant, returning after a few minutes. The waitress arrived at the table with a plate containing a chocolate bar. We were all impressed. Germans were very kind and helpful throughout Judy's pregnancy.

Chris was born on May 23, 1965. Dave and Bryan were staying with friends. The nursing staff asked me to leave and give Judy some time to rest. I went to the PX, bought a few cigars, and went to the mess. I did not have to buy a drink; the lads tried to fill me in. Norm Hull suggested I have dinner with him and his family and I agreed. Norm lived close to us in Rastatte. The meal was great and the wine flowed freely. I drove the short distance to home and fell into bed. I don't think my head hit the pillow when there was a loud knock on the door. I opened the small window to see who it was and there were two MPs saying, "Sir, there is an alert, return to base immediately." I acknowledged the message and, as I was still in uniform, splashed cold water on my face and headed for the base. To this day I do not remember the drive to the base.

I arrived at the squadron and Bud Lawrence said, "My office; lay on the couch." He was one of the culprits at the mess trying to fill me in; I guess they succeeded. I was dead to the world when my buddy Harry Stroud shook me awake, and said, "Don, you are airborne in thirty minutes"; it was 0430 hours and dark out. I walked to the washroom and splashed more cold water on my face. I gathered my gear and headed for the aircraft. Once I was in the air I selected the autopilot on, put my feet in the ejection position and my hand on the ejection handle. If the engine so much as farted I was going to eject. My stomach did not feel the best and, unlike an airline, there was no convenient bag to put a deposit into. I flew my assigned navigation trip and returned to 4 Wing on a very long, straight-in approach. After landing and parking the aircraft, I climbed down the ladder and headed for the bushes, where I bent over and proceeded to leave a deposit for the animals. I then heard a very American voice say, "I goddamn see it, but I goddamn don't believe it." My stomach felt much better after my visit to the bushes. I turned around and there was a Canadian wing commander and an American lieutenant colonel looking at me. I said, "Good morning," and walked back to the squadron. I flew four more trips that day and felt like a million dollars.

The "alert" was our final evaluation by observers to see if the base, squadrons, and aircraft had reached the standard to qualify for the nuclear role. We passed with flying colours. All squadron pilots were given a special nuclear clearance, which allowed the pilot and "only the pilot" near the nuclear weapon.

QRA (quick reaction alert shelters), similar to a Quonset hut, but open at each end, were built to house and shelter the aircraft. Each aircraft had the two guards I mentioned. In addition, the area surrounding the QRA area was double-fenced, about twelve feet high, topped by razor wire. Between the two fences was an area about twenty feet wide for patrols with dogs. In the event of a launch, a large wire gate would open and we could taxi out to the runway and be airborne in four minutes from a dead sleep. Security was very tight. When we were assigned QRA duty we were screened as we entered the secure area, badges checked. We were behind the wire for twenty-four hours. A QRA building had cots for the pilots and ground crew and meals were supplied. Most of the time we either read or played chess. Some preferred bridge but I never enjoyed playing cards.

Early one morning we had a scramble alarm. The aircrew slept in one end of the building while the ground crew were at the other end. In the mad panic to reach our aircraft, both groups passed in the hall leaving next to no room to make a quick exit to the aircraft. One of our pilots was jostled and fell to the floor breaking his arm. Luckily the scramble was just a practice. Routes to and from the aircraft were changed so that we all did not meet in the hall again.

All the pilots were issued with a Dosimeter Badge, which we

CF-104. All external tanks and practice weapon attached; my favourite picture.

were required to wear. The Dosimeters were read at regular intervals to see if we were exposed to any nuclear material. To my knowledge no one was ever affected.

Oran Webber was the doctor who delivered Chris. He knew Judy had had a hard time before and after the delivery. He suggested that I take her and the boys to Italy for a much-needed rest. He and his wife had just returned from Italy, where the weather was spectacular during their visit. Oran and his wife said they would gladly take Chris while we were away. They were newly married with no kids of their own. I started making a few plans.

We borrowed a tent and sleeping bags from Harry Stroud. The first day, we drove through Switzerland and stopped for the night near Lake Lugano. The day had been sunny and bright. We were all settled into the tent for the night when it started to rain. It came down in buckets and, when the wind picked up, I was certain the tent would blow away. I got up and tried to steady the centre pole, but it shook back and forth and I was just hanging on. Finally, I woke Judy and asked her to get the boys into the Volkswagen bug, as well as all our belongings. Once Judy was in the car, I let go of the centre pole and stepped out towards the car. The tent took off in the wind wrapping itself around a fence and bushes. By this time I was soaked. I gathered the tent up, wrapped it the best I could and placed it on the roof rack. Judy had the car going but, as usual, the Volkswagen put out very little heat. It was now about five in the morning, so we decided to leave our campsite and hopefully drive out of the weather. We approached the gate but it was locked. The sign stated the gate would be opened at 6:30 am. We were stuck.

Finally, the gate was opened and we were able to leave. The rain stayed with us most of the day. Late in the afternoon, as we approached our campsite on Lido Beach, north of Venice on the Adriatic Sea, the weather started to clear. It was obvious that the same weather that we had had at Lugarno had hit the area hard, causing wind and tree damage. We did learn that the wind was so strong during the previous evening that it uprooted a tree that fell on and destroyed a car. A collection was made from all the campers and enough was collected for the family to replace their damaged car. It was reported that it was the worst storm since 1945.

We found our campsite and proceeded to unpack. Every piece of clothing was wet. The tent was drenched. I put it up hoping that the sun and breeze would dry it enough so we could use it. We attempted to squeeze the water out of the sleeping bags with little success. About this time campers, mostly German, saw our situation and brought dry sleeping bags and clothes for us all. Words cannot express this show of generosity from our fellow campers; it was truly remarkable.

By the afternoon of the next day we were pretty well dried out. We returned our borrowed sleeping bags and clothing, with grateful thanks. We spent the afternoon on the beach, and the boys had a wonderful time, as did Judy and I. During the evening as we snuggled in our dry bags, Judy started to shake quite badly. I felt her forehead and she was burning up. She took some aspirin and put cold compresses on her forehead with little effect. The next morning she was no better so I packed everything up and we headed back to Baden-Baden. By early evening, we were somewhere in Austria and I was having a hard time staying awake. I spotted what looked like a motel; thankfully it was. I got the boys into our room, wrapped a blanket around Judy, and half carried, half dragged, her into the room. She fell asleep immediately. I rounded up some food for the boys, but I was too tired to eat. Once I put my head down I immediately fell to sleep. The next morning Judy still had a fever. We were on the road early and arrived back in Rastatte in the late afternoon. I contacted Oran and he diagnosed that Judy had pneumonia. Oran ordered medication and said that he and his wife would keep Chris until Judy was back on her feet.

Our trip to the wonderful weather on the Adriatic lasted a total of five days. I was exhausted and the boys were now so full of energy I had a hard time containing them so Judy could rest. By the time I went back to work Judy was back on her feet, Chris was home, and everything was back to normal. The squadron could hardly believe our experience. Quite a vacation.

During our time in Europe we planned a trip to the Costa Brava in Spain on two different occasions. Each time we had to cancel because either Judy or one of the boys became sick.

We knew that if we bought an American-made vehicle and kept it for one year before we returned to Canada there would be no taxes on the vehicle. Many of our pilots bought vehicles through the American PX. We drove to Karlsruhe, stopped at the U.S. PX and ordered a four-door Rambler. The vehicle was delivered in about three months. There were no trade-ins allowed so we sold our Volkswagen to another squadron pilot. It was fun driving a bigger car after the Volkswagen.

One trip we took as a squadron was to the Mercedes-Benz plant in Stuttgart, Germany. We were wined and dined and shown many of their early racing cars. These vehicles had been hidden underground during the war to protect them. The German workers were very interested in the Rambler and looked in every nook and corner of the vehicle. I do not think they were impressed with the quality. On our drive back to 4 Wing, just as we entered the Autobahn, I noticed a rather large truck tire heading straight for us. I managed to move to the right and up an embankment as the tire whistled by. The tire did not miss us by much; it ended up crashing into some trees. The rest of the trip back to Baden was uneventful.

A vacancy opened up in the base PMQ (permanent married quarters). We moved from our apartment in Rastatte. The PMQ was only a two bedroom but the boys now had more kids to play with.

Chapter Sixteen

Sick Kids – Decisions to Be Made

Our squadron planned a dinner party, pilots only, across the Rhine in France. The base provided a bus and driver. We knew no one would be in any shape to drive. The dinner and wine were great. One highlight of the restaurant was the washroom. It was located in a separate building, one door had "*pissoir*" over the entrance while the other had "*shittoir*."

We headed back to base in a very thick fog. On approaching the guard house for identification, one of the guards came on board asking for me. I was advised that my wife and son were on the way to the U.S. military hospital in Heidelberg.

I was instantly sober and quite concerned. I went directly to our apartment and found Bryan and Chris were being cared for by Oran Webber's wife. She explained to me that David was having difficulty breathing and that Judy had called Oran. Luckily, he was attending a party in one of the PMQs. He checked Dave over and said that Dave needed a tracheotomy. They bundled him up and headed for the base hospital.

The rest of the story I learned over the next day or two. When they arrived at the base hospital they found out that trachea trays were only available for adults. Oran told Judy that because he was a new doctor he had never performed a tracheotomy. Judy advised him that during her nursing career she had witnessed such an operation. She then proceeded to give orders to the base nurses, who looked at Oran for direction. Oran told them to do whatever Judy asked.

Judy held David's head, while Oran made an incision in his throat, installing a tube from the adult kit. Oran said that Dave should be in a major hospital, so a call was made to an American base, and a helicopter was dispatched to pick up Dave and Judy. The fog was so thick that the helicopter was unable to land. The decision was made to use the base ambulance for transport to the U.S. army hospital in Heidelberg. Shortly after entering the Autobahn, the ambulance lost power and was forced to pull over. Luckily, the radio still worked and the base hospital was advised. They, in turn, called the town of Baden-Baden and explained the situation. They were happy to dispatch an ambulance. The two ambulances found each other in the fog. Judy and Dave were transferred to the German ambulance and they proceeded to Heidelberg and the U.S. army hospital.

In the meantime, Dave had haemorrhaged through his throat. It was later learned that one lung had collapsed. He was one sick little boy. On arrival in Heidelberg, Dave's lung was re-inflated and a proper tube placed into his throat. He was placed in intensive care. Judy explained she was a nurse, and that she was going to be with him at all times. Judy was awake for about two days when the staff insisted she get some sleep. They gave her a sedative and placed her in a bed next to Dave.

I visited Dave in Heidelberg when he was in intensive care. He was still in an oxygen tent and hooked up to many tubes. He looked so small. He managed a smile when he saw me. I was near tears seeing him so fragile. I told Judy that the other boys were fine. After his time in ICU, Dave was placed in a room with other children to fully recover. Judy drove with me back to Baden for a rest and a change of clothing.

While Dave was still in Heidelberg, we invited Oran and his wife for a "thank you" dinner. Judy commented that she was concerned about Bryan. Oran picked Bryan up and played with him on the floor stating he was fine. Bryan was put back in his crib and we sat down for dinner. We all heard the cough from Bryan. Judy and Oran gathered both he and Chris up and headed for the base hospital. They were placed in oxygen tents and observed rather closely. They were both fine in a day or two and we had no repeat of David's experience.

We did learn that the locals referred to the Rhine valley as "Death Valley." Pollutants from the Ruhr industrial area would settle in the valley. Any German children who had breathing problems were immediately taken out of the valley until they grew out of the problem. We were told that after the age of five children would have outgrown the chance of getting "croup" again. David was five when he had his first attack. He had another when we lived in Montreal when he was seven. By then we knew how to deal with the problem, a change of air usually did the trick. Bundle him up and go outside.

After about a week we were advised Dave could return to Baden. It was so good to have everyone together again. The recommendation of the U.S. doctors was to get the children out of the Rhine valley, and our base doctor concurred. We had some major decisions to make. We had to go back to Canada.

My squadron commander, Bud Lawrence, agreed that we should go home. He thought there would be no problem getting the family back but that I might have some problem convincing the higher echelons that I should go with them. I was mentally prepared for a bit of a fight. I approached the base administration officer and explained my family's problem in great detail and advised him I wanted seats on service air back to Canada, the following Friday. He replied that the military had spent a great deal of money on my 104 training and I was too valuable to let go. I then told him if service air was not provided, I was prepared to board a Trans-Canada flight out of Frankfurt with my family. I stated I could care less what happened to me but we, as a family, were leaving for Canada. He pondered my position and was waffling. I advised him to call METZ, headquarters for the air division, and brief them of my predicament and my intentions. I left his office and went home to pack.

Our *telefungen* radio was quite large. I had to build a rather large crate in order to ship it back to Canada. We had trunks that we had brought from Canada and we soon had them packed. Another problem was that we had not owned the vehicle we had purchased through the U.S. PX for a full year. We were short by nine months. The base administration officer did try to get a special dispensation so we could bring the vehicle home tax free but no answer was ever received. I drove to Karlsruhe and explained our problem to the PX outlet. Without hesitation, they said bring the car back and they would refund the money I had paid. I could not believe our good fortune. I actually ordered another vehicle through the American

PX to be picked up at the factory in Brampton, Ontario. At least we would have a vehicle waiting for us in Canada.

I was advised by the base administration that service air was approved for the following Friday and that I was to be transferred to headquarters in Ottawa, Department of Postings and Careers. I had no clue what my new job would entail and at that moment I could have cared less. We were going home.

In order to leave for Canada, a customs officer had to inspect our personal effects and stamp the appropriate documents. I explained what we had and why we were leaving and that we were already packed. He asked a few questions and stamped our documents. In addition, I had to clear the base, which meant I had to return my parachute as well as several other items. A signature was required from each section on the base. I did not have the time to waste running around from section to section so I signed the form myself. No one questioned my signature next to all the different sections. A squadron friend returned my parachute and hard hat to flight safety.

Transportation was arranged by the base and we headed for 1 Wing Marville, France, for our flight home. Another problem that came up was that Chris was too young to have the necessary inoculations for entering Canada. The problem was solved by a Marville base nurse, who pretended to administer the vaccine and fudged the dates, with our promise to have Chris receive the proper needles as soon as possible on arrival in Canada. Naturally we complied. Chris received the proper vaccine when he reached the appropriate age.

I can honestly say that I do not remember much of the flight home; we were all exhausted.

Chapter Seventeen

Home – New Challenges

We arrived in Trenton, Ontario, December 18, 1965. I arranged train transportation to Saint John, New Brunswick, and we arrived home in time for a wonderful Christmas. It was the first time any of the family had seen Chris and everyone marvelled at how much Dave and Bryan had grown over the past two years overseas.

We had a marvellous Christmas and saw both sides of the families. It was good to be home. I was curious and anxious as to what awaited me in Ottawa. I received a telegram advising me to go to the local armoury for orders and travel documents.

The orders included a train-travel voucher as well as the date I was to report for duty. I said my goodbyes and proceeded to Toronto. I caught a bus to Brampton to pick up our new vehicle, a four-door Rambler. The drive back to Ottawa was uneventful, but I could not find the airport or the associated RCAF base. When I was stopped at a traffic light, I asked the car next to me if he knew where the base was located. He said, "Follow me," which I did. We soon arrived at the main gate and I waved a thank you. I entered the base and soon found the officers' mess. The duty officer provided me with a room. Officially, I was not entitled to a room, but I acted as though I was to be stationed at Uplands and no one was the wiser. I needed a place to stay, cheap, until I could find a place to live for Judy and the boys.

I reported to DPCAF (Department of Postings and Careers) and was warmly greeted. It was explained to me that I would be responsible for 1,500 flying officers and flight lieutenant pilots. In addition to postings and cooperating with the other commands and their demands for warm bodies, I had to deal with individual stations. I was expected to manage individual careers as well. My new job sounded next to impossible for one individual. I was also told that I was required to have the staff school course, in Toronto. The course proved to be very beneficial in completing my assigned tasks.

After my initial briefing, I was given a few more days to find living accommodations, which I eventually found on the west end of the city. I called Judy, and she bundled up the boys and caught the train for Ottawa. All our immediate personal effects had been sent by train to Ottawa station, now the Congress Centre. I found everything but our crated stereo. The staff at the rail station was very cooperative. I eventually spotted the crate I had made in Germany, standing on its end on a trolley near the back of the enclosed yard. I was afraid that it was probably damaged but I was pleasantly surprised to find, when I opened the container, that it was all in one piece.

Europe uses 220 amperes electrical power, while North America is 110 amps. Consequently, I had to get a technician to convert the power source. Once he was finished, I turned the stereo on and everything worked. The technician actually said that he would buy the stereo if I wanted to sell it. I declined his offer. I also advised our orderly room of our new address and they contacted the storage company in Winnipeg to move our stored personal effects from Gimli to our new address.

While I was waiting for everyone and everything to move in, I spent time at DPCAF to get a feel for my future job and get to know the officers I was to be working with.

I had about a month for everyone to settle in before I started my course in Toronto. The course lasted from April 25, 1966, to July 29, 1966. I managed to get home every weekend.

I travelled back and forth to Toronto with another chap on course from Ottawa. We took turns driving. In the summer months, Judy and I arranged a camping spot on Silver Lake, a provincial park, west of Perth, Ontario. My driving buddy would drop me off late Friday afternoon and pick me up on his way back to Toronto late Sunday afternoon. The system worked well. The province had allowed a maximum of thirty days on any particular camp site. When our month was up, Judy and the boys moved back to town. The boys were sorry to leave; they were really enjoying the camp and all it had to offer.

The staff school course was arranged to improve our writing, reading, and public speaking. We were given a series of books to read. We were to write a critique on each book and present it to the course. The instructor would then review our critique and our presentation and offer ways to improve. We also did a speed-reading course, and then we had to answer questions on what we had read to see how much we actually absorbed. This new way of reading was initially hard work but, as the course progressed, we became quite proficient in speed reading and answering questions on what we had read. The system really worked. I still use the craft when I want to browse something quickly. It is not a good system to use when reading a novel or a technical manual.

We had navy as well as RCAF personnel on course. One of the navy students was a hard hat diver. Once we started talking it turned out he knew my family. Small world. I took Mike Fontaine home with me for the weekend. It was a break for him to get away from Toronto, even for just a weekend.

We had a neighbour, Laurie Fry, a navigator, who was working in DPCAF. He arrived at our door one day when Mike was visiting. He told us he had a buddy arriving from Greenwood, Nova Scotia, who was to have a vasectomy on Saturday and Laurie wanted to play a joke on him. He asked me to pretend that I was the doctor who would be performing the operation on his buddy. I was to knock on his door, tell him who I was and that I was in the area and thought I would drop in to see the patient and get some preliminary information and questions out of the way to save time in the morning. I told Laurie that I probably would not be able to keep a straight face but that Mike, who had been listening, would make a perfect doctor since he had lost most of his hair and looked the part. All was agreed to.

Judy, Mike, and I arrived at Laurie's door about seven in the evening. Laurie greeted the doctor, complete with glasses and briefcase, and invited him in. He left the door open and Judy and I entered and went up and sat on the stairs out of sight of the "buddy." We could hear the introductions and the small talk and then the good doctor asked Laurie and his wife to leave the room while he talked to the patient. They joined us on the stairway.

Judy, who is a nurse, had briefed Mike on the operation and had given him a few medical terms to use during the conversation. Mike asked the patient if his wife was in agreement with the operation. He answered that they already had three children and did not want any more. Mike took out a pad and proceeded to make a small drawing of the operation, explaining the whole procedure.

It was about this time that Mike said, "To save some time in the morning, why don't you just drop your pants and I'll do my preliminary examination now. The patient did as the doctor asked. Mike threw out a few medical terms and then in a very serious voice, said, "My God, man, there is not enough there to cut!" The patient finally caught on and said in a very loud voice, "You bastards," whereupon we all left the stairs and entered the living room as the patient pulled his pants up. We had a great laugh and a few beers, giving tribute to our "doctor" and a job well done.

Another student on the course was "Goose"—his last name escapes me. Goose was a navy pilot, who had lost his leg in a car accident, but was able to return to active flying. He was hoping to be the first naval pilot to fly the CF-104, artificial leg and all.

One morning, we were gathered into the briefing auditorium to hear lectures and briefings from royal navy brass. Most of the information was interesting, but we all agreed that the British navy was in love with itself. During the afternoon classes, a rear admiral described the Canadian effort to supply Britain during the war and how we would continue to supply Britain in the next large conflict. At this point, Goose stood up and said that he doubted that Canada could care less what happened to Britain in any future conflict. Silence spread through the hall. The British officers were incensed with Goose's position. Canadian staff tried to soft-pedal the remarks but the Brits had had enough and left the stage. A formal complaint was filed and Goose was ordered to apologize to the British delegation, which he did, with tongue in cheek. We all got a great laugh over the whole incident.

Course completed, I was now ready to leap into my new assignment.

My immediate boss was Jim Simpson who, in turn, answered to Wing Commander Maury Hlady. Our overall boss was an air commodore. The A/C was a wartime pilot and ace, having destroyed seven enemy aircraft.

When I arrived back at my desk in Ottawa headquarters (which we referred to as "the only place in the world run by the inmates"), my in-basket was full with files. My day would be spent reviewing files and writing release forms for those who were leaving the air force. Many of the files I saw were of individuals who were in some sort of trouble or were having problems and their station commander wanted to get rid of them. I also coordinated with other commands when they wanted to move people. Normally, on review, I would concur with their request. Other times I had to say no, usually because the individual concerned was approaching the time for a transfer to or from flying duties. Usually a pilot with a permanent commission completed two flying tours and then, if he showed promise for promotion, he was given a ground job to expose him to the wider experience of pushing paper. There were many pilots who made it known that they did not want any part of a ground tour and that they were happy in rank to remain on flying status.

I recall one flight lieutenant, a wartime retread, who told his kids that flight lieutenant was the highest rank in the air force.

The job kept me busy and, while interesting in many ways, I must admit I would rather have been on a flying station instead of behind the "mahogany bomber"—my desk. I was required to retain my flying status. It was necessary to fly thirty hours in each ninety-day period to retain my proficiency. I was required to have a base checkout on the T-33 at Uplands, the military side of the Ottawa International Airport. Once the checkout, a mere formality, was complete I was authorized to request an aircraft for proficiency purposes. Usually another pilot on a ground tour and I would arrange to fly together to put in the time. Often I could not find anyone to fly with me. I would either fly solo or ask one of the airport ground crew to come along. Most were only too happy to have a trip. We would fly north into the Gatineau hills and buzz the different radar sites. Generally I would just throw the aircraft all over the sky; loops, rolls, and lots of low flying. These trips kept me sane while looking forward to another flying posting.

On one occasion, another pilot and I flew to Gimli on Friday for beer call. Gimli was my old stomping ground so it was like going home. Once word got around I was in DPCAF I received many requests for transfers. I never had to buy my beer. On Saturday morning an old friend, Clive Loader, an instructor, gave me my one and only trip in the Tudor aircraft. The Tudor was very easy to fly, almost too easy, compared to the T-33.

When dealing with files I had to explain my reasons for granting a request or refusing. The files would go to Jim, Maury, and the air commodore for final approval. One individual who had been out of the air force for quite some time requested that he be re-instated. He wanted the air force to grant him permission to attend university, and pay his tuition, leading to his BA. His argument was that he would be more valuable to the service.

The request arrived on my desk from the air commodore. He wanted me to complete the necessary paperwork to "make it happen." I did not agree with him. I wrote that serving members were more entitled than a previous member, who, finding "Civvy Street," not to his liking, tried to make the system work for him. I knew the person involved and I was never impressed with him. My write-up requested that the individual's request be denied. The air commodore agreed with me.

There were times I would receive signed cheques in the mail, asking for a transfer for one reason or the other. I would tear up the cheque and ignore the request. On one occasion, I received a phone call from a padre from one of the flying stations begging me to transfer a certain individual because he was causing great disruption on the station by having sex with every woman on the base, including wives. I granted his request. I had the individual transferred to instructor school. His history followed him to his next station and the riot act was read to him. I often wondered what became of him.

During the summer months, we would get together with air force friends and enjoy a barbecue. One very hot Saturday, we were gathered in our postage-stamp-size condo backyard—two pilots and a navigator, wives and kids running about. We noticed a young couple moving their belongings into a condo kitty-corner to ours. I approached them and invited them for a cold drink. They thanked me and said they would soon be over. When they arrived, introductions were made and I asked them if they would like a beer or wine. The chap's wife was fine with a soft drink, but then her husband said, "I will have a Coke as well. I am a pilot and I do not drink." Well, the three air force guys started to laugh and the wives joined in. We could not help ourselves. It just sounded so funny. Once we had some composure we explained what our backgrounds were. Apparently he was flying for Spartan Airways. He eventually joined Air Canada. I never did run across him during my time with the company.

I never had a nine-to-five job before and I hated going to work with my lunch in a brown bag and driving with the masses each day. John Balsar, at the time, was in communications at headquarters and he hated it as well. He was always asking me to transfer him to helicopters. Eventually, I managed to get him a helicopter course and, when he completed it, I even managed to arrange an exchange posting in the U.K. He was one happy camper.

Early in his tour in the UK, John was airborne in a helicopter with a full complement on board. They had engine failure and were too low to auto rotate. The aircraft crashed and all were killed. I know John would never want me to feel guilty. He was doing what he wanted to do. I have to admit I shed a tear and wondered if I did him a favour after all. Strange, even after all these years, it still affects me.

I was not enjoying myself. The work at times was interesting and I knew that if I stuck it out that at the end of my three-year tour I could post myself to wherever I wanted to go and probably be promoted as well. Paul Hellyer was the defence minister at the time and his claim to fame was integration of the different services. The change was made to save money from duplication. Mr. Hellyer only succeeded in ruining morale and making everyone wear a green uniform. During the transition period, I was one of a group of officers who tried on various shades of green uniforms. Normally, this was an early Friday morning exercise; it was a great way to ruin a weekend. We would give our preference as to colours, rank, braid, etc. Not one officer wanted a change. The army, navy, and air force wanted to keep our present uniforms. Mr. Hellyer was successful in his mission, much to the displeasure of all service members.

I was tired of processing release forms for pilots I knew, who were leaving the service to join airlines around the world. I kept telling Judy that I was not happy with integration and that I was thinking of applying for an airline as well. Week after week I would repeat myself. Judy finally said, "I am tired of hearing the same old story. Shit or get off the pot."

The next Monday I applied to Trans-Canada Airlines. I received a letter in a relatively short time asking me to come to Montreal for an interview. Garth Edwards was the "hire, fire" individual.

I had my interview with Mr. Edwards and, apparently, I was the kind of person the airline was looking for. I was advised that after I had a medical and completed Stanine-type testing that I would again see Mr. Edwards for a final decision on my being hired. It was a long day of interviews, medical, etc. When I entered Mr. Edwards's office, he shook my hand and advised me that I met all the airline requirements and asked when I would like to start course. I was offered a second officer's position on the DC-8 starting in May or a first officer's position on the Viscount. I naturally elected the Viscount position. I wanted to fly. If I had only known about the seniority system in TCA I would have chosen the second officer course. Live and learn. Then again, I would never have had the opportunity to fly the Viscount. In the end it worked out as it should.

On my return to DPCAF my immediate boss knew something was going on but, as yet, I had not put him into the picture. I wrote my resignation and submitted it. My memo was circulated up the ladder. I knew it had reached the air commodore, because he hollered for all to hear, "McKay, get the fuck in here!"

I had worked hard to obtain my permanent commission. Competition was keen at the time I received mine, and I was one of less than ten pilots who had received it out of approximately two hundred. A few years later, anyone who wanted a permanent commission could have one, which left a bad taste for those of us who worked so hard to prove ourselves worthy of it.

Up to the time I walked into the air commodore's office, I was still waffling and wondering if I was doing the right thing. The A/C started by reviewing my record, which was pretty good. I then said that I was not happy with integration and that, in my position, I was going to be one of many serving officers who would have to make integration work. In addition, I stated that those in Grade 8 now would be the ones who benefited from our work.

The air commodore then said he knew many TCA pilots and, as far as he was concerned, they were poor citizens, who showed disloyalty by not staying in the RCAF after the war. I was shocked by his outburst. These pilots fought during the war and had a right to do as they saw fit for themselves during the postwar era. He ranted on about my career and how much I was needed. After his first outburst, I said to myself, "If I ever had doubts about leaving, the A/C proved me otherwise."

Over the next few weeks, I was taken aside by all of my superiors, who tried to convince me not to leave. Wing Commander Hlady had the decency to tell me he was ordered to work on me. Just before I left the service he told me, "If I was your age, I would leave as well." After I left that position to join Air Canada, I was replaced by seven officers of major rank.

Several months after I left the service, the air commodore left the air force early as well. He took a job with Canadian Tire. So much for loyalty.

Chapter Eighteen

Trans-Canada Airlines – Air Canada

The plan was that Judy and the boys would remain in Ottawa until I completed the Ground School Viscount Course. Once the course was completed, I could be transferred to Vancouver, Winnipeg, Toronto, or Montreal. We would make our final moving arrangements at that time.

We were fortunate to have a neighbour who was a jeweller with Birks. He and his family were recently transferred to Montreal and would be living in the NDG (Notre-Dame-de-Grâce) area of Montreal. They advised me that they had an extra bedroom that I could use while on course. I gratefully accepted. One of the requirements for joining TCA (Trans-Canada Airlines) was that I must have a civilian commercial licence, which I had allowed to lapse when I joined the RCAF. I gathered the necessary study material and arranged to write the exams. I was a lot more familiar with all subjects this time around compared to my initial writing for a commercial licence.

It turned out I did not have to write all the exams. The Ministry of Transport was of the opinion that we were well-trained pilots already. We were only required to write one exam; air regulations. The exam was written at the Ottawa International Airport. Once I had written the exam it was graded, and I was advised that I had passed the requirements and given my airline transport pilot's licence, number YZA-001181.

I was talking to the Ministry of Transport representative when we both heard a loud explosion. We could see a large plume of smoke near the approach to Runway 32. Apparently, a TCA DC-8, on a training flight, was attempting an approach with two engines out on one side. Control was lost and the aircraft crashed, killing the four pilots on board.

The TCA course was located at Dorval International Airport, in the TCA maintenance facility. We were greeted by the chief of flight operations and introduced to the different instructors. The syllabus was similar to that of the air force—meteorology, navigation, etc. Since I was to be a Viscount first officer, I had to learn all about that aircraft. Like the air force, we had to build them before we could fly them. It never ceased to amaze me that we were required to absorb all this information even though, in the event that something went wrong in the air, there was nothing we could do to fix it anyway. The instructor's favourite statement when explaining things was, "Attached by a series of linkage and gears." It was not until Boeing aircraft arrived that "need to know info" was introduced. The Boeing system was more pilot-oriented and practical, without the need to build the aircraft before we could fly it.

One surprise on my first day was seeing Paul sitting in the front row. If you recall, I tried to "cease training" him and his two left feet at Gimli. I approached him and said I could not believe that he was still alive. He just smiled. Paul had a successful career as an Air Canada pilot retiring as a captain.

I recall going into a washroom to get rid of some coffee. The room smelled quite bad. I made the comment to another student that someone must have died. A voice from the "throne room" came back with a statement: "Yes, and the body is still here."

One part of the course was that we all had to pass a Morse code test. We were required to be able to copy and translate the code received at about ten words per minute. Most of the people on the course were ex-air force, and we had done some Morse code during our Harvard training. It was recommended that we do the exam every Friday morning. Most of us failed the first few attempts. The air force had the Morse code on the charts, and we would listen and check against the chart to confirm the station beacon. In other words, our Morse code skills were lacking. We would sit at a console, headsets on and listen to the dit-dahs. One Friday morning I passed my test. The instructor checked it and told me I passed. I was surprised, but happy. This bit of the course proved the hardest, but it was a requirement that had to be achieved. Two of our coursemates finally passed the test on the last day of the course.

Once the ground school was completed we started simulator. Several new "hires" failed the ground school and had to leave the program. There were two ex-air force pilots who failed the simulator portion of the course. They were shown the door as well. Three of us were sent to Winnipeg for flying conversion on the Viscount. We received lots of practice on three- and four-engine instrument approaches.

In addition, we did a lot of aircraft handling work. We were expected to maintain our altitude, plus or minus 100 feet, and to maintain the airspeed at 250 knots while doing 45-degree bank turns. We did similar exercises in the air force but on one engine. Four engines took a bit more concentration to do the exercise correctly.

Our final trip was with a Ministry of Transport inspector. Our instructor put us through everything he could think of. The inspector also had us do some tracking and intercepting of different tracks. The trip finished with an instrument approach on three engines. I had no difficulty with the "check ride."

My instructor, Dick Cartlidge, planned a passenger flight out of Winnipeg. We flew to Regina, Calgary, and Lethbridge, returning to Winnipeg via Calgary and Saskatoon. Dick flew one leg and I flew all the rest. It was a very good introduction to passenger flying for me.

Course completed, I headed for home. It was a beautiful, hot summer day. As I approached the DC-8 for the trip to Montreal, I observed the pilots standing on the boarding platform; there were no gates in those days, just trucks with stairs. One of the pilots was Jim Garr, my survival course lean-to mate. I jokingly said in a loud voice so other passengers could hear me, "Are you flying this aircraft?" Jim answered, "Yes, sir." I said, "Well, I am getting off." People looked around wondering what to do. I then shook Jim's hand and we had a good chuckle. Other passengers smiled and we all boarded the flight.

One of my first trips out of Montreal was with a captain I had never met. He asked me how long I had been flying the Viscount; I told him this was my fourth trip. He looked at me and said, "I have been scared before. You fly the first leg." I learned later that he had

Viscount—the first aircraft I flew for TCA, 1967.
Reproduced with the Permission of Air Canada

a bit of a reputation and was always in trouble with supervisors. He was eventually fired for a whole list of things, and, with his attitude, it was no wonder he was fired. I heard he started a dry cleaning business.

Prior to flying into New York, Boston, and even Toronto, we had to write a summary of the route. We were required to know all the navigation aids, radio frequencies, and magnetic headings to and from each en-route station as well as all the approaches. Most ex-air force pilots questioned the reason for this. We had charts with all the information and committing all this extra information to memory was just asking for trouble. The standard answer from the TCA supervisors was, "You military pilots think you know it all. TCA has been following these procedures for years." In other words, keep quiet and do as we were told. Enough of us made a case to cease having to memorize all this information that, with subsequent courses having the same complaint, the practice was eventually stopped.

I flew with Reg Jordan on several occasions. He was a soft-spoken man but a very competent pilot. He also liked to play jokes on the flight attendants. When Reg would order coffee, he always asked that the girls serve his coffee on a silver tray. Once the coffee was delivered and after the stewardess left the cockpit, Reg would polish the tray and set it on the floor in front of the centre pedestal. When one of the girls showed up, he would look down and say, "Pretty pink panties," or something along those lines. The girls in my early airline days were a good group and most just laughed off remarks. Today they would report you and have you charged for sexual harassment. Things have certainly changed. The dirtiest jokes I ever heard were told by the flight attendants.

On one trip with Reg, we were flying from Fredericton to Montreal. The stewardess brought us coffee and said there was a passenger who wanted to see the cockpit. Reg said okay. A young man, probably in his mid-twenties, entered the cockpit. He looked like he was just out of a lumber camp with his heavy wool pants, red-chequered shirt, and gum rubber boots. He just stood there, not saying a word, looking all around the cockpit. Finally he spoke. "Jesus Christ, you got more buttons here then I have on my fly!" As you can well imagine, we all burst out laughing.

Reg retired early, sold everything, and moved to an island in the Caribbean. He purchased a boat and set up a small charter business. Reg's oldest son took pilot training and got involved with the drug cartel from Colombia. On one trip to Canada carrying drugs, they ended up forced to land on an old budworm strip in New Brunswick. He was in big trouble. The authorities promised him immunity if he spilled the beans on the cartel. He agreed. Once word got back to Colombia, there was an immediate contract out on him and all his family. Reg was informed and he packed up his family and they sailed for Miami. The whole family was put into the witness protection program where they were given a new identity. I assume they are all still alive living somewhere in the world. Heck of a price to pay for a son's dream of wealth.

Pablo Escobar, the head of the cartel that put out the contract, was himself shot and killed by the police.

On the Viscount there were two pilots and two stewardesses. On our layovers in Fredericton and Sydney, we had a vehicle to drive ourselves to and from the airport. In Sydney we sometimes bought lobster and went to the beach for the afternoon.

One Sunday morning, we were scheduled to fly from Fredericton, to Saint John, and Moncton, finally landing in Halifax. We departed Fredericton with a total of five passengers out of twenty-eight available seats, all heading for Halifax. We approached Saint John and were advised by company radio there were no boarding passengers. We were about to turn towards Moncton when they advised they had no boarding passengers, either. We went direct to Halifax. Scheduling was a little more flexible in the early days. Today you would never be allowed to overfly a station, even if they had no one boarding.

We arrived in Sydney on Christmas Eve 1968. Our planned departure was Boxing Day. The crew was wishing that we were home for Christmas. We drove our vehicle to the Wandlyn Motel, where we normally spent our layovers. The girl at the desk gave us our room keys and told us the restaurant was closed but there was a room set aside with sandwichcs, chips, and the like. We were told where the bread was so we could make ourselves some toast in the morning. We were also advised that the manager and his family would be out Christmas Day to make us a turkey dinner. At least we would have a good Christmas dinner. In spite of the fact we were not home for Christmas, the Sydney motel manager and family went out of their way to make our Christmas away from home memorable.

We were up early Boxing Day for our trip to Halifax. As we drove to the airport, the vehicle stopped running and refused to start. Here we were—two pilots and two stewardesses, standing on the side of the road, with our luggage and flight bags. The wind was howling and a light snow was falling. The temperature was -20F—it was cold. We were far from being properly dressed. Luckily, we did not have long to wait. A van stopped and picked us up and delivered us to the airport. He was a passenger on our flight to Halifax. Our vehicle was towed and repaired for the next crew to arrive.

George Brown was a delight to fly with. He always had a joke and he was well known at all the Maritime stations. We landed in Saint John from Fredericton. I knew all the ramp staff, having worked with them before and after high school; I was always greeted warmly by the gang. One of the customs officers approached us and asked us to pick him up a particular brand of pipe tobacco in Boston; apparently it was not available in Canada. He also told us to purchase a bottle for our own use with no questions asked. I remember many trips when the customs staff often asked for a "tobacco run." It was understood that as long as we did not abuse the privilege we could always bring a bottle from duty-free in Boston. When landing back in Saint John, Jimmy Heighten, a ramp attendant asked George how the girls were in Boston. George replied that they were just like birds; "all feathers and no tail." We all got a chuckle out of George's one-liners. George transferred to Vancouver and not long after he suffered a fatal heart attack. I often think of him and his wit.

Boston was one of my favourite places to have a layover. We were in a hotel near the Common, the centre of everything. The fish food restaurants were unbelievably good. A favourite for beef was Durgan Park, a converted warehouse. There was always a line-up to get in. We were told by other crews to just go to the bar, order a beer, and advise the waiter we were airline. They knew that our time in Beantown was short. Soon he would return and advise us that a table was ready for us. He would then show us the back stairway to the second floor; I never did have to stand in line.

On one Boston layover, we, as a crew, decided to take in a Red Sox ball game at Fenway Park. One of the stewardesses was new to the airline, having moved from France to Canada with her family. Our seats were in the bleachers and we were surrounded by Boston fans. The girl knew nothing about baseball, so we tried our best to explain the game. Suddenly she looked around at the fans and in a loud voice said, "We are surrounded by n—" I put my hand over her mouth and told her that the term is not to be used. We had some dirty looks from some fans but the game soon captured their attention. We left before the game was over so as not to give any provocation to some fan. That night we all went to Durgan Park. We were seated in the usual way. I had a nice steak but could not finish it. The French stewardess looked at me and asked if she could have what was left. She ate like she had never seen food before. Thankfully, I never had to fly with her again.

Captain Pierre Charbin was on one flight from Montreal to Val d'Or, the backend crew and passengers complained that the cabin was cold. We checked our switches and all were in the correct position to be delivering warm air. Pierre took out the aircraft manual and decided he could fix the problem by moving valves manually. The problem was they were located in the main cabin, under the carpeting. Pierre left his seat, leaving the cockpit door open so I could observe him, and proceeded to remove the cabin carpet and lift a panel in the floor, with passengers looking on. He proceeded to explain the heating system of the Viscount. He loved the rapt attention of the passengers. He advised that he could fix the problem by manually moving valves, which he proceeded to do. Nothing happened. The cabin got neither warmer nor colder. Pierre replaced the panel and carpet, mumbled something to the passengers and returned to the cockpit. He wrote in the log book, "Heating system not producing sufficient heat." He made no mention of the fact that he had manually tried to fix the problem.

Friday trips to Val d'Or and Rouyn were always very interesting. We would have several, attractive, alert young ladies on board; some disembarked in Val d'Or and the rest at Rouyn. Friday was payday for the miners in both towns, and the ladies were hoping to collect as much of their paycheques as they could. If you were lucky enough to operate the return flight to Montreal on Sunday afternoon you would see the same ladies again. They were not as attractive or alert anymore, but exhausted from their weekend of work.

We landed at Val d'Or and were told that the Canadian Old-Timers had just completed an exhibition game and would be returning to Montreal with us. Doug Harvey was among the group. The scheduled time arrived for departure, but there was one player missing. Harvey entered the cockpit and said, "See the Buick with the lights on? He is having one last "piece for the road." The car door opened and the missing player raced towards the aircraft stuffing his clothes back into a more normal position. Quite the group.

Another favourite for the ladies was Sept Isles. Friday was also payday for the iron ore workers. On two occasions I had a layover in Sept Isles. At night it was really not safe to go for a walk, particularly over the weekend. The workers were usually drunk, and any provocation would start a fight, even if you looked at them the wrong way. We would eat in the hotel and hit the bed early to avoid any problems.

I also enjoyed layovers in Moncton. I would usually rent a car and drive to Sackville to visit my older brother and family. I always enjoyed these visits. We, as a family, had visited Lorne many times over the years, but now I seldom saw him unless I had that layover.

When I was growing up in Sackville, it was a big thing to travel to Moncton. During the Christmas season, everyone travelled to Moncton to shop at the large Eaton's store, now long gone. I also enjoyed watching the tidal bore. The bore was literally a wall of water that filled the Petitcodiac River at high tide in the Bay of Fundy. It was quite a sight then, but less spectacular today due to dams and bridge-building along the river.

Another highlight was Magnetic Hill, where you can put your car in neutral and the car will actually accelerate uphill. When you see it for the first time it makes you wonder how the car can go uphill without any power; apparently it is an optical illusion. Try it sometime.

On one trip to Halifax we were scheduled to return to Montreal on the Vanguard, another British-built turbo-prop aircraft. The novelty of the Vanguard was that the first-class cabin was in the rear of the aircraft. It is the only aircraft I ever saw in that configuration. All the others had the first-class cabin in the front of the aircraft.

On the completion of one year of flying, all pilots had to complete a probation ride with a supervisor. The ride was important because if you had not reached the TCA standard, you could lose your job. I was scheduled to fly with Jim Rowan. Our route was Montreal, Ottawa, Earlton, North Bay, and back to Montreal.

After landing in Ottawa, the flight attendant entered the cockpit and said there was an elderly passenger who would like to shake the pilot's hand who landed the aircraft, saying, "It was the best landing he had ever experienced." Jim looked at me and said to the stewardess, "Have the gentleman come to the cockpit." Jim introduced himself and then me. "This is the pilot who landed the aircraft." The gentleman, probably eighty, shook my hand and congratulated me for a landing well done and wished me luck in the future.

The stewardess escorted the gentleman from the cockpit. Jim said, "What can I say? With that endorsement, you passed your probation ride." I turned towards the stewardess and said, "Will you thank Dad for me?" The expression on Jim's face was worth a picture. He was not certain if I was pulling his leg or telling the truth about "Dad." I smiled at him and he knew. "You bastard; I must admit that was a first." He also told me he never had a passenger come to the cockpit to shake the pilot's hand. We completed the trip without incident. After landing back in Montreal, Jim said words to the effect of "good ride, no problems, enjoy your career." I saw him a few weeks later and he asked if I was still flying relatives around. We both had a good chuckle.

I thoroughly enjoyed my eighteen months on the Viscount and flying to the "swamp," as the Maritimes were affectionately called. We faced all kinds of weather conditions; fog, rain, hail, freezing rain, snow, and winds that came from every direction—seldom down the runway. We all improved our crosswind landing technique. I was treated very well by most of the captains I flew with and I absorbed a lot about the airline passenger business. I was fortunate to have worked on the ramp in Saint John. I now had a good knowledge of both sides of the whole business.

Chapter Nineteen

DC-8

Each year there was a bidding process, where we would request our personal choice for our next flying assignment. I bid to fly as a first officer on the DC-8; however, all bids were based on seniority. I had to be an "oiler," or second officer on the DC-8. Initially, I was disappointed, but in the airline you live by the seniority. It dictated what aircraft you would fly, when you would be promoted and even when you could have vacation. I knew my time would come.

The course itself was similar to all the courses I ever had. We had to practically build the aircraft before we could fly it. My duty as a second officer was to manage all the aircraft systems, ensuring that during refuelling, the fuel went to the proper set of fuel tanks to ensure proper balance throughout the aircraft. More important, to me, was to observe the captain and first officer to ensure they were doing the right thing. On more than one occasion, I would observe the wrong beacon being tuned in or the wrong communication frequency selected. I observed mainly to learn about the DC-8 and overseas procedures; picking up the errors was bonus. I guess I was reverting to my days as a flying instructor, knowing that you could learn a great deal by observing. Second officers were not normally given time to fly the aircraft. This condition changed during our ground school course and I was fortunate enough to get a takeoff, a few steep turns and a landing. It gave me confidence, knowing that I could fly the four-engine aircraft if and when it was ever required.

Part of the training was an overseas checkout with a supervisor. The duties on the Atlantic included monitoring that the clearances copied by the two pilots were correct. In addition to balancing the fuel to ensure it was being consumed in a proper sequence for aircraft balance, I was also responsible for getting the latest weather

Douglas DC-8 taxiing.
Reproduced with the permission of Air Canada

both for destination and alternate, as well as Canadian airports, in the event we had to return for some reason or other. The radios for reception on the Atlantic were high frequency. They worked when they wanted to; it all depended on atmospheric conditions. Some nights they were loud and clear—other times nothing but static. Eventually, the addition of satellites made radio transmission and the all-important position report much easier.

After takeoff from Canada we would proceed eastbound. Once in contact with Gander Air Traffic Control, we would receive our ocean clearance, which included a "track." The tracks for a crossing were normally issued by Gander for eastbound traffic and Shanwick for westbound aircraft. Aircraft on northern routes would receive their clearances from Winnipeg or Scottish Air Traffic Control. The tracks took weather into consideration—mainly the winds. Speeds to fly were either a true air speed or Mach number. Most airlines used a Mach number: "Maintain Mach 80," which represented 80 percent of the speed of sound. Some aircraft were slower and some a bit faster. The control centres tried to get all aircraft to use the same Mach number on any given track for easier control and separation, which was ten miles in trail. The introduction of inertial navigation and satellites allowed for closer separation.

Normally, on any Atlantic night crossing, there were a minimum of 500 aircraft heading to and from Europe, the United States, and

Canada. Aircraft were always transmitting position reports; at times it was hard to get a word in. Sometimes, when we were unable to contact either Gander or Shanwick, we would ask other aircraft to forward our position report.

North American flights usually left in the early evening to allow for an early morning arrival in the UK or Europe. The crossings were made in total darkness. Occasionally, you could see the navigation lights of other aircraft. Most pilots did not like the sunrise, but, personally, I relished it. The sky ahead would gradually get brighter, then the sun would appear on the horizon, and, as if by magic, it would rise and be bright on your face, the start of a new day. After sunrise you could usually see other aircraft, the same ones we had shared the night sky with over the Atlantic. To me the whole experience of an Atlantic crossing was magic; I never tired of it.

In the early days, a navigator would use his skill to "navigate" the aircraft. The introduction of inertial navigation made navigators redundant. In addition, there were weather ships every 300 miles across the Atlantic. Theirs was a lonely existence, bobbing up and down with the ocean. Normally they were at sea for three months.

On a quiet crossing we would say "hi" to them and exchange a few comments. One evening United Airlines was talking to a ship when a stewardess's voice was heard. The ship's radio operator asked where she was based. She responded New York. He, in turn said, "I live in Brooklyn" and asked for her phone number. She declined, saying, "I better not, someone else may be listening." The radio operator managed to convince her that they were on a discrete frequency and that they were the only two on the frequency. She gave her number and, right on cue, every aircraft responded with a "repeat the number," or "was that 678?" The stewardess had no idea that there were dozens of aircraft listening to her conversation. The frequency was 121.5mh, or the emergency channel, which all aircraft monitored on the Atlantic. No one complained of the conversation being held on the emergency channel.

On occasion, the weather ship would take a position report. One evening, *Alitalia* gave his position, stating he was ten miles south of the weather ship. The radio operator, who had radar replied, "*Alitalia*, estimate your position 100 nautical miles south of our position." The aircraft answered with, "Thank you." He now knew his exact position. Like navigators, the weather ships soon became redundant with the introduction of better navigation aids and radios through satellites.

We left London one clear beautiful day, and our route took us over northern Scotland, Iceland, and Greenland. The Greenland glacier was unusually clear. We knew there was a weather station smack in the middle of the ice cap, so we gave them a call to say hello. We had chatted back and forth when the radio operator said if we had a few moments, he wanted to tell us a story of a recent experience at the weather station. One early morning the radio operator was alone at his station. He could see the cook preparing breakfast for the station complement of twelve, who were sleeping or getting ready for their shift, when he heard a knock on the door.

He said the cook and he looked at each other, knowing that all the station crew were inside the building on the middle of the ice cap. Then, another knock. He and the cook slowly headed towards the door not really wanting to open it. Another knock and voices could be heard, in spite of the wind. Slowly, the door was opened and there stood four men asking to come in. Once in the building, they removed their heavy winter gear. Over coffee, the four explained they were all Norwegian students and, as a summer project, they had decided to walk across the Greenland ice cap. They saw smoke from the weather station and stopped by to get warm and have a hot meal. The radio operator said, "Looking back it was funny but, at the time when the knock on the door came, we didn't know what to do. We are in the middle of nowhere and we were not expecting visitors."

Flight 871 operated from Paris to Toronto. The captain was giving a position report to Scottish control. The operator said the transmission was not clear. "Would you please round out your vowels." The captain replied, "Asshole; is that round enough for you?" With that, we continued on our way laughing.

Air Canada had different series of DC-8s: -40, -54, -61, and -63. All were different, some in many ways. The -40, for instance, had Rolls Royce engines, while all the other series had Pratt and Whitney. When the -63 series arrived, looking down the aisle from the front of the aircraft, it was hard to believe that that entire fuselage was coming with us. Of course, we had to be familiar with each series. I made it a point to review a chapter on each Atlantic crossing, so I became quite familiar with all the systems of each series.

The -40 was used as a freighter and the -54 usually half freight and half passengers.

The freighter operation always left late in the evening and was usually late leaving, so it made for long days and nights. After departing Winnipeg for Vancouver, we were advised by flight dispatch that we were to divert to Edmonton to pick up a load of shovels for Vancouver. A snow storm had caused havoc and stores had no shovels to sell. We filled the gap.

On one trip Vancouver direct to Montreal I developed a bad toothache. I hung in and asked flight dispatch to advise my wife of my problem and to make a dental appointment for that afternoon. In spite of the fact it was Saturday, Judy found a dentist for me and I had a root canal completed before we went home.

The DC-8 had four compressors to pressurize the cabin. On descent, we normally turned two compressors off to avoid a racket in mid-cabin with the compressors gasping for air at reduced power settings. One captain, I will call him Ben, did not think this was necessary. The back-end crew would come to the cockpit wondering why there was such a racket in mid-cabin. I would ask Ben again to turn numbers two and three compressor off. He would ignore me and the passengers' comfort. Once at lower levels the problem solved itself. This proved to be a bone of contention with Ben and me on many flights. I was going by the book. Ben, I was told, was a very intelligent man. I never saw any sign of intelligence, just stubbornness.

I was on a freighter with Ben and a new first officer. Ben landed the aircraft in Frankfurt and asked for reverse. Instead of selecting engines two and three first, the first officer selected all four at once. Ben started giving him a lecture on the proper way to select reverse on the -40 series. In the meantime, we were weaving back and forth along the runway. I called out that we were going to end up in the grass unless someone paid attention to keeping the aircraft straight. Ben realized the problem and corrected our weaving. I received quite a stare from him when we parked at the ramp.

Ben had a reputation and, in my mind, it was not a very good one. During a layover in St. John's, Newfoundland, his television was not receiving what he wanted to see (there was no cable in those days). Out of frustration, he picked up the TV and threw it out the window, which was closed at the time. He proceeded to the front desk, explained what happened and that he would pay for any damages. He also asked for a new room; his was cold.

I observed on my trips with Ben that, on final approach, he had a tendency to keep the throttles near idle, which is a "no, no" on a jet airplane. Others noticed the same thing. I have explained earlier, that in a piston engine aircraft you received instant power when you opened the throttles, while in a jet aircraft, the engine has to "spool up" before you get the power you need. When jet aircraft were first introduced, many aircraft were landing short. The crews had always flown piston aircraft and were slow to adapt to the differences in jet engines. As far as I am concerned, Ben never did understand the differences. I never understood how he lasted as long as he did.

On another freighter trip to London, Ben was flying. The weather was foggy, with mist and very low ceilings. We completed an instrument approach and, as Ben rounded out to land, we floated and floated using up good runway. The first officer did not say a thing. I knew we did not have much runway left so I hollered at Ben to put the damn aircraft on the ground. Crunch, we hit the pavement; full reverse and braking was applied and we stopped with less than 300 feet of runway remaining. Ben told me to never tell him what to do again. I told him it was either holler or go off the end. I was not impressed.

Ben had a habit of not opening his flight bag, which carried all the approach charts. We were always receiving amendments to different airports and we had to update our charts accordingly. He would just reach over and take the first officer's charts. Knowing Ben never opened his flight bag or amended his charts, two pilots opened his bag in the mail room, took out all his charts and inserted an equal weight in bricks. He carried the bag for quite a while before he realized the change. He started amending his charts again. He got the point.

My association with Ben came to a head with another freighter to Frankfurt. Ben did his usual of not turning off compressors and, instead of getting his own approach charts out, he reached over and grabbed the first officer's. I gave the first officer my charts to monitor the approach. Another lecture followed on proper reverse technique on landing. I had had just about enough of Ben, but I bit my tongue.

That evening we were going to meet at the beer tavern for supper. I arrived early and had finished two white wines before Ben and the first officer arrived. Ben rambled on about the trip and that I kept reminding him to do things and he was not happy about it. I had enough wine in me to tell Ben I was not impressed and that he probably flew piston aircraft the same way he did jets and that he did not know how to fly jets. As I said, I was feeling no pain and I was fed up with him. Before I finished, Ben stood up. He was a big bugger and I thought he was going to hit me. The first officer said, "Leave," which I did. That was the only time the first officer actually said something meaningful.

I left and headed back to the hotel. I had a good night's sleep and had just finished showering when I heard someone knocking on doors in the hall. I assumed it was a porter trying to wake Ben and the first officer. They obviously did not answer their phone crew call. I opened my door and sure enough the porter was banging on each door in turn. Then I heard the elevator go "bing" as the doors opened. I turned and saw Ben and the first officer arriving from their night out. I closed my door, finished dressing, and went to the lobby, where the navigator for our flight was dressed and ready for the flight home. He asked me if I had seen the other two. I told him I had. I was in a quandary as to what to do. Should I call the company or not? The navigator asked me if I could fly the aircraft, and I told him I could. He said, "Okay, let's do the flight; it's only a freighter." When Ben and the first officer finally arrived in the lobby, not a word was said. We arrived at flight planning and headed for the aircraft.

Ben was to do the flying home. Once we were airborne, he passed out. I reached up and engaged the autopilot and slid his seat back and into recline. I tapped the first officer on the shoulder and told him to go lie on a pallet and sleep it off. I occupied the first officer's seat, monitored the systems and made all the necessary radio calls and, when the navigator was ready, he took control of the aircraft from his position and navigated us home. Approaching

Labrador, Ben woke up, wondering where we were. I told him and then woke the first officer. Not a word was said. I returned to my second officer's position and we landed in Toronto. The navigator and I exchanged glances and we went our separate ways. When I reported for my next flight, Ben was again captain. He had switched flights with another captain. I gave a quiet groan and did my share of the flight planning. During the trip, Ben was as good as gold. He had nothing but praise for me. He turned the compressors off, as per the manual, and said, "In deference to the second officer I will do it his way." In other words as laid down in the flight manual.

He and another senior captain developed a very dangerous habit. It was necessary at times to "hold"—fly a race-track pattern at a specific altitude and speed. The hold was necessary in an area of heavy traffic density or weather. When aircraft below you were cleared to a lower altitude, you, in turn, would be given a lower altitude. Normally, when cleared to a lower altitude the pilot flying reduced the power and set up a rate of descent to arrive at the new assigned altitude. Not Ben; he would select the speed brakes. The aircraft would enter a rather quick descent and Ben would deselect the speed brakes nearing the new assigned altitude, chuckling the whole time. The passengers must have had their hearts in their mouths.

Ben's friend did the same thing but with a twist. Spoilers and speed brakes were the same airfoil; when selected panels on the upper wing popped up to disrupt the lift in the air, to help slow down, they were called speed brakes. When selected on the ground to help slow the aircraft they were called spoilers.

During the before-landing check, gear down, the spoilers were selected to the arm position. On touchdown they would automatically deploy, decreasing the lift and speed helping to put weight on the wheels to assist bringing the aircraft to a stop. Ben's friend, let's call him Joe, would sometimes pull the spoilers partially back to get a smooth landing. This took a very delicate touch. On an approach to Toronto and over the approach lights, near the end of the runway, Joe's first officer accidently pulled the spoiler lever back full. The aircraft stalled and hit the runway hard enough to dislodge an engine from the aircraft. The crew attempted a go around and managed to get airborne but soon lost complete control of the aircraft, which crashed, killing all on board. Non-standard procedures as per the manual were used by both Ben and Joe. In Joe's case, not briefing the first officer on the use of the spoilers on landing proved fatal. The first officer had flown with Joe before and probably assumed he wanted the spoilers selected in the air, as he had observed him doing on different occasions. The first officer's mistake was pulling the lever all the way back.

Ben was in a panic, knowing he was using non-standard procedures as well. He started to read the manual and applied standard procedures as per the manual the rest of his career. Ben passed away several years ago.

As a former air force pilot, I knew something about flying. There were some captains who told me not to touch anything except my panel. Some even said, "You are not to use the radios." I just shook my head. Most captains were great and included me in all decisions, which I appreciated.

London, England, had several listening stations around the airfield. Their purpose was to ring a bell in the control tower if noise abatement procedures were not followed. One senior captain "rang the bells" on more than one occasion and a fine was levied to the company. Knowing my background, he asked me, on departure out of London, to observe his take-off technique to see if I could see what he was doing to ring the bells. I observed that, instead of following the charted lift-off speed, he was delaying the lift off by about ten knots and ringing the bells. I found a note in my mailbox, thanking me, and saying, "You were right."

On the take-off roll out of Miami we received a call on the company frequency. I waited until we were airborne. Both pilots were busy flying, so I answered the company call. They advised me that they had received a call that there was a bomb on our flight. Once the aircraft was cleaned up and we started our departure procedure, I advised the captain of the company call. He said, "Are you sure they said a bomb?" I replied, "Yes, and they want to know our intentions." The captain then proceeded to call the company to confirm what I had told him. I wondered if he thought I made such a thing up. Once confirmed, the captain said, "I think it is nothing but we will return to Miami, anyway." The back-end crew were advised that we were returning to Miami but the captain never told them why. We landed and were told to taxi to a specific area on the field. We shut down the engines and I expected the captain to advise everyone to evacuate. Portable stairs were already placed against the cabin doors. I opened the door and noticed not one person was heading for the exits. The captain did nothing and the first officer just sat there. I grabbed the PA and advised everyone to evacuate immediately and to leave items in the overhead.

People moved rather fast. We were met by the FBI and bomb-squad personnel. Everyone was told to move away from the aircraft. All luggage was removed except for a coffin in the forward baggage compartment. I thought, "Great place for a bomb." George Murkowski, an Air Canada navigator, was a passenger on our flight. He approached us as we were talking to the FBI. George said he had been in the bar having a beer and overheard a couple talking about their Air Canada flight back to Montreal. He advised he had not seen the couple among the passengers. The FBI had George accompany them to the terminal. They went to the original departure gate, finding the missing couple sitting and looking out the window. The couple admitted to making the call, thinking that the aircraft would return to the gate and they could board. The FBI arrested them and took them away. George was delivered back to the aircraft. People and luggage loaded and we proceeded to Montreal. People can make some stupid mistakes. I could never understand the captain or first officer not taking control of the situation. The captain did not believe me when I told him what the company had said. He said it was probably nothing but returned to Miami anyway. Neither man told the people to evacuate. I just shook my head. I wrote and submitted an incident report but never heard anything back.

On another flight, our schedule was to take us from Toronto, landing at Halifax, St. John's; destination Prestwick, Scotland. The flight attendants advised us that two gentlemen were travelling together and that one appeared to have been drinking. It turned out he was afraid of flying, and his buddy had him pour some courage down his throat. After we left St. John's, we were told all is well and our passenger of concern was sound asleep. Halfway across the Atlantic, a frantic flight attendant entered the cockpit telling us that the passenger had woken and gone to the washroom, bent over to make a deposit, and his false teeth had fallen into the toilet. Apparently he did not flush.

We had the flight attendant block off the washroom and we advised Prestwick of the incident, asking them if they knew of a way of possibly retrieving the teeth. After we landed, one of our Prestwick ground crew arrived wearing a rubber glove up to his shoulder. He fished around the toilet, came out of the washroom with a set of false teeth, dripping in sanitation fluid. The gentleman took his teeth, entered the washroom and ran the teeth under tap water. He popped the teeth back into his mouth and entered the cabin, all smiles. We could not believe that he did not sanitize his teeth. The ramp attendant just shook his head. The word “gross” was heard a lot.

On the same route, different flight, again halfway across the Atlantic, a gentleman requested a visit to the cockpit. He was sober and well dressed. He introduced himself as the president of the Newfoundland Wine Growers Association. It was the funniest thing any of us had ever heard—grapes growing on “The Rock.” Once we had our chuckle he said he was serious. He was making wine from concentrate and on his way to a wine-tasting contest in Portugal. The wine was called “Newfy Duck.” Brights Winery had taken him to court over the similarity of their label, “Baby Duck.” He won the court case and was able to continue using his label. It was just the way he came out and said, “I am the president.”

Perhaps one of my most interesting flights was Toronto to Copenhagen and then on to Moscow. We had a layover in Copenhagen, where we toured the Tivoli gardens and had a good tour of the city. The next day we operated to Moscow. On arrival, a uniformed official, I assume police, took all of our passports, no doubt to photograph them. The passports were returned as we left Moscow. We had several hours in Moscow and spent it with our local agent Aggie Kukkovich (I probably have his name spelled wrong). Aggie had a good reputation and was the translator for the Canadian hockey team when they played team Russia in 1972, during “the game of the century.” It was memorable for the Canadian fans calling out, “*Da*, *da*, Canada, *nyet*, *nyet*, Soviet.”

Aggie had arranged for us to take some cabs downtown; it took three for the whole crew. The trip to the city took us past a memorial that marked the farthest advance of the Germans into the Moscow suburbs during World War II. Personally, I was excited to be in Red Square and observe all the surrounding history; Lenin's tomb, the changing of the guard, and the Kremlin. One highlight was visiting the GUM department store in Red Square, a huge complex of stores of all kinds. It was famous for its ice cream, so we all had one. The store was four to five stories high and was very busy.

We watched one woman buy a pair of shoes. She tried them on, and the man helping her gave her a slip of paper. She obviously was buying the shoes. The lady presented the paper to another worker behind a wicket where she paid for the shoes. She again was given another piece of paper or chit and went to another wicket to finally collect her purchase. This was a classic example of full employment in communist Russia. The small purchase required three workers and several minutes to complete compared to a Canadian store where one employee would complete all transactions in half the time.

Our flight attendants at that time wore long red coats, high black boots, and red pill-box hats. They certainly looked sharp. During our tour around Red Square, we noticed the same male faces kept walking by us. They were admiring our well-dressed, blue-eyed, blond flight attendants.

A visit to a washroom was next in order. We found that none of the toilets had seat covers. Aggie advised us that the next five-year plan would ensure that seat covers would be available. The Soviet government frequently operated on five-year economic plans. Our group even had a ride on the famous Moscow subway. I had read that each station was decorated differently. Our boarding station was full of statues of all the heroes of the revolution. The whole façade was marble. The next station had a Roman theme—it was completed in marble as well, and very beautiful. The one thing that really stood out in each station was the smell. I now knew what the smell was that I experienced as a young boy, when all the students of Saint John were taken on a German submarine at the end of the war. It was body odour. Deodorant had yet to be discovered by the Russians.

We noticed women sweeping the snow off the street with brooms made from branches, similar to our witches' brooms at Halloween. The buildings were very drab, lacking any colour. We could see one lonely light bulb hanging from the ceilings. The people offered no smiles and the streets had very few automobiles.

Montreal's Cardinal Paul-Émile Léger founded a leper colony in the French Cameroons, Africa. I was fortunate to operate a flight to that country with the cardinal. We flew to Paris for a short layover before proceeding to the Cameroons. The flight took us over the Sahara desert, which was absolutely huge. It took hours to cross before we started to see any vegetation. Our job was to get the cardinal to the Cameroons where we, as crew, had about five days to explore. Each day, we rented a van with a driver. The driver spoke only French, but all the flight attendants were French-speaking so we had a lot of translators. The countryside was lush with heavy vegetation and the people appeared friendly.

One stop was at a local market in a small town. As soon as we started to look around, all the locals kept pushing items to buy in our faces. Each of us was surrounded by ten to twelve hawkers showing off their products. I was interested in an ebony carving, which is now in the basement family room. I was given a price in local currency, which was meaningless to me. I pulled my Jeppesen hand computer from my pocket to convert the price to dollars. I noticed that when I pulled out the computer everyone took a step or two back, giving me a bit of breathing room. This was new to them and they were not certain what I was doing. Each time we stopped at a local market and I used the computer, everyone stepped back.

On our return trip to Montreal we landed in Dakar, Senegal. The approach to the airport was very picturesque; every building was painted white with the Atlantic Ocean in the background, in stark contrast to the jungle we had been flying over. After refuelling was completed, we took off and were immediately over the Atlantic Ocean on a direct route to New York. We made our normal position reports but never received a reply from anyone. All our transmissions were "blind." (When unable to contact an air traffic authority, we would transmit our position so that other aircraft in our vicinity would know where we were; other aircraft would do the same. We always tried to keep a mental picture of where other aircraft were in our vicinity—hence, transmitting blind and hoping someone hears you.) Transmitting blind was good airmanship. We were well south of the track system and in an area where there were very few aircraft, if any.

When we approached North America, the New York centre answered our call, saying, "Good day, Air Canada, we figured you would be along soon." Once in contact with the centre, we were able to receive weather updates and they informed us that there was a strike of air traffic control in Montreal. As we approached the Montreal area, we made blind transmissions to make other aircraft aware of our position and intentions. Approaching Montreal airport we observed a small aircraft over the city but we were well clear. We landed without incident. Next day the *Montreal Gazette* carried a story, "*Airliner and Small Aircraft in Near Collision*." What a crock. Someone was taking advantage of the air traffic strike situation to create a sensation.

On completion of a Frankfurt, Germany, layover, we were scheduled to fly to Warsaw, Poland, to pick up a group of Canadians of Polish descent and return them to the Edmonton area. As usual, after we landed our passports were taken and guards were posted around the perimeter. The Warsaw charter had arrived with 150 people to visit relatives and friends.

After everyone was boarded, luggage checked and boarded, an officer did a head count and came up with 151 souls not 150. He recounted and again counted 151. Crew and passengers were ordered off the aircraft. Another count was made, this time 150 souls were counted. We were allowed to board the aircraft. Once more, with everyone in their seats, there was another head count, and you guessed it, 151 not 150. Everyone was deplaned again and the luggage was also taken off the aircraft.

The authorities were certain someone was trying to be smuggled out of the country. Identification and all credentials were checked and double-checked. Attention was focused on a woman with a baby. It turned out she arrived in the country pregnant and had her baby during her visit. The authorities said she could leave but not her baby. The baby belonged to the state. Naturally she was very upset. Through our interpreter we contacted our embassy, who dispatched a representative to the airport. When he arrived, the situation was explained to him and, after much conversation and waving of hands, which lasted at least thirty minutes, all passengers including the baby were allowed to leave. Everyone was boarded once again and when the luggage was loaded we left before someone could change their minds. The delay was well over four hours. This coupled with our trip put us well over our duty day, but we had to get the folks out of Dodge.

Frankfurt was a great city to have a layover. The food was great and the wine was as good as I remembered it from my military days in Europe.

After another Frankfurt layover, we were scheduled to operate a flight to pick up another charter group in Kiev, Ukraine. We were required to have three Russian army personnel on board. Two were radio operators who would be making all radio transmissions. None of our crew spoke Russian. The flight was to leave late evening. It was surmised that the reason we operated during darkness was so we could not see the countryside and report what we had seen. Airborne cameras at that time would not photograph at night.

We departed around ten in the evening and proceeded east. The two Russian radio operators sat in the cockpit while the senior of the three sat in first class and proceeded to drink the plane dry. Initially the flight proceeded normally, but it soon became apparent that we could not acquire any radio facilities for proper navigation, beacons, etc. The captain told one of the Russians that we would return to Frankfurt unless we started to receive proper radio facilities. The one Russian who spoke some English realized the problem and went to his superior in first class. The officer came to the cockpit smelling of liquor. He grabbed a microphone and rattled off a Russian message. After a short time we suddenly had radio facilities. Apparently, the Russian authorities had all radio facilities shut off at night for security and conservation reasons.

We did learn that the charter group were told that they would be picked up at 7 p.m., but we did not land until well after midnight. The group was told when we were in the circuit, and apparently a loud cheer and much clapping occurred. When boarding they hugged every crew member they saw. The group was more than ready to return to Canada. Everyone asked for good Canadian coffee—airline coffee, no less. They were one happy group to be leaving.

Kiev airport had many Russian aircraft parked all over the field. One feature of the runway was that it was made up of poured concrete, in a diamond formation. None of our crew had ever seen such a layout before.

I thoroughly enjoyed the Vienna, Austria, layovers. The city was beautiful and full of history. I was lucky enough to have a weekend layover on two occasions, and I would spend the day in a park close to the centre of the city. During the summer months, there was always an orchestra playing Viennese waltzes—truly magical.

We received our flight plans and fuel requirements from London dispatch. My job as second officer was to ensure the fuel on board was correct and to fill out a take-off chit, giving speeds and runway length. On this particular Vienna departure, I advised the captain that we required more runway than was available. The aircraft was too heavy because we had boarded too much fuel. The captain checked my figures as did the first officer, and they both agreed that London had given us an incorrect fuel load. London was contacted and we explained our problem.

London rechecked their calculations and advised we were correct and they had made an error. We had to defuel to reduce weight, in order for us to be able to have sufficient runway for takeoff. Dispatch offices made very few errors but when they did it was a "biggie." It was up to us, as crew, to ensure safety at all times.

One interesting trip was to Prague, Czechoslovakia. Early in 1968, Alex Dubček became leader of that country. During the early months of his tenure, he eliminated many restrictions that had been placed on the population by former leaders, who had submitted to Soviet rules and regulations. The movement became known as the "Prague spring." Leonid Brezhnev, the leader of the Russian Soviet state at the time did not like the lifting of Czech restrictions. He viewed them as a threat to Russian influence in the whole Eastern bloc countries. By August, Warsaw Pact countries invaded Czechoslovakia and overthrew Dubček and reinstated restrictions to the press and freedoms in general. Dubček ended up as a clerk in a lumberyard.

Soviet occupation ended in 1990. In the early '70s our trip had us landing in Prague. We were escorted to Wenceslas Square, which had become the centre of resentment towards the Warsaw Pact invasion. The country was still occupied by armed soldiers and tanks parked in the streets. It was uncomfortable walking around the area; we were soon escorted back to the airport and we flew to Frankfurt, Germany.

Trips to Los Angeles were always interesting. On more than one occasion I experienced earthquakes, a first for me. Most of the time they were quite gentle, but you could feel the building move and on two occasions we were actually told to leave our hotel and stand in the middle of the street until things settled down.

On one L.A. layover, we, as a crew, went out for dinner. After returning to the hotel the flight attendants went to their respective rooms. The three pilots went for another beer. I had my fill and said goodnight to the other two crew members. I arrived on my floor to find one of our flight attendants standing there in her baby-doll pyjamas. She was actually on course in Dorval the same time as I was and we had often talked over lunch. I said, "Hi," but received no response. The girl was sleepwalking, and her door was open. I took her arm and escorted her to her room, put her into bed and covered her up. The next day, I told her what happened and she could hardly believe it. She said that she did sleepwalk quite often and was undergoing medical help to try to correct the problem.

I always enjoyed flying in and out of L.A. There was lots of aircraft traffic, both in the air and on the ground, taxiing around. We had to be very vigilant. Due to the volume of traffic, the air traffic control had to be very professional. When they asked you to reduce airspeed or speed up you had to comply immediately. One of our senior captains on the DC-8 was given a specific instruction to keep his speed at 250 knots until the outer marker. He advised he could not comply with the instruction. Air Traffic Control told him to go direct to a certain navigation beacon and hold until he could comply with their requests. The L.A. controllers did not fool around. The supervisor asked the first officer to complete the approach since he was more current than the supervisor. (A supervisor is also a captain who did check rides and pushed paper. He did not fly as frequently as a normal line captain.)

I flew with the same supervisor on two Trans-Atlantic trips. I will call him Bill. In the late '60s and '70s the food on the Atlantic was great. The flight attendants would ask us if we wanted a cup of consommé. It normally arrived with a splash of sherry. Bill let his glass sit in the cup holder while we proceeded to consume ours. Bill finally picked his cup up and took a sip. It was about this time he lost his cool, telling us not to drink the consommé. When he discovered it was too late, he asked for the in-charge. He wanted an explanation as to why our consommé was laced with sherry. The in-charge, being rather astute, said, "There must have been a mix up with the passengers' cups." Bill accepted the explanation. The in-charge left winking and nodding at us.

First class would receive soup, fish, pasta, or baron of beef. After serving the passengers, the cockpit door would open and the first class serving wagon would be rolled in, so we could help ourselves. The whole meal service was really "first class." Today's meal service is not comparable.

On my second trip on the Atlantic with Bill, he appeared bored. He looked around as if looking for something to do. There was a rudder trim tab at the rear of the console between the captain and first officer. The top of the trim knob was easily removed, and jokes or meaningless notes left for all to read. Bill removed the top, took out a piece of paper, read the contents, and threw it in the garbage. Naturally, the first officer, navigator, and I were curious as to what the note said. I kept a close watch on the piece of paper as the flight progressed and the bag of garbage filled up. After landing in London, Bill was anxious to leave the cockpit. Once he left I dug into the garbage and retrieved the note, which said, "Bill aaaa, is a fink." We could not have agreed more.

In my early days in the airline, my luggage and flight bag were quite heavy, and wheels on luggage had yet to be invented. Usually after a trip, if we saw a luggage cart, we piled our luggage on board, rather than carry it all over the airport. Bill, in his wisdom, published a memo stating that luggage carts were for passengers only. The next day every pilot who spotted a cart grabbed it, even if they were just going for coffee. There are supervisors and there are supervisors.

We were flying along on our way to L.A., when a flight attendant asked us if we wanted coffee. We all said yes. She returned to the cockpit in a short time and gave us our coffee. When she was giving the captain his drink he said, "My, you smell good, what have you got on?" Her answer was, "Chanel No. 5." In the same breath she said to the captain, "Hmm, you smell good, too; what do you have on?" Our wily captain said, "I have a hard-on, but I didn't think you could smell it." There was laughter and chuckles all around, including from the flight attendant.

Johnny Cross was a very senior pilot. He reminded me of character actor Adolphe Menjou, from the '40s and '50s movies, right down to the thin moustache. John flew many trips to L.A. He was always met at the airport by a lady in a convertible. We never saw him until we returned to the airport for our trip home. One time we were returning to Toronto from an L.A. trip with John flying. He always wore white leather gloves. He flew the approach well but the landing left a bit to be desired. The cockpit door flew open and the senior stewardess said, "What a terrible landing, Johnny, were your gloves dirty?" The first officer and I started to laugh. Johnny taxied in and not a word was said.

We were departing Montreal for L.A. with John, one beautiful summer day. We, as crew, were enjoying the sun on top of the truck stairs (remember no gates?). John arrived a bit late, and was asked by a flight attendant, "Tell me, John, why do you wear white leather gloves when you fly?" John did not answer. He put his flight bag down, opened it, put on his white flying gloves, and grabbed the stewardess by the crotch, saying, "So my hands do not get dirty." Try that today; you would end up being charged.

Judy accompanied me two or three times on trips to L.A. Johnny was the captain on two of these trips. As we flew along, Judy asked John where the Grand Canyon was, and he said, "A bit south of us." Judy said she had always wanted to see it. John replied, "So you shall." He contacted Air Traffic Control and asked if, traffic permitting, we could detour south and do a turn over the Grand Canyon. Response from control was, "No problem. Let us know when you want to head direct for L.A." Judy, as well as all the passengers, had a great view of the canyon.

Another time, shortly after takeoff from L.A., John asked the air traffic control if they could give him radar vectors to a specific town, down the coast from L.A. He explained that he was about to retire in the area and wanted a good look of the surrounding territory. Air Traffic Control provided the vectors and advised us of any conflicting traffic. After we circled the area a couple of times, John thanked them, and we proceeded en route to Toronto. L.A. Air Traffic Control wished John well in his retirement. He was quite the character.

I approached the captains I would be flying with to L.A. on two separate occasions and received their permission to bring Dave on one trip and Bryan on another. Dave and I spent a wonderful day at Disneyland. On the next trip, Bryan and I spent the day at Marineland of the Pacific, where we were splashed by a whale. It was memorable for all concerned.

On one trip, we were to operate a freighter from Mirabel to Toronto and ferry a DC-8 back to Mirabel, all of which was fairly routine. We landed in Mirabel and the three crew members went to our vehicles and drove home. Shortly after returning home, the phone rang. The in-charge customs officer advised me that I was to be fined $400 for not clearing customs at Mirabel. My immediate thought was, "When did Quebec separate?" We had operated the flight within Canada—no big deal. Apparently, and unknown to us, the aircraft was in bond. Perhaps we should have known but we did not. We complained to our supervisors. The fine was reduced to $100 for each pilot. It all seemed ridiculous.

On arrival at the freight terminal in Montreal on another trip, we were advised we had a very special cargo for the Munich, Germany, zoo. On board was a killer whale, which had been caught off the California coast. The first flight leg was from L.A. to Montreal. We were to fly the whale to Munich. The animal was in a waterproof sling and unable to move. Water was continually circulated and sprayed on the animal to keep it wet at all times. An animal trainer accompanied the whale and his job was basically to ensure the animal stayed wet and advise us of any problem. No problems were encountered and we delivered the whale safe and sound to the Munich zoo. It was one of my more interesting and enjoyable flights.

In addition to whales, we also ferried many cattle to both the Caribbean and Europe. On one early cattle flight we were operating to Europe, additional fans were installed to assist the aircraft cooling and air conditioning. The animals always had handlers to keep them at ease. The fans and aircraft systems did not do the job. Sweat from the animals fell from the ceiling all over the aircraft. We were drenched and starting to smell like the cattle. It was back to the drawing board for those who planned these flights.

Charters were flown from Montreal and Toronto to Vegas. These trips were paid for by the casinos. Patrons were expected to have $10,000 for gambling. Food and lodging was included. High rollers from both Canadian cities loved the challenge. I often wondered how many returned broke.

On one Vegas trip, we were pushing back from the gate for our trip to Toronto, when we were advised by the company that Toronto airport was closed, due to heavy snow. We were pulled back into the gate and the passengers advised they would be spending another night in Vegas. In less than thirty minutes, transportation to hotels was arranged for all passengers and crew. The crew hotel gave us each a $25 gambling chit, which we all lost. There were slot machines everywhere, all over the airport, including the washrooms.

One memorable captain was Garth Dundas, a gentleman in every way. He had a daughter who flew as a flight attendant. Garth completed three tours, flying Lancasters during World War II. Sadly, he passed away shortly after he retired.

Another memorable character was Mad Dog Mulford. He lived in Ontario next to a family that had large dogs. The dogs were forever jumping the fence into his yard. Conversations with the dog owners did not help. His family was young and he was afraid that the dogs might attack them. Every time he was in the yard he would place one rifle at one end of his yard and a shotgun on the other. One afternoon, one of the dogs jumped the fence, a rifle was selected, and a shot fired, killing the dog, hence the nickname Mad Dog. He had some problems with the neighbour and the police and was eventually forced to move.

Mad Dog was also cheap. Normally, after we arrived at our overseas destination we would have four to five hours of sleep, agreeing to meet in the lobby of the hotel at a specific time and go for a beer before dinner. Mad Dog always bought the first round, usually at the train station, the cheapest place to drink in town. We would then proceed to another bar, a bit more upscale, where the first officer would buy a round, at double the price from the train station. Off we would go again to Mad Dog's favourite place for a beer—my turn to buy. The price was triple the station price and I was the one making less salary then the other two. He did not succeed in conning me a second time.

Fletch Fraser was another senior captain who had seen wartime service. He was actually shot down, evaded capture with another crew member, and ended up in Switzerland. After about six months, they were both bored with sitting around and anxious to get back into the war. One early morning, they left the embassy where they were staying, telling no one of their plan. They decided to leave Switzerland and walk across France to Spain. They succeeded. I only wish I knew the full story.

Fletch loved his cigars. He took sheer delight in blowing smoke in your face and generally smelling up the cockpit. Smoking was the norm at that time. Over time Fletch decided to quit and, where before he allowed anyone to light up, he now refused, telling one and all how bad smoking was for your health. A convert.

Andy Proulx and I did several L.A. trips together, with Andy as first officer. On one flight, I introduced Andy to one of the flight attendants as Mr. Liepshits. I was Don Pisswhistle. Suspicions confirmed—she was blond and thereafter referred to us by our new last names, Messers Liepshits and Pisswhistle.

During layovers in Santa Monica I used to jog along the beach, before my knee started swelling on me. I would go to Sambo's restaurant for breakfast. One morning, I spotted Lee Marvin, the movie actor. I approached him and told him I enjoyed all his movies. He invited me to sit, bought me a coffee, and asked where I was from. He spoke highly of Canada and we had a good chat. I told him I had to return back to my hotel for pickup and a flight to Toronto. He wished me well.

I saw him on different occasions at Sambo's. He would wave and say, "Hi, Canada."

Another frequent passenger on our flights to Toronto was Bill Cosby. He always travelled first class and had a different white, stunning blond on each trip.

There is the story of an Air Canada pilot landing at Frankfurt. He was advised by the tower to exit on "Charlie" taxi-way. He missed the exit and the ground controller was a bit upset, saying, "You were asked to clear Charlie and used Delta, were you never here before?" Our pilot answered, "Once in 1944, but I didn't land." Radio was now quiet. Most airlines claim the statement. I was on a Frankfurt layover with another World War II captain and, as we walked along, we came to the railway station. He said, "I blew that place to pieces in 1944."

There was one World War II pilot who did not like Germans. His language was much stronger and he probably had his reasons. On the return flight to Toronto a flight attendant entered the cockpit, and the captain asked her name. The girl replied, "Ingrid." The captain said, "How the hell did I miss you?" I did imply he was not very nice.

Chapter Twenty

DC-9

In this chapter I was just going to write about my time as first officer on the DC-9. On reflection, I have decided to include my time as a captain on the DC-9 as well. I spent three years as a first officer on the Boeing 727 before I was promoted on the DC-9. My aircraft sequence was, first officer, DC-9; first officer, 727; promoted to captain on the DC-9; followed by three years as captain on the Boeing 727. At this point, I could have gone on the airbus as a captain but my eye was on the Boeing 747.

I knew, because of my age and seniority, I would never get to fly the 747 as a captain, so I elected to fly the aircraft as a first officer. I had planned to be on the 747 for two years with the election to go on the Boeing 767 as a captain. It was at this time the company purchased the Boeing 747, 400 series. It was bigger, flew further, and I wanted to fly this aircraft. I decided to stay as a first officer, flying the 400 series for one full year before returning to the Boeing 767 as a captain for my last two years before retirement.

In all, it took twelve years before my seniority coincided with a captain promotion. I was not really concerned; I knew it would happen sooner than later, although there were times in the late '60s that I thought I would retire as a very senior second officer. The industry had slowed down considerably in the late '60s and early '70s.

My Douglas (DC-9) course started in November 1973. Again, we were required to build the aircraft before we were allowed to fly it. The course itself was quite straightforward. Two training pilots were assigned to be "mutual partners" throughout the simulator and flight training.

Bill Young was to be my mutual partner. Normally, the pilot with the higher seniority does the first session in the simulator while the

DC-9 taxiing for takeoff. This plane was fun to fly.
Reproduced with the permission of Air Canada

other pilot sits in the observer seat. Each pilot receives two hours at the controls. Bill and I elected to toss a coin, and Bill won, so he had first crack at flying the simulator. Ken P. was our simulator instructor. Ken proved quiet but thorough.

I observed Bill do a takeoff, climb to altitude, do steep turns, stalls, and just about everything else that Ken thought up. Bill did a super job. Now it was my turn in the right seat while Bill sat in the observer's seat.

We completed the required checks for takeoff, applied power and, as I lifted off, there was a loud bang and the simulator moved to the right, resting on the hydraulic jacks. Ken said, "You just crashed; let's try it again." Same result, another crash. Ken said this time he would do the takeoff to demonstrate the proper technique. I was to put my hands lightly on the controls to get the feel of the simulator. We took off, and there was a loud noise again. "What the hell?" came from Ken. "We crashed again—the simulator must be broken." The simulator was indeed broken. There had been nothing wrong with my technique, but for a moment I was beginning to wonder. The next day I took the controls first, and all exercises were completed normally. It helped to have a fully serviceable simulator and not some computer saying, "You crashed!"

On our last simulator session we had a Ministry of Transport official on board. He observed all aspects of our two hours on the controls and we were considered instrument-qualified on the DC-9.

Ken took both Bill and me on a training flight. We each flew a couple of instrument approaches on two engines and on one engine, followed by landings and takeoffs. Neither Bill nor I had any problem. Ken was happy with our progress, and we were told to report to the chief pilot of the DC-9.

We introduced ourselves to the chief pilot, who welcomed us to the DC-9 family. In addition, we were each given a flying assignment with one of the DC-9 supervisors. My flight was a scheduled passenger flight to JFK airport in New York. I thoroughly enjoyed the trip and the professional attitude of the American controllers. Instructions were crisp and rapid. We were expected to complete instructions in an accurate and efficient manner. I always liked flying into high density airports; it was hard work at times, but very pleasant. The professionalism and respect of both the air traffic controllers and the pilots towards each other made the flying that much more enjoyable.

The supervisors wanted to see for themselves that we could fly the aircraft before we were released on the unsuspecting public.

I was fortunate to fly with some very good captains on the DC-9. I was able to observe—my instructor days showing again—the different approach each had to their flying. I was able to pick out the good points of each as well as the ones that did not fit my personality and approach to flying.

Whenever I made a request for weather or passed on a message to maintenance, I always replied with a "Thank you, sir." To me, it was common courtesy and, no doubt, my military training. Upon receiving and reading back a revised clearance from Air Traffic Control, I did my usual, "Thank you, sir." One captain I was with went ballistic, ranting about my using "sir" to a bunch of no-good air traffic controllers. He advised me not to use "sir" again. I still did, followed by an, "Oops, forgot." The captain married late and he could not understand how I had teenagers when he had a boy in diapers. We were the same age; it was all rather pathetic on his part.

We landed in JFK airport in New York with a planned twenty-four-hour layover. Our arrival was late afternoon. We proceeded to the hotel, changed, and all agreed to meet in the lobby and go for a brew and dinner. There were three flight attendants and two pilots. All were keen for a short walk before we went for dinner. We strolled along Fifth Avenue with our heads on a swivel. There was a lot to see and the aroma of food was everywhere.

Our first stop was a pub just off Fifth Avenue. We ordered beer all around and started to talk about the day, wives, and boyfriends. Suddenly, one of the flight attendants looked around and commented, "Guys, the place is full of men and we are the only three girls in the bar." We had stumbled onto a gay bar. Trying not to stare at everyone looking at us, we finished our beer and left as quietly as we arrived. Once we hit the street, we walked fast and far before stopping for dinner. It was the first gay bar any of us had ever been in.

During a short layover in JFK, we would stay at one of the airport hotels. The flight attendants always wanted one of the pilots to go into their room with them. There had been incidents of men entering and hiding in rooms waiting for an unsuspecting female to arrive. We would look behind the curtains, in the closet, and even under the bed. One of our pilots noticed a terrible smell as he entered the room with the flight attendant. He looked under the bed and there was a dead body. The management was notified, who in turn called the police. I could never understand how the maid cleaned the room, made the bed, and never detected odour from the body.

Our flight operated from Toronto, Montreal, and Moncton, with a twenty-four-hour layover. We went to the employee cafeteria for something to eat, and I ordered a hamburger and milk. We proceeded to the aircraft, completed our checks and, once the passengers were on board, we taxied out and got airborne. Half way to Montreal, I broke out in a cold sweat and started to feel dizzy. I was not sure what was happening. When we landed in Montreal, I advised the captain I was going to get some fresh air and hopefully clear my head. My stomach was growling so I proceeded to the washroom, assuming the appropriate sit-down position; suddenly I realized whatever was in me was coming out but not from my present position. Before I could remove myself from the seat I vomited, half on the floor and the rest on my uniform tunic. What to do! What to do!

I cleaned the floor and opened the cubicle door and proceeded to the sink, retrieving lots of paper towel in the process. I cleaned my tunic as much as I could, all the while trying to ignore the stares from passengers, who, no doubt, were wondering if this character was operating their flight. I felt a little better and returned to the cockpit, explaining my predicament to the captain. He was somewhat sympathetic but was more concerned with my ability to continue to operate as a first officer. I advised him I felt much better and that I was happy to press on. Shortly after takeoff, I broke out in a cold sweat and my stomach was not too happy. I explained my problem to the senior flight attendant and she gave me a glass of warm ginger ale. I was amazed how quickly my stomach settled down.

When we arrived in Moncton, I was still feeling lousy and actually fell asleep in the vehicle to the hotel. The arrival at the hotel room is still a blur. I awoke about sixteen hours later feeling one heck of a lot better. My uniform had been cleaned and pressed and was hanging on the door. Apparently, I had had a good dose of food poisoning, an occupational hazard. Two of the flight attendants had put me to bed and had sent my uniform for cleaning. I was very grateful. I have recommended the warm ginger ale to many crew members over the years. It really works.

One flight was operating Toronto, Winnipeg, Regina, and finally, Calgary. Passengers were loading when a flight attendant entered the cockpit and told us that the Winnipeg football team was on board and that every one of them left their equipment bag on the loading bridge. They had told the in-charge to stow them away. The captain went to have a look. He asked to talk to the coach and showed him all the equipment bags on the bridge.

The coach wanted to know what he was supposed to do about the bags. The captain told him that all the bags should have been checked and stowed in the belly. The coach said, "Well, get some ground crew to put them in the belly." At this point, the captain told the coach, "You advise your team to put their equipment bags on the ramp. Our ground crew will then put them in the belly. If this is not done, the flight will be cancelled." The coach, now agitated, said, "You can't do that." The captain replied, "Watch me."

The coach, having second thoughts, advised his team to do what the captain had suggested. We had a bit of a delay before all the bags were recorded and stowed. I was privy to the whole conversation, having the cockpit door open. Back in the cockpit, the captain chuckled to himself. That day, I learned a very good lesson. The captain of an aircraft has power and can use it in the best interests of all concerned. He did well and certainly earned my respect.

We proceeded to the Sydney airport for an early morning departure one day. During flight planning, one of the front passenger agents arrived with a good story. His duty was to be the first agent to arrive, turn on the lights, and generally get ready for passengers. The time was 6:00 a.m. and the flight left at 7:15 a.m. After turning on the lights, he noticed an elderly lady, who obviously had been sitting in the dark. He approached her and asked if she was all right. The lady said she was fine and was waiting to board the flight to Halifax. The agent took her ticket and told her she was confirmed on the flight and asked why she had arrived so early. The lady said, "I am seventy-three years old, so I arrived early to make certain I received a seat. I did not want to stand all the way to Halifax." The poor soul had never been on an aircraft before and she thought if all the seats were full she would have to stand and hold a bar or strap, as on a bus.

We did invite her to the cockpit but she declined.

During another layover in Sydney, I was advised my dad had had a heart attack. I called crew scheduling and asked them to have a replacement pilot in Halifax on our arrival as I was booking off the flight and proceeding to Saint John. I was advised that the flight would be delayed so a replacement first officer could be flown to Sydney to replace me. I thought this was a bit ridiculous. I was quite capable of operating the hour flight to Halifax but they would not accept my suggestion. It turned out to be a very long day.

Air Canada had two series of the DC-9, the DC-9-15 and DC-9-32. The -15 series was shorter than the -32 and about 10,000 pounds lighter. When flying the -15 series, you had to be aware that the aircraft was lighter than the -32 series. It had no leading edge slats, which made for higher landing speeds. Airports like Rouyn, Quebec, had a short runway and you had to keep the proper speeds on final to ensure a safe landing. Luckily we had engine reverse capability, which helped immensely.

The -32 series was a pilot's airplane. Everything about the aircraft felt right. I always felt that you could roll that aircraft and not even spill the coffee. The addition of the leading edge slats made life much easier for the pilots, particularly when landing in winter conditions.

It was about this time I elected to fly the Boeing 727 (more on the 727 later). After my three years as a first officer on the Boeing 727, I returned to the DC-9 for captain training.

My mutual partner was Bill Long and our instructor was Bob Gordon from Toronto. All our simulator training was completed in Toronto. Bill came down with mononucleosis and was unable to complete his training until later. Bob and I completed the required training in a fairly short time.

Bob had a sailboat on Lake Ontario. We would finish our simulator sessions early, Bob's wife would prepare lunch for us, and he and I would go sailing for the afternoon. Bob was not only a good instructor and sailor but a very nice person. We got along very well.

The training was quite straightforward: many trips in the simulator, reviewing all the procedures, and all in the left seat. The training required that I fly with a Ministry of Transport inspector for an instrument ride.

I returned to Montreal and met the new DC-9 supervisor. As a prospective new captain, I was required to fly so many hours with established captains.

One fellow trainee was Pete. He was a know-it-all and, when he flew as a first officer, he was not well liked by the captains he flew with. Pete asked me if I had been asked many questions during my left-seat training. I told him I was asked one question. He was upset and said that he was asked questions every time he flew with anyone. It was the last chance for the captains he flew with to get back at him for being a not-well-liked first officer. Once you were promoted you were an equal and the powers-that-be would never admit they made a mistake.

I was flying a departure out of JFK with the DC-9 chief pilot. It was on this trip that I was asked my one and only question. As we climbed through 17,500 feet, he asked me, "When do we set the altimeter to standard pressure?" I answered, "Now." In Canada, a standard pressure reading of 29.92 millibars was set at 18,000 feet. Most other countries set standard pressure at 18,000 feet but there were exceptions, so we carried charts to indicate when standard pressure was to be set. Standard pressure was used so that all aircraft were using the same pressure. All altitudes above 18,000 feet in Canada were based on 29.92 inches of mercury.

On our layover in New York, the chief pilot showed me a few of his favourite haunts. Our departure was midafternoon, so we had breakfast and walked around Central Park. I suggested we had better return to the hotel to get ready for cab pickup, he agreed and said, "Follow me, I know a shortcut." We became really lost, finally asking a mounted police officer for directions to Fifth Avenue and our hotel. We arrived back in time for a quick change before our cab to the airport arrived.

I recall a New York layover a few years later. We were picked up on schedule at our hotel by a new driver. Neither the first officer nor I paid too much attention to where we were going. We had been in the cab for about thirty minutes, when I looked up at a stoplight and realized we were still in the city. I looked down a side street and saw our layover hotel. I asked the driver if he knew where the airport was; he did not. We had been going around in circles as he looked for signs to La Guardia Airport. We gave him directions to the airport and we just managed to arrive in time to have a scheduled departure.

Prior to promotion, we were required to complete one final simulator with a training captain. He occupied the right seat and completed anything I asked him to do, but offered no direction or input in the way I was doing things. I was the captain and he was the first officer doing what I directed. When we completed the check ride we had a debriefing, where the supervisor pointed out a few things I could do a bit better. All in all, the check ride went very well.

The next part of the captain's training was with a check pilot. Our trip took us through the Maritimes and Newfoundland and back to Montreal. When the trip was completed, Bob Tucker, the supervisor, shook my hand and handed me my captain's epaulets. I was now promoted.

When I arrived home, Judy had invited folks over for a promotion party—she knew I would pass the check ride.

Throughout a career for Air Canada, every three months you were required to complete a simulator ride. Medicals were once a year until you reached the age of forty, and then they were twice a year. In addition, you were required to fly with a supervisor on an annual check ride.

As a new captain, your landing limits were raised to 400 feet and one mile visibility until you reached 100 hours as captain. This

DC-9 cockpit. I flew as both first officer and captain.

restriction posed problems flying in the Maritimes, whether it be spring, winter, or summer. Snow, fog, and low ceiling were prevalent. I solved the problem very easily. The first officer's limits were 200 feet and a half-mile visibility. When the weather was below 400-1, I let him fly the approach. Strictly illegal, but we got the job completed with no inconvenience to the passengers. I reached the 100-hour mark in a very short time so the problem was not long lasting.

In the simulator, we were required to do maximum rate descents; power off, select speed brakes, and, when the speed is reduced, select the undercarriage down. It was not necessary to lower the gear but it certainly added to the descent, and the extra drag kept the airspeed from increasing. Roll over and straight down.

I was operating a ferry flight from Halifax to Montreal, without passengers, although we had three flight attendants on board. It was a great opportunity to practice what we did in the simulator. I briefed the flight attendants that we were going to do a maximum-rate descent; the same procedure would be completed in the loss of pressurization. Air Traffic Control advised us that there was no conflicting traffic and we could enter the procedure when we wanted to. We started the descent about thirty miles from Montreal at an altitude of 35,000 feet. I asked air traffic what our profile looked like on radar. He stated that we were descending so fast that we did not show up on his radar. In total, we lost 25,000 feet in about fifteen miles and levelled out at 10,000 feet to enter the normal profile for approach and landing at Montreal. We seldom had the chance to complete these exercises, but I usually managed to do something on a ferry flight. It was always a good exercise and learning experience, not only for the pilots but for the flight attendants as well.

I received a phone call from crew scheduling late one afternoon, advising me that I was being drafted to operate a wheels-down ferry flight from Quebec City to Montreal. Apparently, on landing, one of our pilots had gone off the side of the runway and over a mound of earth. The bottom of the fuselage was covered in muck, as was the undercarriage. Maintenance was completing checks on the aircraft. I was told that the ferry flight was scheduled to depart Quebec and that we would be landing in the dark in Montreal. I replied to crew scheduling that I would not operate a ferry flight in the dark, particularly one that had been involved in an incident. I was a first officer on the equipment at the time. I was told I had to. I refused. I was informed that the chief pilot would be advised of my refusal. I said, "Fine, have him call me." Once the chief pilot, DC-9, was informed, he agreed with me that a night ferry contained certain risks. Within days, a directive was issued stating that there would be no night ferries, period.

The sad part of the whole incident was that the pilot who ran off the side of the runway and over a mound of earth did not report the incident or put any mention of it in the log book. Maintenance on a routine after-landing check found the damage and muck and reported it. The pilot concerned was now at his layover hotel. He was contacted and stated he felt a bit of a bump on landing but thought nothing of it. The gentleman concerned never flew for Air Canada again, retiring to the East Coast.

The Maritimes had just experienced the tail end of a hurricane, with the associated rain and high winds. I was operating from Montreal to Fredericton after the storm had passed. It was early evening and windy on approach. We were advised that the runway was wet. The runways at Fredericton are fairly short and, with the wet runway, we wanted to "plunk" the aircraft onto the ground to break any water adhesion and avoid aquaplaning. With aquaplaning, the aircraft literally would stay on the film of water without the wheels even touching the runway. This has led to aircraft running off the end of the runway. Anyway, we "plunked" the aircraft onto the runway, selected reverse and we were decelerating quite nicely, when I noticed chunks of cement and asphalt littering the runway. I was able to avoid the chunks and come to a stop. I turned the aircraft around, and we could see that one side of the runway had lost quite a bit of its former size. Apparently, the winds were very strong and had lifted the pieces of cement and deposited them on the runway. What made matters worse was that no one had inspected the runway when the airport re-opened after the storm passed. We did it for them. We had a bit of a departure delay waiting for the runway to be cleared of debris.

The flights from Fredericton to Saint John were always a lot of fun. The trip took about twenty minutes. We would take off, make an immediate left turn to avoid the military camp at Gagetown, climb to 8,000–10,000 feet, and level off, request descent into Saint John, and perform the "in-range check" followed by the "before-landing check." I asked a new first officer how he liked the short leg. He said, "It all happened so fast that my brain was still on the runway in Fredericton."

On the drive to the airport after a Halifax layover, one of the flight attendants did nothing but complain. She complained about the hotel, the time away from home, and her job in general. After takeoff and approaching Houlton, Maine, the flight attendant who did all the complaining entered the cockpit. I gave her my headset to listen to a tape of a gentleman identifying the navigation facility, "Houlton VOR" (very high frequency Omni-directional radial). I told her to consider herself lucky that she didn't have to do an eight-hour shift of repeating, "Houlton VOR." She actually believed that was what the man did; not even thinking it might be a recording. By the way, she was a blond.

The drive from downtown New York to JFK Airport passes some very large graveyards. One particular morning, one of the girls commented about the huge graveyards. I told her that New York was running out of space and that they were considering burying people vertically. She pondered the problem and wondered if they would be buried heads up or down. I could not contain myself, so I said, "It depends on which way they are going, heads up for heaven and heads down for hell."

Winter operations can present some especially tricky problems.

Landing in Montreal, the braking action was reported as poor. That was no big problem; "plunk" the aircraft down, select full reverse and hard on the brakes, releasing brake pressure as necessary to keep the aircraft straight.

The tower asked the aircraft that landed ahead of us for his assessment of the braking, he said, "Braking action is nil." Yet, he managed to stop his aircraft and taxi in. His statement posed a real problem for me. In theory I should have overshot and gone to our alternate, yet, he had landed okay. I elected to land. If I had gone off the end or side of the runway I would have had a problem with management. The other pilot should have said, "Braking action is poor." This would have allowed me to land and not have to worry about management action. If I landed and found that the conditions were really bad I still would have plenty of time to overshoot. We landed without incident.

The flight was full of passengers and another pilot was in the jump seat hitching a ride to Halifax. The Maritime weather was not the best and we were required to have fuel to return to Montreal, our alternate. We were 106,000 pounds for takeoff. Normally we were a lot less. The ramp taxiways were slushy and slippery, and I assumed the runway would be the same. There was a lineup for takeoff on Runway 24L. The aircraft ahead of us was a large aircraft 1011, and a DC-8. Their take-off roll was quite long and their exhaust threw up lots of slush and water. I reviewed a rejected takeoff once more with my first officer, just in case.

We were finally cleared for takeoff. Power was applied and we started to accelerate, slowly, initially, because of our weight. As we approached V1—in effect the "go—no go speed," both engines started to crackle and pop, and I knew we had ingested slush. I called for "reject" selecting throttles to idle and activating the reverse and selecting the spoilers up. All these actions were to slow us down. The runway was close to 9,600 feet and we did not seem to be slowing down. I advised those in the cockpit that I thought we would be going off the end. If this happened, I asked the pilot in the jump seat to use the PA and advise the passengers to brace themselves. The first officer and I were busy trying to stop the beast. We had about 1,500 feet of runway left, when I could feel we were getting full control of the reject, and the aircraft started to decelerate at a faster rate. We were able to stop before the end of the runway and cleared the active runway on the last taxiway available.

We had used most of the runway to stop the aircraft. I then made a PA announcement to the passengers advising them what had happened and that we were returning to the ramp. The in-charge advised that items had flown all over the cabin but everyone, while concerned, was all right.

On return to the ramp, the company advised that another aircraft was available and that luggage and passengers would be transferred to the new aircraft. By the time we taxied out for takeoff once more, the runway had been swept of slush and most of the water. This takeoff went smoothly. All the passengers elected to continue with us to Halifax.

The manual stated that reverse on the DC-9 was not to be used while taxiing. One evening, taxiing in at Montreal, the taxiway was very slippery and the wind was causing us to drift off the taxiway. I immediately selected reverse to stop the slide. The first officer shouted, “We are not to use reverse while taxiing.” I told him to use his head. If I had not used reverse we would have ended up in a snow bank.

Rules and regulations are for the guidance of wise men and obedience of fools.

I always tried to get my first officers to think ahead and not be only in the moment. Most first officers were very good, but the odd one thought he knew better than the captain. I would let him go as far as I dared and then ask him what he was trying to accomplish. Usually, he was not completely certain. They did learn a valuable lesson.

I always briefed that when the other pilot was making the PA announcement to the passengers, never, never mention the fact that there was fog at our destination. We have all seen and read newspaper articles about an aircraft crashing in the fog. Just tell the passengers it is cloudy. The word fog makes them nervous.

When I flew with first officers for the first time, I always told them that flying together is “a mutual admiration society.” I told them we were here to get the job done well, but also to enjoy and have fun with the experience.

In addition, I always told them that if they saw me doing something they did not understand or like, tell me and I would explain. I also told them that if I saw them doing something I did not like I would ask for an explanation. I always thought this cleared the air and everyone knew he was free to speak up, always ensuring a safe operation.

During an upgrade to captain, a pilot must fly so many hours in the captain's, or left seat. The qualified captain would occupy the first officer's or right seat. The captain "to be," in effect, was flying on the captain's licence. I had one ex-navigator, who had obtained his pilot's licence. He thought he knew it all. On one occasion, I was copying a clearance from Air Traffic Control when the company called on the company frequency. I asked the trainee to see what the company wanted while I copied the clearance. He said, "That's not my job." I told him to stop the aircraft on the taxiway and set the parking brake. I asked him how many hoops I had on my shoulders, and he said, "Four." "Correct," I said, "and they mean I am the captain of the aircraft and if I ask you to do something, do it." I was really cheesed with his attitude. He never impressed me. He did, however, manage to pass his captain's course.

During the summer months, we seemed to carry many passengers from Germany to Thunder Bay, Ontario. I often thought that if the authorities were looking for war criminals in Canada, the Thunder Bay area would be a good place to look. I enjoyed Thunder Bay layovers. Quite often they would have an act playing at the hotel. We would arrive in time for the last show, and the hotel staff always let us in a side door; we never did pay.

On one occasion Roy Orbison was headlining. I always enjoyed his singing and music. He sang his "Pretty Woman" song the night we were there.

Windsor layovers were also a favourite for the same reason—music or comedy acts at the hotel. At one show, Lou Rawls was the performer. He was very good and just becoming known in the music business. Phyllis Diller was the comedy act. I have never heard such foul language coming from any person like I heard coming from her. I could never understand why people with talent thought that every second word should be a swear word.

Chicago, as well as New York and Los Angeles, were favourite airports to operate in and out of. Chicago had parallel runways, and takeoffs happened about every twenty seconds, and at the same time the parallel had an aircraft taking off. Everyone had to be mentally sharp and do as they were advised by the air traffic control. One mistake could lead to an overshoot or worse. After landing, due to gate congestion or traffic density on the taxiways, we would be sent to what was known as the "penalty box." We could wait ten minutes or an hour with the engines running until we were cleared to the gate. The Air Canada gate was very central and was great from a passenger point of view. I heard at different times that other carriers were willing to pay Air Canada for the use of the gate, but Air Canada never accepted any offer.

The Palmer House was the hotel of choice for layovers. They also had headliners and we, as crew, were either given a ticket or ushered through a side door to see the show. One time the performer was Gordon MacRae. I always admired his tenor voice from the movie *Oklahoma*. The show was late starting, and then it was announced, in complete disgust, that Mr. MacRae was unable to stand let alone perform. He was drunk. Personally, I was disappointed. Another attraction was the Chicago Philharmonic. In the summer months, they would perform over the lunch hour in a square close to Palmer House. It reminded me of Vienna—most enjoyable.

One time I had been flying all day with a trainee captain. He was doing most of the work and was not performing to much of a standard. I tried talking him through approaches, but he would still make one error after the other. It was obvious he was becoming very frustrated. On the layover in Thunder Bay, we had a late beer and called it a night; crew call next morning was 7:15. During the night I was woken by knocking on my door. My clock said 5:30. I staggered to the door and looked through the peephole. There was the trainee captain, completely dressed in his uniform. I thought, initially, I must have the wrong time and he was waking me up. I opened the door and he said, "I quit." I brought him into my room and he started to review how miserable his flying had been and that on return to Montreal he was going to resign. We talked for quite a while. I agreed that his flying was not of an acceptable standard at the present time but that he was not to resign, or he would lose a lot of his benefits. I told him to approach a supervisor and advise him that he was having some difficulty and request extra time with a check pilot to iron out some problems. I always found that the supervisors were very approachable and once they knew of a problem they were more than willing to help.

I sent him for coffee while I had my shower. The flight home operated to Toronto then onto Montreal and Halifax. I was displaced from the Halifax leg by the chief pilot on the DC-9. He had heard from other captains the problems my co-pilot was having and wanted to see for himself. Extra time was granted both in the simulator and extra air time. The individual concerned did progress and was eventually promoted to captain. I would like to think that I helped him along in some small way.

I had been away on vacation and returned to find my first trip was to Val d'Or, Rouyn, and back to Montreal. I was flying with a very senior first officer. I flew the first leg and my first officer flew the leg to Rouyn. On landing, the first officer selected reverse and applied the brakes but we did not seem to be decelerating. I also got onto the brakes and selected full reverse. The runway at Rouyn had been quite short but a small extension had been completed. We passed the only exit off the runway before we finally brought the aircraft to a stop. We probably had about 100 feet of runway left before we would have gone off the end. When we turned on the runway to taxi to the terminal, I noticed the runway had an oily appearance. A rain shower had preceded our arrival and the runway was wet. After parking the aircraft, the ground crew mentioned that it looked like we would not stop but go off the end. We were then advised that the runway had just been resurfaced. That, coupled with the rain, had us aquaplaning most of the runway. There had been no notices to the resurfacing in any of the data we had checked in Montreal. The first officer had done everything correctly, but it took the two of us to stop the aircraft.

When we arrived in Montreal, I looked for a DC-9 supervisor. It was late Friday afternoon; none were in sight. Bob Coneen, a B-727 supervisor, asked what the problem was. I reviewed what transpired in Rouyn and asked that a memorandum be attached to the pilot bulletin board to make them aware that when wet, the runway at

Rouyn was very slippery. He thought I should file an incident report because it would get quicker action, which I did.

Approximately two weeks later, I received a note in my mailbox to see the chief pilot DC-9 at my earliest convenience. I was walking down the hall to his office when I spotted Bob Coneen coming the other way. He stopped me and asked if I remembered the incident report I had filed. Naturally, I did. He said that another captain had actually gone off the runway at Rouyn but was able to get back on the runway. I had filed the incident report on Friday afternoon and the other pilot had flown the trip the very next day. Bob told me that the chief pilot, DC-9, had planned to fire him. Because I had filed an incident report that had not been actioned, the chief pilot was unable to fire him, so he kept his job.

By this time, I was really curious about the reception I would receive from the chief pilot. He was very pleasant when I entered his office and asked me to explain what had happened at Rouyn, which I did. He then started to say if it had been him he would have had no problem stopping the aircraft in any conditions. At this point, I had had enough. I stood up and said, "Jack, you were not there, I doubt if you could have done any better." I left and never heard another word from him. He was not a likeable person to start with.

My very favourite airport to fly into was Saint John, New Brunswick. I had started my flying career at the Fundy Flying Club and I worked as a ramp rat with Trans-Canada Airlines. I knew everyone on the ramp and they were always happy to see me. I often saw George Legere in the coffee shop at the airport and he was still telling everyone that he had taught me everything I knew. I really loved the man; he was a true spirit.

During layovers in Saint John, I would take the first officers home to have dinner with my mum. I would let her know that I would be in Saint John and she would have a chicken cooking and a batch of cookies made. Over the years, these same first officers often asked about Mum, and Mum would ask about them. They all enjoyed their short time together.

Judy and I had been doing downhill skiing. She was better than me in the sport but we both enjoyed the outings. We were skiing at Calabogie, west of Ottawa. During the morning, we had completed some runs when we decided to go down Black Donald as the hill was called. It was not particularly steep or fast. I was ahead of Judy when, suddenly, I was face down in the snow. One ski slid about ten feet from where I fell, and the other was under a root that I did not see on my run. Once my skis hit the root—face plant for me. Judy retrieved my ski, and I untangled the other ski from the root, put both skis on, and we completed the run.

When we arrived at the bottom of the hill, I mentioned that my leg was beginning to hurt. Judy gave me a couple of aspirins and proceeded back on the hill. I thought I should walk and work the kink out of my leg but it still hurt. Judy finally arrived back and we loaded up the car, planning to have lunch at a truck stop en route. When we got home, Judy, being the good nurse, told me to go have a bath and soak my leg. I called her to take a look at my leg, which was far from its normal colour. Her immediate reaction was for me to get dressed; we would have to go to emergency. I was x-rayed and a lot of blood drained from my leg. It was broken. The doctor wanted to know why we took so long to have someone look at my leg. Heck. I had skied down the hill with the leg broken, driven the car, gone to lunch, and walked into the house and it never entered my mind that my leg might be broken.

A cast was placed from my heel to my upper thigh. I could only ride in the back seat of the car. I had to advise Air Canada of the incident and told them that I would be off work for about three months.

Going to the bathroom posed a bit of a problem. I could not sit down normally on the toilet; I had to lean back and fall towards the porcelain receptacle. In the process, I cracked two toilet seat covers. I knew Judy found one of the cracks when I heard her scream from the bathroom; it pinched.

The cast was removed in about eight weeks, but I needed crutches and a cane to get around. Judy suggested we go to Barbados for a week or so to get some sun. Away we went, with me struggling with a cane trying to keep up with Judy. The first few days we would cab to the beach. After a while, I started walking on the beach and before long, I could walk from our room to the beach. Walking in the sand strengthened my leg dramatically. All good things must come to an end, so we proceeded home. I no longer needed the cane.

If you are off flying for ninety days you are required to have a simulator ride as well as a check-ride with a supervisor. I hated the thought of having to complete both. I checked with the doctor and he gave me a clean bill of health. I advised the company that I was available for flying and was awarded a flight the next day. I flew the trip with no problem. Thankfully, I did not require the simulator or check ride. It had only been eighty-nine days since I broke my leg.

Judy and I planned a trip to Hawaii with another couple. It was obvious very early in the vacation that we had little in common. We tended to go our separate way during the day and met now and then for dinner.

Honolulu had lots of attractions. We enjoyed Waikiki beach but it was very crowded, towels almost overlapping. The view of Diamond Head from the beach was spectacular. The Kodak show had several dancers in Polynesian costume wiggling their hips to the drums. The highlight was a visit to the USS *Arizona*, which had been sunk by the surprise raid on Pearl Harbor, on December 7, 1941. The trip was very enjoyable, but we promised ourselves that next time we would go alone and visit the other islands.

We were operating a flight from the west, landing in Ottawa and then to Montreal. Passengers started to board when the purser came to the cockpit and said. "René Lévesque just boarded. Will the no smoking light be on throughout the flight?" I reached up and ensured the light was selected "on" and replied, "Yes, it will." René Lévesque was the leader of the Quebec Separatist Party and a very heavy smoker. Normally, in the after-takeoff check we would turn the no smoking sign off. Smoking was allowed on aircraft at that time. The purser came to the cockpit and said, "René has a cigarette in one hand and a lighter in the other with both eyes glued to the 'lit' no smoking light." It was our way of getting a bit back on René for his advocating the breakup of Canada. The flight is only about twenty minutes, so he did not suffer for too long.

On another flight from Ottawa to Montreal, the weather was cloudy with showers and the odd thunderstorm cell was showing on the radar but well south of us. Suddenly, "bang!" we were hit by lightning. I swear that if I hadn't had my shoulder harness on I would have gone right through the top of the aircraft. The suddenness of the hit put our hearts in our mouths for a second or two. The flight attendants advised that all the passengers jumped as well but all were strapped in and all right. On landing we looked the aircraft over, and there was a rather large hole in the radar dome.

Another phenomenon that happened occasionally was the presence of St. Elmo's fire. It was nothing but static electricity dancing off the forward windows. It gave quite a show but never lasted very long. Those who experienced it for the first time thought it was fire and that something really bad was happening. Passengers, on occasion, would report "sparking" on the wings and we would reassure them that it was harmless. Ships with masts often experienced St. Elmo's fire. It was often reported that flame was shooting out the top of the masts.

Caribbean trips in the winter were always enjoyable, and while the trips were mostly turnarounds, we did manage to enjoy the warm weather. Judy often accompanied me on Barbados layovers.

We were operating from Montreal to the Bahamas. The in-charge was having some problems with a couple of unruly passengers. They were loud and made for an unpleasant trip for those around them. I asked the in-charge to move people around so that the unruly couple were isolated a bit more. We had open seats so this was not a problem.

The flight seemed to settle down when the in-charge again entered the cockpit, stating that the unruly (read "drunk") couple refused to fill out the Bahamian landing card because it was not in French. I advised her to inform the couple that the form was a Bahaman legal document and had nothing to do with Air Canada or the Canadian government. I further told her to advise the couple that if they did not complete the landing card they would not be allowed to remain in the Bahamas and, furthermore, I refused to have them on board on the return to Montreal in the event they did not complete the documentations.

The couple continued to be loud and disruptive. I advised the company in Nassau about them and asked that the local authorities meet the aircraft and explain the facts of life to them. When we arrived, two local police officers were positioned at the bottom of the stairs. The in-charge pointed out the two passengers and, as they proceeded to walk away, they were intercepted and escorted by the officers to the airport police office. I never did hear what happened to them. No loss.

The part I did not like on layovers was the cab rides to and from the airport. It seemed each driver wanted to impress us with his skill. Most seemed budding race car drivers.

On one drive to the Winnipeg airport, the driver was all over the road. I asked him to pull over twice before he actually stopped. I reached over from the back seat, took the keys, and threw them in a snow bank. He was a little upset. The first officer and I hailed a cab and proceeded to the airport. On arrival, I called the company that had the contract to drive crews and explained what had happened. I was advised the matter would be looked into. I doubt if it ever was.

Several locations provided a crew bus or our hotel layover provided transportation. These drivers were competent and friendly.

Chapter Twenty-One

Boeing 727

After flying as a first officer on the DC-9 for three years, I elected to fly the Boeing 727. Instead of 98 passengers on the DC-9, the 727 held 150.

Jim Todd was to be my mutual partner. We knew each other from the RCAF days. Our instructor was John Catley, and all of our simulator and flight training was completed in Vancouver. The simulators belonged to Canadian Pacific. Canadian used General Electric engines, while Air Canada used Pratt and Whitney; consequently, the engine instruments reflected Canadian's operation. We had no difficulty using the Canadian simulator.

John mentioned that if we had a good simulator trip the following morning, meaning no simulator "breakdowns," we would go sailing for the rest of the day on his sailboat. We were up early and completed our simulator session in record time. John drove us to his home, where we picked up a lunch basket that his wife had prepared. On the way to the yacht club, we stopped at the local liquor store and stocked up with beer and wine. We probably had enough for ten people.

We set sail about eleven in the morning and went all over English Bay, where many tankers and transport ships were waiting for their dockside assignment. It was great fun weaving in and around these large ships. John wanted to know if we had done any sailing; Jim had not. I told John of my experience with Bob Gordon in Toronto during my DC-9 training. I was assigned the steering for the next while. Lunch was served and some liquid consumed.

It started to get dark and we continued to weave our way between the big ships. Jim started to talk about his girlfriend and how much he missed her. He mentioned that she was training to be a stewardess with United Airlines in California. John felt sorry for him; we were all feeling no pain. He suggested we call her on the ship-to-shore radio. After several attempts, contact was established and Jim had a conversation with his girlfriend, with the entire world listening in. He felt better after the call and by now it was very dark, so we decided to head back to the yacht club. John took control of the operation and away we went.

On entry to the yacht club a very loud voice called out, "Is that you, John Catley?" John answered in the affirmative. The other gentleman said, "Then I guess we can call off organizing a search for you." Then John remembered that his wife had invited us back for dinner that night. When we did not show she became worried and called the yacht club. The club was organizing a search when we arrived. John had some explaining to do, both to his wife and club. Jim and I laughed our way back to thc hotcl.

The next day we started our flight training with John, out of Vancouver airport. Jim won the toss while I observed. He did a super job and now it was my turn. We completed the normal air work and returned to the airport for some touch-and-go landings. On my first landing, I greased the aircraft onto the runway. John said, "Enough of that crap." As I overshot, he simulated loss of an engine by pulling the throttle back. The Boeing 727 had three engines in the tail of the aircraft and it was quite easy to maintain a prescribed heading on the loss of an engine; press the required rudder and trim out the forces. I never had any problem with heading control but John would pull a throttle back when I least expected it. I still held the heading. He told me that while the Boeing 727 was easy to fly, he had never seen anyone maintain the heading as well as I did with an engine out.

Training complete, I returned to Montreal while Jim remained in Vancouver, his home base. I introduced myself to Bob Coneen, the 727 chief pilot. He arranged a line check for me and I was once again released onto an unsuspecting public.

I knew many of the captains I flew with from both the Viscount and the DC-9. I got along with the majority very well, but there were always one or two who seemed to have an agenda. I do not think they even knew of their hang-ups. One continually asked the girls for diet

Pepsi, not Coke, but Pepsi. More than one referred to the aircraft as "my ship." I took it all with a grain of salt and soldiered on knowing that I would soon be captain on the aircraft and the first officers could talk about my hang-ups.

Initially, I was not happy flying the 727 but I came to love the aircraft. The 727 was built by Boeing and, consequently, was very strong. I always referred to the aft cabin door as comparable to a watertight door on a submarine. The aft cabin door could be opened and stairs lowered for loading and unloading. This was the same exit Mr. D.B. Cooper used after he had hijacked a U.S. carrier, landed, and demanded $100,000 and two parachutes.

On departure, he told the crew where to fly and somewhere along that route he opened the aft door, lowered the stairs and bailed out; never to be heard from again. There is speculation to this day as to whether he could have survived the jump.

Landing the 727 required a different landing technique, which took a bit of time to get used to. Normally, prior to landing, the pilot pulled back on the control column. On the 727, just prior to touchdown, the pilot would push the control column slightly forward; ground effect assisted in the landing. Simply put, air displaced by the aircraft wings when close to the ground tended to keep the aircraft in the air. By pushing the control column you were using that air to make a smooth landing. Each aircraft is different, but the 727 is the only aircraft I ever flew that required the slight push forward.

Another feature of the 727 I liked was that we could carry lots of fuel. There were times on the DC-9 that an alternate field could not be found for diversion purposes due to extensive bad weather. I never had that problem on the 727.

One major difference on the 727 was that it required three pilots rather than the normal two. The third pilot acted as the flight engineer, controlling fuel and pressurization. Another pair of eyes in the cockpit never hurt.

The third pilot was referred to as the second officer. When I was captain on the 727, I often picked up one of my second officers at his home, waving to his wife as we left for the airport. The pilot was a nice young family man, who appeared to be happy. I never had any problem with him; he always carried out his duties in a very good manner.

Boeing 727 that I flew both as a first officer and captain. Nice aircraft.
Reproduced with the permission of Air Canada

One afternoon, he waited for his children to arrive home from school, a boy and a girl. As they arrived home he killed them, each in turn, using a knife. When his wife arrived home from her work he also killed her. Then he got into his car and at high speed attempted to kill himself, by hitting the partition leading into a tunnel in Montreal. He suffered serious injuries, but survived. The investigators discovered the bodies of his family, and he was charged with murder. When he recovered he was tried and convicted. I heard that he served his sentence and was released on parole. I have no idea where he is today. There were rumours that he owed a lot of money from gambling. I still feel bad about his family. He now lives with the memory of the crime he committed. A very sad story.

We were operating a flight from Calgary to Chicago, when we had a delay without any explanation. I asked the gate agent to find out what was causing the delay. The agent soon arrived back, chuckling to herself. She said that a passenger had been asked by U.S. Customs (Calgary had U.S. pre-clearance) what country he was from. The man said, "Quebec." The officer again asked him what country he was from and he again said, "Quebec." He asked a third time and received the same answer, "Quebec. The officer then stamped the passenger's boarding card "Entry Denied." He advised the passenger that the United States does not recognize any country called Quebec. The passenger then loudly proclaimed he was a Canadian and wanted to board the flight. U.S. Customs and Immigration told the individual he was asked three times what country he was from and each time he stated, "Quebec." We all had a good chuckle over the stupidity of the man. We proceeded to Chicago without him.

On another Calgary to Chicago flight, just prior to descent into Chicago, a flight attendant asked if she could bring a young boy and his mother for a visit to the cockpit. I naturally said yes. I loved to have young people visit the cockpit. It was a crystal clear night, and we could see the "big city" before us. Just as we initiated our descent, the young boy and his mother arrived and the whole panorama of the city filled the windscreen with its abundance of lights. The young boy without hesitation said, "I guess we're almost there; I can see the bottom." One never knows what anyone is going to say, but I always loved this lad's first impression of looking out the windscreen.

One very cold winter night, just before Christmas, we were operating to Sudbury and return to Toronto. On our arrival in Sudbury, the second officer said he would go in and get the latest Toronto weather. We knew the weather was clear and cold but he was keen and wanted the latest for the first officer and me to see. He arrived back with the weather and told us that the station agent told him that there was a young woman with a baby kitten, a Christmas present for her mother. The agent, knowing that the animal would never survive the cold temperatures in the luggage compartment, asked if it would be okay for the young lady to sit in first class with the kitten. The first class section was not being sold. I told the second officer to call the agent and advise him that it was okay for the lady to bring her pussy to first class. He picked up the radio and halfway through his transmission he realized what I had said. "You set me up!" We all had a chuckle, and the kitten arrived in Toronto in time for Christmas.

We were scheduled to pick up a flight from St. John's, Newfoundland, and operate to Toronto. On our arrival in Montreal we met the operating crew. The captain said that he thought they had hit a wingtip on landing in St. John's due to a strong crosswind. He further said he checked the wing and it looked okay. I thanked him for the information, dropped my "brain bag," and proceeded to look over the aircraft. I found the navigation light on the right wing was broken and looking down the wing, I could see that it was rippled. The other crew had indeed hit the wing tip on landing. Why they did not see the damage is beyond me.

I contacted maintenance and told them I was grounding the aircraft due to the wing being rippled. Maintenance arrived and concurred with my decision. After a short delay, another aircraft was towed to a nearby gate and passengers and luggage were transferred to the new aircraft. The trip to Toronto was uneventful.

Two days later, while at home, I received a phone call from the chief pilot wanting to know why I flew a damaged aircraft from St. John's to Montreal. He advised me that an incident report had been forwarded to him from maintenance. I explained that I did not operate the aircraft to Montreal. I gave him the captain's name who did, and explained that the captain had advised me on landing in Montreal that he thought they had hit a wingtip on landing in St. John's but, on his inspection of the aircraft, everything looked okay. I did my own external of the aircraft and found the wing tip navigation light broken. Looking down the wing I saw that there was obvious rippling of the skin of the wing.

I told the chief pilot that it was me who grounded the aircraft and that I had advised maintenance of this fact. Upon inspection, they had concurred with my decision. I further requested that my name be removed from the incident report and another initiated with the proper captain's name attached. The changes were made and I never heard another word.

Chapter Twenty-Two

Boeing 747

I had completed about four years on the Boeing 727 as captain, and I was looking for a change. The company had just introduced the Airbus, and I gave serious consideration about bidding for a captain's position. Then I started to think that, with my age and seniority, I would never see the 747 as captain. But I always wanted to fly the "big bird," so I elected to fly the 747 as a first officer. My plan was to fly the 747 for two years and then bid on the Boeing 767 for my last four years before retirement.

The ground school courses were normally given by ground staff. Air Canada was going modern by introducing computers containing the course curriculum. We would review chapters, sitting with our earphones on, and then write an exam on that chapter, using nothing but the computer. If we did have a question there was usually an instructor nearby to answer our queries.

On all previous courses we were expected to build the airplane before we could fly it. Boeing introduced a "need to know" system. Their philosophy is; what is the point of learning the electrical system? If something went wrong, you could not fix it anyway. Boeing introduced a logical system, which was well received by all pilots.

Toronto had some very experienced 747 instructors; some did double duty in the simulator and in flying training.

The 747 had four engines. It took awhile to get used to a handful of throttles, but we soon settled into the routine. Our last simulator was an instrument ride with the Ministry of Transport observing our flying.

Even though the 747 base was Toronto, Judy and I elected to continue to live in Ottawa and I would commute to Toronto for my flights. The ticket agents at the Ottawa airport soon began to know

Aluminum overcast, Boeing 747. I flew as first officer.
Reproduced with the permission of Air Canada

me as a commuter. If a first class seat was available I would be assigned that seat. Quite often I rode on the jump seat in the cockpit. Occasionally, I would have to ride steerage.

All the 747 flights were long range so it was necessary to carry extra clothes. Our flight attendants were very experienced on what and what not to pack. I would pack enough uniform shirts for each day of flying. It was their suggestion that I only take two shirts. On arrival at the layover hotel I would call the concierge desk and someone would pick up my laundry. It was always returned in lots of time for me to dress for a flight. I always packed too many sets of underwear. One of the senior girls told me to buy silk undies, wear one pair and wash it at the hotel. It was always dry by morning. Their suggestions left room in my suitcase for purchases.

On overseas trips, most pilots bought a bottle of liquor; one was allowed. There were always those who abused the system and would try to bring in more than one bottle. There was one case of a very senior captain who, on landing in Shannon, Ireland, with a very good duty-free shop, would proceed to the duty-free with a sports bag. He would fill it up and stow it on the aircraft. On arrival in Montreal, he would proceed to customs with the rest of the crew, but without his sports bag. It was discovered that the captain had an arrangement with a ground-crew person, who would retrieve the sports bag and drive to the captain's car using an Air Canada tug vehicle. This individual would open the captain's trunk, take a bottle for his trouble, close the trunk, and continue with his duties.

The captain was eventually caught and he was restricted from flying the Atlantic for three months. He had been doing his sports bag trick for years. On his first trip back on the Atlantic he carried his sports bag with him. His logic: They caught me once but not twice. They never did, and the ground crew gentleman was never caught, either.

Usually, when flying into the Caribbean, it was understood that we could purchase a bottle, usually rum. Naturally, an individual was caught with six bottles and was reported to the Montreal base chief pilot. A memo was placed on the bulletin board stating that the privilege of bringing back a bottle on a turnaround flight was terminated. Few pilots abused the privilege and, rather than punishing the guilty, we all suffered from one person's greed.

After a period of about three months another memo stated that the privilege of bringing a bottle back was reinstated. The memo went up on Friday. On a Saturday return trip, one of the navigators on the DC-8 arrived in customs with a full case of rum hidden below his flight bag, which was on a wheeled luggage carrier. The privilege was once again cancelled never to be re-instated.

I recall on the DC-8 we landed at Orly airport; this was before the Charles de Gaulle Airport was open. I had a fibreglass suitcase and it was heavy; there was no wheeled luggage in those days. The suitcase did double duty; it not only carried my clothing but it would also carry seven bottles of French wine. I would pick up my wine in the city near our layover hotel. At Orly, I would pick up some cheese and a French baguette. Clearing customs, I always told the officer I had red wine (never mentioning the quantity), cheese, and a baguette for my wife. I was always told, "Enjoy," and my suitcase was never opened.

I thoroughly enjoyed flying the 747-200 series. Flying into Tampa with 500 passengers on board, the tower operator made the comment, "Must be a load of snowbirds if your company is flying the big boat into Tampa." Of course he was correct.

The aircraft, while big, was easy to fly. It was very responsive to our inputs. Although I was a first officer on the aircraft I still wore captain's bars on my shoulders. Most captains were happy to have an experienced captain on board. When I was flying, I was left to make all the decisions necessary to have a smooth flight. There were, however, one or two captains who thought that I should wear first officer's bars. I thought they were a bit insecure in their own minds and they wanted one and all to know that they were the captain.

When the 747 was landing, the front of the aircraft was about thirty-five feet in the air when the main wheels or "bogeys" touched the ground. Initially, it took a bit of getting used to—sitting so high before touchdown—but it soon became natural. Once the nose wheel settled onto the runway, reverse was selected, and was very effective. Icy conditions or strong crosswinds were a bit tricky. The wind would hit the large tail surface and try to push you or weather cock (force the aircraft to go in the direction of the wind, like a windsock) the aircraft. We had to be aware and react as necessary.

The 747 was a long-range aircraft used mostly on long hauls: London, Paris, Frankfurt, and, eventually, into India and Singapore.

Flying in and out of London was great fun. Traffic was very heavy, with aircraft from both the East and the West. London had two parallel runways; one was used for takeoff and the other for landing. Everyone flew the aircraft by the numbers. If Air Traffic Control wanted you to fly 210 knots, you flew that speed. Not 205 or 215, but 210. We were given heading and speeds to fly by the air traffic control so that they could vector all aircraft safely to a landing or a departure point on takeoff.

One morning, we had completed our cockpit checks, and passengers were on board. A very British voice in London control tower said, "Ladies and gentlemen, there will be a slight delay in issuing clearances. The tower is on fire and we are evacuating to an alternate site." The tower was up and running in about ten minutes from their alternate site.

One evening, we were departing from Toronto to London, England, with a twenty-four-hour layover, and then proceeding to Bombay (now Mumbai). Shortly before departure, one of our flight attendants, a male, was helping an Indian lady to get settled. She appeared anxious about flying and the attendant did his best to make her comfortable. The lady's seat was next to the entrance door so she had lots of leg room. Our attendant knelt down in front of her to make certain she had fastened her seat belt and to offer her comfort. As he knelt in front of her she threw up all over him. She was very upset with herself and apologized. Luckily, he had a clean uniform and changed, knowing he could have his dirty uniform cleaned in London. The flight then proceeded according to plan. We did inquire if the attendant was all right and we were assured he was fine. After our London layover we proceeded to Bombay with the same back-end crew. The male attendant said that he was still okay.

The flight to Bombay is long, nearly ten-plus hours. We usually crossed over Europe and, depending on the weather, possibly go a bit south to the Mediterranean, slightly east of Greece, entering landfall north of Lebanon. The Lebanese civil war was on at that time, and we had to make damn certain we were well north of Lebanon. The U.S. military had AWACS (airborne warning and control system) aircraft monitoring all aircraft in the area and often told aircraft to move farther north as they were about to enter Lebanese airspace. Most of the time, we would fly over Europe, Hungary, parts of Yugoslavia, Rumania, and Bulgaria, and then enter Turkish airspace over Iran, a huge country, which is very mountainous in the north. This area was famous for its ski hills under the shah, prior to the revolution. After crossing Iran, we would be south of Pakistan, over the Arabian Sea into Bombay, India. On descent below 10,000 feet, you could actually smell the air. It was not clean air but pollution from India's many coal fires.

We landed in Bombay around two in the morning. As we left the aircraft, we noticed several guards in military greatcoats, sleeping on windowsills or benches. Most had an old 303 Lee Enfield rifle, a leftover from World War II, or a 9mm Sten gun. We did learn that our guards had no bullets for the weapons. Their mere presence was enough to keep everyone in line. None appeared under sixty years old.

Customs could be a bit of a chore; paperwork had to be exact. If anyone was carrying a bottle of liquor he or she was made to open the bottle, take a drink and then put the cap back on. We presumed the logic was, with the seal broken and some of the contents consumed, one would not be able to sell the liquor at a profit to a local.

After customs, a bus took us to our hotel, the Oberei. The Oberei was one of the hotels where terrorists attacked and killed many civilians. The bus was a vintage one and had screens over all the windows. We learned that the screens would stop rocks and later we heard the screen was supposed to stop grenades from entering the bus. Frequently, as we approached the hotel, a woman would throw herself against the bus, hoping we would stop and offer her help or money. The drivers ignored the woman and we pressed on. This was a common practice. They knew the bus had foreigners on board.

The hotel itself was made up of two parts, old and new. We stayed in the older section, which was really very nice. The food was good, shops were available, and it even had a roof pool. The newer section was very modern: a very open concept with lots of marble. One could stand in the middle of the foyer and look up and see each circular floor.

This section of the hotel became very special to the local high-school graduates. If their marks were too low for university, several would take the elevator to the top floor and jump to their deaths hitting the marble floor. I was there when it happened but I had no desire to see the body of the young lady involved.

After our layover, we proceeded back to London. I always rose early and had ham, toast, tea, and eggs in the dining room. My stomach could not handle the food boarded for the crew. Departure was very early in order to arrive in London in the morning. We still had the same crew, and the flight attendant we were still concerned about said he was all right.

En route was routine and we landed in London on schedule. We had another twenty-four-hour layover in the big city. The next morning we were on our way to Toronto. Halfway across the Atlantic, the in-charge said the flight attendant we were concerned about collapsed. Many flights seem to have a doctor on board, and this time we were lucky. The doctor reported the patient was asleep and was in no apparent danger. As we approached the Canadian coast we advised the doctor that we could to divert to St. John's, Newfoundland, with no problem, if warranted. The doctor advised the flight attendant seemed all right so we pressed on. Passing north of Halifax, Montreal, and Ottawa, we posed the same question to the doctor. Each time we were told the patient was all right. Well into our descent, midway between Ottawa and Toronto, the in-charge came rushing into the cockpit and advised that the doctor said he was losing the patient and we had to land ASAP. Toronto was closest. We advised Air Traffic Control and the company of our problem and we were given priority. We kept the speed well above normal descent speed, slowing at the last minute for landing. Our company advised that an ambulance would meet us on arrival. We asked the passengers to remain seated until the ambulance crew was with the patient near the aft of the aircraft. Once the aircraft was empty, the patient was put on a stretcher and transported to a local hospital.

Apparently it was touch-and-go for the flight attendant. He spent seven days in intensive care and several weeks recuperating. It was surmised when the lady threw up over him, he must have picked up a germ of some kind. He was a very lucky lad. I actually flew with him about six months after the incident. He was fine.

During layovers in Bombay, we were told that if you were in a cab and the driver had an accident, leave the vehicle and do not look back. Indians believe in karma; in other words, if we had the driver take us to a certain destination and we were involved in an accident, it would be our fault. Their logic was, if we had not asked him to go, to wherever, he would not have been there and would therefore not have had an accident.

Another pilot and I were actually involved in a fender-bender. We just left with the driver hollering at us. A policeman who was close by completely ignored us. We mingled with the crowd and went our merry way. Another strange habit the drivers had at night was not to put on their headlights. They believed it would run down the battery.

Judy accompanied me on a couple of these flights. On one trip, we were in a cab when, suddenly, we were surrounded by seemingly thousands of people. The driver advised that all the jewellery workers were on a one-day strike. He asked us to put our windows up to keep hands from prodding at us. It became very hot very quickly; these vehicles had no air conditioning. Luckily we had brought water with us.

Prior to these trips, Judy would often give me a picture of a particular piece of jewellery she liked. I would take it to a jeweller near the hotel. He would make the piece in a day or less and I would pick it up before our departure. The pieces were very cheap and were of a good quality of gold. An item that would cost $300 in Canada was about $100 in India. Unfortunately, most of the jewellery was stolen when our home was broken into while we were away on vacation.

On one occasion, a second officer joined me on a trip to an outdoor market. The windows were down and as we stopped, hands, palms open, were in every window looking for money. One spoke excellent English and asked why we did not give him money. The second officer, who was a big lad, said in a very gruff voice, "Because we are Russian." Hands withdrew and we carried on to the market.

I was looking for a denim shirt, which I found. It had a Wal-Mart tag and a price of $10. The shirt was locally made. Wal-Mart had the workers price and tag each item; shirts were even placed on hangers. Items were then shipped to a store in North America. On arrival, all the staff had to do was hang them on display.

The streets were literally filled with people. Street vendors were everywhere; barbers, tailors, fruit vendors, and clothing kiosks of all kind could be found.

Many crew members learned the hard way not to buy food of any kind from a street vendor. Normally at home if we had an orange, we would bite the peel and peel the rest by hand. In India biting into the peel guaranteed that you would become very friendly with the porcelain receptacle.

The air was not the cleanest in the world and that is an understatement. There seemed to be little or no control of traffic. Cars pulled out and passed all the time with no thought of the oncoming vehicles. At night, neighbourhoods would watch movies or television on outdoor screens.

If you got off the beaten track, you would come across snake charmers playing their flute and a cobra snake would rise from a basket. I often came across a man and a monkey performing tricks for the bystanders. Any time you wanted to take a picture, the owners would put their hands towards you signifying they wanted money from you to take a picture.

In another area, you could watch women washing clothes in a river and smacking the clothing against the rocks to squeeze as much water out of the material as possible. The clothing was then placed on the rocks for the sun to dry it.

It was amazing to me that there were not more fires in the city.

A myriad of overhead wires went in every direction.

During my visits to both Bombay and Delhi, it was obvious there was no middle class. Locals were either very rich or very poor. The Tata family was probably the richest in the country. A middle class was created by North America call centres offshore; many went to India because of the people's ability to speak English. If you have ever contacted a call centre in India you know how bad some of that English was.

One place I wanted to visit was Mahatma Gandhi's home in Bombay. The house was surrounded by other homes, none of which were lavish. They were very plain, as was Gandhi's work. He always tried to proclaim peace through peaceful means. He was assassinated by a Hindu fanatic in January 1948. He was quite a man and well worth reading about.

In the hotel, there was a shop that made leather jackets. The owner would take your measurements and, in about three hours, the work was completed. The jackets were well made. I had many made for family and friends over the years. The jacket would cost about $35–$50.

Another favourite spot to visit was Bridge Candi. This area had a huge swimming pool left over from colonial rule. The pool itself was in the shape of the Indian subcontinent. Judy and I spent a few afternoons getting wet and keeping out of the very hot sun.

It was interesting to see scaffolding outside our hotel. It was not metal, as we know scaffolding in North America, but bamboo tied with rope reaching up to the twelfth floor.

One morning, one of our female flight attendants had a shower and left the bathroom, towelling her hair. She looked up and saw a man on the scaffolding and she screamed. He panicked and fell ten floors to his death. The flight attendant was nude at the time.

Normally, when we landed, the pilots were the last off the aircraft. We had logbook entries to make and aircraft systems to shut down. On this particular flight, we were surprised to see the whole back-end crew waiting by the exit door. We were advised that the crew had to be escorted to the customs hall. Walking along, I asked our company representative what the problem was. He advised that an Italian crew, on a crew bus, had been mistaken for a Pan American crew. A man armed with an Uzi submachine gun entered the bus while the crew was getting settled. He hollered something that no one understood and pulled the trigger on the Uzi. Nothing happened. The crew hid behind the seats while the captain asked what was going on. He walked down the aisle towards the man, who by this time had cleared his weapon and shot the captain twice. After he exited the bus, the man tossed a hand grenade into the vehicle. It failed to explode. The man was overpowered by security, which came running when they had heard the shots.

We now understood the caution being taken for our crew. We were escorted to our crew bus, the door closed, and away we went. The crazy part of all this "security" we endured was that not one armed guard accompanied us on the bus. We were hoping that there were no more armed individuals lurking in the darkness. At least the window had wire to deflect any thrown grenades.

Naturally we were concerned about how badly hurt the Italian captain was. Although he had been shot twice, he survived his ordeal and returned to active flying a few months later. When I left my room the next morning, I was surprised to see so many armed army personnel on our floor. Someone in authority must have realized the seriousness of the "terrorist attack" and attempted to protect the crews while we slept.

During the period when Ronald Reagan was president there was an air traffic control strike. Reagan ended up firing all those involved and having the military take over the control tower and other duties until such time as replacements could be trained. Many fired employees found work in the Middle East.

On a return trip to London from Bombay, we were talking to Saudi controllers, who were obviously American. They said they were tired of the area and looked forward to returning to the States. They told us that Canadian Air Traffic Control was looking for people for duty at St. John's, Newfoundland, as well as Winnipeg and Vancouver. None of the controllers had any idea where these cities were or what they had to offer and asked for our opinion. Naturally we encouraged them to apply for Newfoundland, telling them they would love it. We all got a chuckle out of the conversation. We did correct our initial selection and advised them that Vancouver was the best choice.

Flying into the Caribbean with the large aircraft took a great deal of concentration. The runways were all short and, if you did not stop within the confines of the runway, you would get wet. Every pilot flew the airspeed to the exact knot to make certain not to go into the water. The runway ended where the water started. Takeoffs were interesting due to the hot temperatures. The aircraft would lumber along, slowly picking up speed. There was never much runway left after we became airborne.

My two years on the 747 went very quickly, and I was thinking of bidding for the 767 and a captain position. It was about this time that it was announced that Air Canada had bought the new 747-400. My seniority dictated that I could have a good position on this new aircraft if I wanted to remain a first officer. I elected to stay another two years flying the newest, biggest, and heaviest aircraft in the world.

All up-weight for takeoff on the 747-200 was 740,000 pounds. The new 747-400 had a take-off weight of 875,000 pounds. Later, the extended range version had a maximum take-off weight of 910,000 pounds. United Airlines actually had a 747 take off with a weight of one million pounds. The aircraft had all the newest technology and I looked forward to the challenge.

Ground school was in Toronto and, similar to our previous course, we used computers to review systems and to test what we had absorbed.

When we completed ground school, we were sent to Minneapolis–St. Paul for simulator training. We each had a suite with two bedrooms, full kitchen, and a fireplace. Judy, on a visit, mentioned that we were spoiled. We were and we loved it. I never had a course with Air Canada that was so enjoyable. The complex was a United Airlines facility. There was every type of simulator imaginable. United Airlines catered to pilot training all over the world. Simulators were available for just about all aircraft flying worldwide.

Initially, we had pilots from United as our instructors. This situation did not last long, and we now had Air Canada qualified Boeing 747 pilots as our instructors.

The 747-400 was leap years ahead in technology, compared to the aircraft we had previously flown with Air Canada. As in the past,

Judy in a Boeing 747 cockpit on our 1994 trip to Bombay.

we buddied up with another pilot for training, one being a captain and the other a first officer, as in my case—having elected to fly the 747-400 as a first officer due to my age and seniority. The 400, initially, flew with two pilots. Once the Far East routes started, a relief pilot was added. The addition of a relief pilot meant we could take a turn in a first class seat to have a short nap or read. Eventually, bunks were provided, and you could lie down and just relax; most enjoyable.

We practiced every emergency in the book and completed many approaches on four and three engines. No one had any particular problem with the conversion. Our last simulator trip was an instrument ride with a Canadian Transport Inspector overseeing our progress.

On return to Toronto, we flew with a supervisor to get acquainted with the new aircraft, flying to Bangor, Maine, where we completed a few approaches each, and many touch-and-go landings. Each pilot had about an hour flying the aircraft, and then we were all considered competent to fly with passengers. Our group had a lot of Atlantic experience so there was no need to have a supervisor show us the Atlantic procedures.

The inertial navigation on the aircraft was state-of-the-art. It was referred to as FMS, flight management system. The whole trip could be programmed on the ground; all departure procedures, en route waypoints, and altitudes. We had offset capability, which means we could parallel a track by a distance of ten miles. This capacity helped our traffic control when they planned the overseas tracks. After everything was programmed all the pilot had to do, once airborne, was plug in our "German friend," the autopilot. The aircraft would level off to the programmed altitude. We could dial up new altitudes, press a button, and the aircraft would climb to the new preset altitude.

Many of the pilots used the autopilot most of the time. Personally, I always hand flew the aircraft to altitude and many times on descent. Once we knew the landing runway at destination we could enter the approach. When it came time to leave altitude, the whole system was activated to the approach. All we had to do was sit back and watch it do its thing. The aircraft could actually land hands-off, assuming the airport had the necessary equipment. Once landed, the throttles came back automatically, as well as the reverse. The brakes would activate all by their lonesome from a preset setting that the crew selected prior to landing. The aircraft would actually track the centre line of the runway, coming to a complete stop all by itself.

Initially, we would be crossing the Atlantic and the aircraft would start a small turn or do something not programmed, and we could not understand why it was doing what it was doing. The standard question was "what's it doing now?" We soon got proficient on the new equipment. It got to the point that we were thinking faster than the computer. We would insert a new heading, and, by the time the computer digested the new input, we could have completed the turn manually.

There are three categories of instrument landings or landing minimums. Category 2 was 200 feet above ground with a visibility of one-half mile. Category 1 was 100 feet and one-quarter of a mile. Category 3 was auto-land, with basically no ceiling or visibility. Crews were asked to complete an auto land once a month. This was to check both the aircraft and ground equipment.

On the 747, due to the long route structure we did not get many landings a month. We were all a bit reluctant to complete an auto land in clear conditions. Everyone just wanted to fly the approach and complete a landing, but we knew it was necessary to ensure all components were working properly. Completing an auto approach in clear weather gave everyone a good look at all the equipment and gave confidence when an actual auto approach had to be completed.

Air Canada had added Singapore to its Far East route structure via Bombay. Initially out of London, we flew the standard route to Bombay, over Europe, Turkey, and Iran. A new route was finally approved, which took us over Europe, Russia, Afghanistan, and Pakistan. This route saved quite a bit of time and fuel.

The Russian occupation of Afghanistan and the war that followed resulted in their defeat by the Mahjadeen. These local fighters were well supplied by the U.S. with weapons; including Red Stone shoulder missiles. Once the Taliban took control, some of us were concerned about what they might do with these missiles. They would have been more than happy to shoot down a Western airliner. Our concerns were not taken seriously. Eventually, British Airways became concerned with the Taliban's intentions and changed their route back to flying over Turkey and Iran. All other carriers soon followed the British example.

We were crossing the Atlantic one day, when a young man of Indian descent asked to see the cockpit. He told us he was living in Vancouver and that his family had arranged a marriage for him and he was on his way to India to see his prospective bride. He was not happy with the arrangement but he was forced to follow family tradition.

We had our layover, followed by a return trip to Singapore, another layover in Bombay and then onward to London. The same young man arrived in the cockpit again. We asked him about his bride-to-be. He told us that he took one look at her and went into hiding until he could get a flight back to Canada. His biggest concern was having to face his family, particularly his father. We understood his concern. We, in North America, have the privilege of picking our own wives, with their permission, of course. Indian tradition was different. The poor guy had lived in Canada most of his life and had adopted North American habits, while his family still followed tradition. I often wondered how he made out with his family.

The route to Singapore took us over the Bay of Bengal, the Nicobar Islands, the Strait of Malacca into Singapore, on the southern part of Malaya. Crossing the Bay of Bengal there were frequent thunderstorms. We often had to divert 100–200 miles from our planned course to avoid these storms, which were as high as 60,000 feet. It was next to impossible to contact Air Traffic Control, so we would transmit blind, giving our position and our intention to divert. Other carriers did the same. At least we knew where other aircraft were and they knew where we were.

Singapore is not very large but it is a republic and sits on the southern tip of the Malay Peninsula. All the facilities, from navigation aids, runways, and terminal, are very modern. The south end of the airport was once the infamous Japanese prisoner-of-war camp, Changi. The prisoners were mostly British and Australian army personnel. They received very harsh treatment at the hands of their Japanese guards.

The terminal is designed in such a way that you are able to buy your duty-free on arrival or shop in many upscale stores. It is an example that all terminals should follow. It would save weight and eliminate a fire hazard from all the liquor being brought on board.

Singapore has very strict laws about smuggling, particularly drugs. If you are caught, the penalty is death. Speed limits on vehicles are strictly enforced. If you were caught spitting or throwing gum on the street, you would receive a heavy fine and might be subject to jail time as well. Not flushing a toilet is also a punishable offence. To my surprise, the city is very modern. I envisioned quaint houses and markets. Instead, it was like downtown Toronto or any North American city. Orchard Road has most of the large shopping stores. These stores are all three to four storeys high and carry every imaginable item at reasonable prices.

We would arrive at our hotel at eleven in the morning. I would call Judy and she would be just going to bed at eleven in the evening, a twelve-hour time change. Although we arrived at 11 a.m., we were scheduled out at 11 p.m. Most of the crew raced to the stores and then tried to get some sleep before we left.

During one of my walks, I came across the famous Raffles Bar. Unfortunately, it was closed for renovations.

One of the back-end crew usually arranged for a "watch party." We would be told to be in room such-and-such at a particular time. When we got there, a local businessman and an assistant would greet us. The bed would be covered with watches, all knock-off copies of well-known watch companies. It was hard to tell they were "fake." Everyone bought one or two or more; they were very cheap and guaranteed to work while you were in the room. I bought several during my trips to Singapore and most lasted quite a while.

One of our flight attendants, a male, brought a suitcase full of these watches, hoping to sell them when he got home. Bombay customs caught him at the airport and confiscated all the watches. He was charged with smuggling and spent a few nights in jail. He missed our flight home.

We learned that he was released and confined to the Oberei hotel until his trial. He quickly made his way to Goa and got out of the country as fast as he could. He eventually arrived in London, no doubt with a story to tell. When he arrived in Toronto and reported to his supervisors, he was advised he was fired. I did learn that the flight attendant union went to bat for him and he was eventually reinstated. I imagine he stayed clear of India.

Early one morning, the captain of a flight in London that was scheduled to leave for Toronto failed to arrive for crew bus scheduled departure time. His room was checked by hotel staff; it was empty and the bed had not been slept in. The crew decided to leave for Heathrow without the captain, assuming he would show up at the airport. The captain failed to show, and another captain was drafted to operate to Toronto, incurring a delay. Later in the morning a body was found in Regent's Park, very near our layover hotel. All entrances into the park are normally locked early in the evening.

The body found in the park was that of the missing captain. He was very physically fit and had earned a black belt in Judo. It was surmised that he found the exit gate locked and decided to climb the iron fence surrounding the park. The tops separating the vertical portions of the fence looked like arrowheads. Somehow or other, he slipped and fell onto the top of a section of the fence. The arrow-shaped portion penetrated his groin, and he then fell backwards back into the park and bled to death.

Another part of this sad story was that he had just married

a younger flight attendant. Unfortunately for her, he had never changed his will, so a home in Montreal and another in Florida, as well as all cash and death benefits, reverted to his former wife. I often flew with her after Rod's death. She put up a good front and did her job but she was a very sad young lady.

Air Canada changed the Indian destination from Bombay to Delhi. I was scheduled to fly with a Vancouver captain on the inaugural flight out of Delhi. We flew as passengers to Paris and then on Air India to Delhi. Prior to leaving for the airport, I had my breakfast in a local restaurant. I had often eaten there, enjoying their omelettes and strong coffee. Departure from Charles de Gaulle was on time and we settled back to read and enjoy the long flight to New Delhi. Approximately three hours after takeoff, I could feel my stomach starting to act up. I rushed towards the bathroom, which thankfully was not occupied. I closed the door and my breakfast made a deposit on the wall, mirror, and sink. I spent the next twenty minutes cleaning my mess and myself up. I returned to my seat. I explained to Bernie Mack, the captain, what had happened and promptly fell asleep. Food poisoning was certainly an occupational hazard and I had my fair share of discomfort over the years.

Prior to our inaugural flight there was an Indian ceremony, blessing the plane and crew. Local dignitaries shook our hands and presented each crew member with a small rug—mine hangs on a wall in our home. I have completed several trips to Delhi. My most memorable was when, as a crew, we arranged for a small bus to take us north to visit the Taj Mahal, situated in Agra.

It was beautiful, with its white marble sparkling in the sun. Without doubt, it is one of the most impressive and beautiful places I have ever seen. It is considered the eighth wonder of the world. The grounds consist of reflecting pools and well-manicured lawns. The structure took twenty years to build and was completed in 1653. The emperor at the time had the Taj built as a tribute to his third wife. Both are buried within the Taj itself. The interior is all white marble as well, and makes for a cool refuge from the hot sun. Another attraction in the Delhi area is the Red Fort made from sandstone. It is famous for its ornamental art work.

Both structures were built by the Emperor Shah Jahan, and reflect the best of Muslim art. There is a story that he planned to build a black marble mausoleum across the river, in sight of the Taj Mahal, but he was overthrown by his son and the structure was never built.

Crews on layover visited the outdoor markets for the sights and sounds. In one particular market, a young boy came running up to us and pointed to my friend's feet. He was wearing sandals and no socks. One sandal was covered with, shall I say, "number two?" The lad took the sandal right off his foot and ran down between two stalls. We followed, and as we approached, the lad was removing the deposit and cleaning the sandal. He put his hand out for money, which my friend gladly paid. This scam was widely used on tourists in markets in Delhi. Kids would use a stick to drop contents on a shoe or sandal, and, for a fee, clean the droppings off. We called it the "shit stick." Luckily, I never experienced the "shit stick" but I know many who did.

Chapter Twenty-Three

Far East

Air Canada was granted flights from Vancouver to Seoul, Korea, and Osaka, Japan. I was looking forward to flying to both cities.

Leaving Vancouver, our route to Seoul took us over the Aleutian Islands, north of Midway Island—of World War II fame—then south of the Kamchatka Peninsula. This was Russian-controlled territory.

Korean Airlines had a habit of taking a shortcut to Seoul by crossing over the southern part of the peninsula. The Russians were obviously upset by this continuous incursion of their air space. They intercepted Korean flight 009 in 1983, shooting down the aircraft and killing everyone on board. The Russians claimed the aircraft was a United States spy plane.

On one descent into Seoul, in cloud, we saw an American fighter aircraft. We asked Air Traffic Control why we were not advised of the proximity of another aircraft. They told us there was no other aircraft in our vicinity. It was obvious to us that the Americans used us as target practice to improve their intercept ability. We were not happy.

There was a note on the approach chart for Seoul airport that said any aircraft that strayed off the assigned path would be fired upon. The presidential palace was just a short distance from the airfield, and they were not taking any chances.

There was a similar notice on the charts we used in Europe about flying over the Charles de Gaulle chateau in France. Charles de Gaulle was the president of France when we arrived in France on the CF-104 aircraft. His life was always in danger.

Seoul is now a modern city, largely newly rebuilt after the Korean War. The 38th parallel is only 40 kilometres north of Seoul and marks the boundary of North and South Korea. The area is heavily armed by both sides and is continually patrolled. Many American troops are still stationed in Korea.

We spent many hours walking the streets and observing the locals. The food was generally very good, although I was not fond of "kimchi"; fermented cabbage. Language was not a problem in local restaurants. All the food available was on display in the window; all you had to do was point at the dish you wanted.

In the early evening, we would see well-dressed men passed out on the sidewalks. We were told that most had stressful jobs and were pressed to succeed. After work, they would drink themselves into a stupor and pass out as they made their way home.

One custom that I enjoyed happened when a large department store opened for business. The staff was all lined up and bowed to the customers, in effect, thanking them in advance for their purchase.

In one area of the city was a large airfield left over from the Korean War. The field no longer had aircraft but thousands of bicycles, stacked in row after row. We learned that the locals come to the field on the weekend and ride their bikes around the perimeter. It was safer than venturing onto the streets. The drivers drove very fast and twisted and turned down the narrow streets.

We soon found a great area for shopping and tended to visit the same area each trip.

On one shopping expedition a very loud siren sounded. We were told that we had to stay inside the store until the all-clear sounded. The streets were soon deserted and only the military was allowed to move around. After about an hour the all-clear was given. We never did learn what the problem was, other than all was okay.

The very next day, we arrived at the airport for our trip back to Vancouver. We observed literally hundreds of U.S. military vehicles heading north. Obviously, there was something going on. It was time to get out of Dodge.

Trips to Osaka followed roughly the same route we took to Korea before we adjusted course towards Japan. We found the Japanese air traffic controllers hard to understand even though they spoke English. There were times we would request a change of altitude or perhaps a heading change, and the answer was never very clear. We assumed we were cleared as requested, but depended on the Japanese air traffic control to monitor our position. After a few trips, it became easier to understand the controllers.

Osaka airport is called Kansai International Airport and is about fifty kilometres from the city of Osaka. The airport is located on artificial islands in Osaka Bay. The airfield is reached by a causeway to the mainland and, once on shore, branches off in many directions.

The terminal is state-of-the-art and is really one of the finest I have ever seen. It contains every amenity a passenger could wish for. We were told that the airfield is actually sinking at a very slow rate due to all the fill used during construction and the heavy aircraft and equipment used to keep an airport operating. The main terminal actually sits on gigantic springs to offset the effects of an earthquake.

The drive to Osaka gave us a wonderful view of the countryside. The superhighway bypassed many large and small villages. All were quaint and colourful. Along the coast, we could see many fishing villages and boats of all sizes and description.

Our hotel, I believe, was the Crown Plaza, a twenty-four-storey structure. It was ideally located and only a short walk to good shopping. The lobby was quite large with a fountain and restaurant. There was a canal nearby with a walking path. I often walked to the train station for breakfast. All I had to do was point to a picture on their menu and be served. There was also a small outlet similar to a McDonald's, which served a breakfast sandwich.

The station itself was interesting—watching the people rush around, going in all directions. I noticed a man giving samples of toilet paper to everyone exiting the train and entering the terminal by an escalator. Out of curiosity, I checked the male toilet for toilet paper; there was none. There were, however, foot indicators to place yourself when squatting. It reminded me of France. Always make certain you bring lots of Kleenex when travelling around Japan. The station had a lot of English signs, which helped orient you in relation to the city.

Three of us took a side trip to Kyoto. This city was the capital of Japan at one time. It had many older buildings and quaint wooden buildings. We walked for many hours and found the people most gracious. When lunchtime arrived, all we had to do was point and say "*Arigato*."

Judy accompanied me on my next flight to Osaka, on January 16, 1995, and John, the captain of the flight, had his wife along as well. During our Vancouver layover, we were able to visit with Judy's brother, Rick.

The trip to Osaka was routine. On arrival I noticed that John looked a bit pale. He said he was all right. John was a tall, good-looking man with salt-and-pepper curly hair. He was due to retire in three months. I had known John for many years; we got along well together and respected each other's abilities.

That afternoon, Judy and I did a bit of a tour visiting Osaka castle, a must-see when visiting Osaka. We were fortunate to observe a couple of men performing kendo, a martial art, using bamboo sticks. Another plus for us was that the two individuals were dressed in traditional costume. The grounds, as well as the castle itself, are kept in very good condition. It replaced an old temple in about 1555 and was quite a sight.

During our walk, we stopped to look at our map just to make certain we were going in the right direction. A gentleman approached us, bowed slightly, and asked, in perfect English, if he could be of any assistance. He confirmed we were heading in the right direction.

That evening, many of the crew went to dinner together, a most enjoyable get-together. It had been a long day so everyone went to their rooms in anticipation of our flight home the following day.

Around five-thirty in the morning, I was literally tossed out of bed. The building was doing "rock and roll"; we were experiencing an earthquake. We later learned it was centred in Kobe, a city across the bay from Osaka, and measured 7.2 on the Richter scale. The building was moving side to side. We found shelter between the closet door frame, as recommended in an earthquake pamphlet we had read. Judy and I were both covered in plaster dust. I told Judy to dress because we were getting out of the hotel to look for a clear area.

As I left our closet area, I looked out the window overlooking the canal and the elevated auto route. Cars on the road were being shoved around by an invisible hand and the elevated road was moving as if it was a snake, slithering through the grass. I finished dressing and looked around for Judy, but she was not in the room. I opened the door to the hall and there she was sitting on the floor tying her shoes, with her passport in her mouth. Before I could say anything, Judy said, "If I die at least they will know who I am."

We headed for the stairs. Our room was on the twelfth floor. We descended perhaps four floors, when we found the stairway blocked, not by debris but by hotel chairs, boxes, folded tables, and lots of other equipment used in a dining room. I started kicking whatever was in my path out of the way, and we proceeded to the lobby. We later learned the staff used the stairway for storage after the New Year festivities.

The lobby was full of people. Some were dressed; others had bedclothes wrapped around them. The once full fountain was now empty of water.

I spotted one of our flight attendants talking on the phone. As I waited for her to finish, I could see that both her elbows were raw and bleeding. Her call finished, and I grabbed the phone, hoping to call home and let family know we were all right. The phone was unique in that it did not have numbers but countries. I pushed Canada and immediately was talking to a Canadian operator. I was connected to family, gave them the news, and asked them to contact the rest of the gang. After I finished my call, I asked the flight attendant what had happened to her elbows. She told us her room was on the twenty-fourth floor and she, like me, had been tossed out of bed. She tried crawling to a corner, but the building was moving back and forth so fast that she was not making any progress. All she succeeded in doing was giving herself rug burns and scratches.

I approached the desk and told them about the stairway being blocked with hotel property. He just shrugged his shoulders and said, "So sorry for earthquake."

John and his wife were in the lobby and he did not look well, but said he was all right. I asked him if he had contacted the company in Toronto, but he had not. Soon, most of the crew was in the lobby. I made my way to the phones once more and called Crew Scheduling in Toronto. I informed them of what had happened and that all the crew was accounted for. My call was the first they had heard about the earthquake.

Later, when we talked to Judy's brother in Vancouver, he said he had called Air Canada and was advised that our flight had not landed yet. He told the staff member that we must then have crashed into the sea because the flight had left the day before and he knew the aircraft did not have enough fuel to stay twenty-four hours in the air. He was upset and told the company representative to find out where his relatives were.

Hotel staff advised everyone that the quake was over and that the building was secure due to the heavy springs that had been used during construction to act as a counter-balance during a quake. We were also advised that a light breakfast was available in the dining room. The crew all had a bite to eat and we arranged to meet in the lobby later on to decide on a place for dinner. Later when we checked out, we found we were all charged fifty Canadian dollars for breakfast. One would have thought that, in view of the earthquake and the limited food available, a free breakfast was in order. Judy and I finally left the hotel and, looking up and around, realized that there was no open area to go to for safety.

There were continual aftershocks, and we braced ourselves as we walked along the canal. Steps had moved about six to eight inches, and small storage sheds had been completely removed from their base.

We walked in the direction of the rail station. Although there was not much in the way of debris on the street, we noticed that windows, vertical to one another, were all broken, while the next row of vertical windows was untouched. Many buildings had window-washing platforms hanging down vertically.

Coming around a corner, we could smell perfume and liquor. The two stores beside each other had just about every bottle in either store broken. The source of the smell was found.

The roads had emergency vehicles only—flights and trains were cancelled. We wondered what damage occurred at Kansai Airport and if a tsunami had hit the man-made islands in the bay. When we got back to the hotel, the phone rang in our room, and I answered. The Air Canada representative at the airport apologized for the earthquake as if it was his fault. He informed me that our flight was cancelled and that he would advise us of our new schedule. We knew we would be in Osaka for a day or two depending on damage at the airport. The agent had tried to reach John and when he could not, he called me.

When we met as a crew in the lobby, I advised John of my conversation with the company. He and his wife had been out most of the day as well, and had not had a call.

Many of the crew elected to have an early night, while the rest of us started to hunt for a place to eat. We did not feel like eating at the hotel. As a group, we walked many blocks, finding that most establishments were closed. Finally, we came across a noodle house, which was doing a booming business. The restaurant was full of rescue personnel but we managed to put a couple of tables together for the crew. The restaurant had one item only; noodles, in large tureens. The noodles and broth were excellent and we all had our fill.

The aftershocks continued all day and into the night. I placed a glass of water on a night stand next to the bed and after each aftershock, the glass moved closer to the edge.

Electricity was restored, and we watched television to observe the damage in Kobe, the worst-hit area. Elevated roads had collapsed as well as many buildings, blocking the streets, which made it impossible for fire and rescue personnel to reach the hardest hit areas. We also saw damage to Osaka mostly in the form of collapsed wooden homes.

The authorities soon confiscated a cruise ship nearby, and it was brought to the Kobe area, docking close to shore. People were rotated back and forth for food and rest as well as to attend injuries. It was reported that the first responders were the local Kobe mafia. They set up a soup kitchen and dispensed diapers and medicine well before the local authorities got their act together.

We finally received notice of our scheduled departure and were advised that all elevated highways had to be inspected for damage. We would be taking a long circuitous route to the airport. The drive was most enjoyable and we were able to see more of the countryside as well as some of the destroyed wooden homes.

The trip home was routine from the flying point of view, but I was still concerned about John. He seemed pale and pre-occupied. I told him to put his seat back and rest; I would look after the aircraft. He declined. Judy told me that she fell into a deep sleep and woke thinking she was in the earthquake again.

When we arrived in Vancouver, John and his wife's room was ready but ours would not be for another forty-five minutes. I went to a coffee shop near the hotel and Judy and I sipped our coffee waiting for our room. John arrived and said he was going for a beer and invited me and Judy along. It was the last thing we wanted at seven-thirty in the morning.

We contacted Judy's brother, and he was happy to hear that all was well with the both of us. It is during this conversation we learned about his efforts to try and find out if we were all right after the earthquake.

The next morning we operated direct to Toronto. Judy and I took a flight to Ottawa as passengers. Normally, John and his wife would have taken a passenger flight to Montreal but they remained in Toronto to visit with one of their sons, who was having a birthday party.

Family and friends were seated around a table enjoying each other's company and good food, when John collapsed. His wife, a trained nurse, immediately started chest compressions while their son dialled 911. John was transported to the hospital. He had suffered a massive heart attack and, due to the length of time without oxygen, he suffered major brain damage.

Here was a man in his prime who now functioned as a seven-year-old. I visited John in hospital in Toronto, and he told me strange stories about priests with guns and people running around. He was eventually transferred to Montreal to a rehab facility. John was taken to his home to see what he would recognize, but he wanted to go "home," back to the long-term care facility. He did not recognize his own home. I learned that medical tests showed that John had had a very low potassium level. This could have led to irregular heartbeat and disturbed heart rhythm.

The Montreal pilots often took John out to lunch and for drives in a friend's convertible, which he enjoyed. At the time of writing, John is still alive but in failing health. I often think of him, and why I kept asking him if he was okay. Perhaps I had a sixth sense that all was not well with him. To think he was only three months away from retirement after having flown for thirty-five years.

Chapter Twenty-Four

Boeing 767

My time on the Boeing 747-400 was coming to a close. I completed two to three trips to Europe before I was scheduled to return to the left seat on the Boeing 767. I never had a return trip to Osaka.

I attended the ground school course for the 767 in Toronto. The aircraft had similar up-to-date electronics as the 747-400, so the simulator transition was straightforward. As with all previous aircraft conversions, I flew with an instructor, completing single-engine approaches and touch-and-go landings.

I can truthfully say that during my years with Air Canada, I had what I would call two "good instructors." The 767 instructor was not one of them. In my opinion, he should have stayed on line, flying to acquire more experience before being selected for an instructor's position.

I was scheduled to fly with a supervisor for my overseas check-out. It turned out that he had had very little time on the Atlantic and I was giving him a few tips on what and what not to do. All in all we had a very good trip.

Once again, I was released on the unsuspecting public.

The 767 is a delightful aircraft to fly; it has few, if any, bad habits. I flew several trips to San Francisco. It is a very busy airport with parallel runways used for landing and takeoff. On final, you would see aircraft close to you, lined up to land on the other parallel runway. Things tend to happen very fast at a major airport and everyone is expected to be very professional.

My favourite flights on the 767 were from Ottawa to London–return. I bid for these flights as often as I could. These trips saved me from going to Toronto to operate a series of flights. The summers

Captain, Boeing 767. Last aircraft flown before retirement. Great fun.
Reproduced with the permission of Air Canada

of 1995 and 1996 were busy for me. I was operating lots of flights overseas. In the back of my mind, I could not help but think that in two short years I would be retiring.

Many of the first officers were very senior. One individual, who had plenty of seniority and could hold the 767 as a captain, elected not to get promoted. He had been through a messy divorce and if he made more money as a captain he would be forced to share his income with his former wife. He was not prepared to give her one cent more. There were others with similar stories.

I was fortunate enough to do a few Vienna trips. The city seemed to have music everywhere. Like my days on the DC-8, I would walk to a central park and sit and let the music surround me.

Layovers in Frankfurt during my time on the DC- 8 were at the Intercontinental Hotel, near downtown Frankfurt. I was happy to learn that the layover hotel had been changed to the Hilton, in the town of Mainz. The town of Mainz is about a thirty-minute drive from Frankfurt. It is situated on the banks of the Rhine River, and the town boasts many wine festivals, spring through fall.

On one trip, with Judy along for the ride, we were pleasantly surprised to see the town was having a wine festival. We soon learned that it was best to buy the glass with the wine, and then at the next stop, just hold out the glass and it was filled at a much cheaper rate. Judy wanted a few extra glasses to take home. Of course we bought them full of local wine.

My favourite warm-weather walk in Mainz was to cross the

bridge, walk parallel to the Rhine to the town of Bebrich, cross over another bridge across the Rhine, and walk back to Mainz. It probably took me four to five hours to complete, but was well worth the effort. Some first officers accompanied me while others did not. I still had the reputation of taking long walks. Naturally, we could stop and have a glass of beer or wine along the route.

A new first officer on the 767 flew with me to Mainz. He had had very little Atlantic time. I advised him that the best way to get over the time change was, on arrival, go to bed for four hours. When you wake you will feel pretty lousy but once you are out just do things that the locals are doing. If it is lunch, eat lunch. If you sleep late you will have a very hard time sleeping in the evening.

On arrival, I told him to meet me at the bar for a cold beer at five in the afternoon, and that we would go to Margo's for dinner. Margo's is a nice German restaurant with wonderful food at a reasonable price. The original Margo married an Air Canada captain and sold the business. The new owners kept the original name.

I had told the first officer that if he was not there at five, I would not call him, and that I would leave for Margo's on my own. I finished my beer and there was still no sign of the first officer, so I left. He had obviously overslept and would learn quickly from his mistake and plan differently on future overseas trips.

When I arrived at Margo's, it was full of American Airline crews. I looked for a familiar face but did not see anyone I knew. As I was about to leave, I saw an older gentleman sitting alone near the kitchen. He had his hand in the air and was beckoning me to join him. It was the only seat left. I made my way towards his table, and said, "*Danke.*" I introduced myself and he asked in excellent English, if I was with the airlines. I told him I was flying for Air Canada and I was on a layover, but that my first officer had slept in, so I came to Margo's alone.

The gentleman bought me a glass of white wine. It was obvious by the way the staff treated him he was a regular, although I had never seen him there before. He said he had just ordered, so I followed suit. While waiting for our meals, we bought each other another glass of wine.

Half way through our meal, he told me that he had been a Luftwaffe pilot during the war. He was wounded during the Russian campaign and after his recovery he was transferred to North Africa. The Malta siege was being fought, and his job was to fly, in a flying boat, near the battle area looking for downed German pilots in the Mediterranean.

He said that they used to listen to the British on their radios and pretty well knew where they might find a downed pilot. One of his spotters, a medical corpsman doing double duty, advised he had spotted a head bobbing in the sea. They landed near the downed airman and pulled him on board. The corpsman advised that he was a British officer and that his leg was in a bad way. The corpsman did what he could but the pilot needed immediate medical attention.

The gentleman then told me he asked if the airman still had his dog tags. He did. He then asked his radio operator to contact the British on his radio, and advise them that they had a British flight lieutenant in need of medical attention. The airman's serial number was given. They told the British that, if they could be guaranteed safe passage, they would land in Malta so that the pilot could get proper attention.

After several minutes, the British confirmed that the pilot was one of theirs and that they would give the Germans safe passage so they could deliver the wounded airman. The gentleman told me they were given specific instructions to follow, to guarantee their safety.

They landed and the pilot was removed. Their aircraft was allowed some precious gasoline. In addition, a thermos of tea and sandwiches were given to them. They were then told to get the hell out of there and that after thirty minutes they would be fair game for British fighters. They escaped back to North Africa without incident. I had never read or heard a story like this gentleman told me. It was a true act of bravery and showed remarkable chivalry towards a fellow pilot, albeit an enemy.

Shortly after the Americans landed in North Africa, he was taken prisoner and spent the rest of the war in a POW camp in the U.S. The war finished, and he was released and travelled back to Germany to help resurrect his family's glass business. With tongue-in-cheek he added that there was a great need for glass after the war. The business flourished and he was now retired.

After he retired, he started to wonder what had happened to the British flyer. For some reason, he remembered the dog tag number.

He wrote to the British foreign office in Bonn, explaining the circumstances of how he acquired the dog tag serial number, and asked if they could provide any information on the downed pilot.

He told me he had no expectations, when, after a few months, a letter arrived from the British explaining that the pilot in question was indeed alive and living in London. Included in the letter was an invitation for him to come to London and meet with the pilot, and he was asked to provide a convenient date to travel to London. After a few exchanges, a date was finally settled. He was to travel to London, where a room at the Royal Air Force Club would be provided. He was to meet the pilot in one of the rooms in the mess at a specific time. He told me he was very excited and anxious and curious about the reception he would receive.

When he entered the room, he saw a large man leaning on a cane; he had obviously lost his leg. Standing next to him was his wife, who immediately approached the German, kissed him, and thanked him for saving her husband's life. He told me the emotion he felt was overwhelming. He cried that day from the joy of a life saved in all the horrors of World War II.

The gentleman and I shook hands and parted company. I saw him on two occasions after that, sitting at his favourite table, and I always joined him.

During my last two years, there were plenty of rumours about Canadian Airlines going bankrupt. There was some talk about amalgamating with Air Canada. I recall Canadian Airlines employees in uniform, marching on Parliament Hill with placards reading, "Better Dead than Red." I will never forgive them for their actions, particularly in view of the eventual amalgamation of the two airlines. Happily, I was retired by this time.

Canadian Airlines ceased to exist as an airline in July 2000. Air Canada had hoped that the government would let Canadian Airlines go and that we in Air Canada could pick up what was left. This was not to happen.

The government forced Air Canada to absorb Canadian's debt. In addition, Canadian employees were to be absorbed into Air Canada. A layoff clause guaranteed the employees jobs for four years, and they all received a 20 percent pay raise. Several senior Canadian Airlines employees elected to take retirement rather than be forced to move from Vancouver.

Since the two seniority lists were merged, I have heard many stories of former Canadian captains telling Air Canada first officers not to touch anything unless they were told to. Great for cockpit co-operation. I know of some Canadian pilots who had actually failed the Air Canada course and were later hired by Canadian. The merging of the list actually made some of the failed pilots senior to Air Canada pilots who were on the same Air Canada course. It just did not seem fair.

I was on a layover trip to Frankfurt and as a crew we were in the Hilton hotel in Mainz. My phone rang in the early morning and I was advised that my older brother was seriously ill with congestive heart failure. Rather than tell the company, I elected to operate our flight to Calgary the next day. If I had reported the situation, I would have been taken off the flight and returned to Canada as a passenger, seriously delaying passengers and crew.

I was naturally concerned with my brother's health. As we proceeded to Calgary, I advised the company of the situation and that on landing in Calgary, I would be booking off my next flight on compassionate grounds.

I informed Air Canada Calgary of the situation and, knowing that a flight was leaving from Calgary to Toronto close to our arrival time, I asked the radio operator to explain to the outgoing captain my desire to make his flight and, if necessary, absorb a short delay. Normally, in similar situations, the crew would have given an "on-time" departure. I also asked the operator if she would contact customs on my behalf; explain the situation, and that I had nothing to declare so that I could go immediately from one aircraft to the other.

Upon landing in Calgary, I observed the Toronto flight pushing back from the gate. I asked the operator if she had even talked to the captain about my request. I was rather upset when she said she had not. Her excuse was she wanted an on-time departure.

We cleared customs and I delayed my departure for the airport hotel. I wanted to speak to the agent. I did not mince words with her and she knew I was more than a little angry. She threatened me by saying she would report me to the company. I told her to go ahead, because under the circumstances I knew the company would have been on my side.

I proceeded to the hotel, rose early, and caught the first flight to Toronto. I was able to arrange a seat on the Moncton flight. When I arrived, I rented a car and proceeded to the Moncton hospital. I spent a few minutes with Lorne, my older brother. He was lucid but very groggy. I know he was happy to hear my voice. The rest of the evening was a waiting game. Lorne passed away about six hours after I arrived. It was February 1997.

After Lorne's death, I started to think of my own future. I was due to retire in October 1997. I knew that my last summer would have been great with lots of good overseas flying, but I elected to retire July 1, 1997. I thought, one never knows what the future may bring, and I decided I wanted another full summer with my family.

Prior to my last trip, I bought three magnum bottles of champagne. Bottle number one was for the Ottawa ground agents who always ensured I had a seat when I was commuting to Toronto for a flight.

Bottle number two I presented to the central flight dispatchers based in Toronto, with thanks for all their help and assistance over the years. I had contacted these individuals if I wanted extra fuel or to perhaps add an alternate to a flight plan due to weather at a destination.

Bottle number three I presented to the central crew schedulers, based in Montreal, thanking them for their help and understanding over my career with Air Canada. This was the office I would call if I had to book off sick, either at home or away. They also awarded blocks of flights if I was on reserve or wanted extra flying.

I left a note with each bottle, advising all recipients that they could drink, raffle, or draw, but to please enjoy it in the spirit it was given.

I was advised that my final trip was to be Bombay. I was not particularly happy about the trip knowing of some of the diseases one could catch. I saw firsthand what had happened to the one flight attendant who had ended up in intensive care, and I knew of other cases as well.

Last flight. Boeing 767 Vancouver to Toronto, June 28, 1997.

It would be just my luck to catch something.

On reflection and, with Judy's encouragement, I called crew scheduling and advised them I did not want to do the Bombay flight and requested a European trip instead. Crew scheduling advised me that a trip to Vancouver, Zurich, Vancouver, and back to Toronto was available. I accepted the trip.

Jim was to be my first officer and we had flown together once or twice before. We got along well. The Vancouver trip was uneventful. Jim and I went out to dinner together and had a glass of wine or two in celebration of my forthcoming retirement.

On our flight to Zurich, we reported a massive forest fire in northern Manitoba. Air Traffic Control was aware of the fire, but had been advised that it was so remote, not enough fire equipment was available to fight it, and the authorities had decided to just let the fire burn itself out.

Jim had told our flight attendants about my retirement and everyone planned to get together for dinner. I had been in Zurich many times and knew it did not matter where you ate. The food was always very good. The in-charge suggested a backyard restaurant he was familiar with. The setting was ideal; very private, with tables under trees. We had not even ordered, when a bird let loose and pooped on my head. Everyone had a great laugh and I was told it meant good luck. I cleaned myself up in the washroom and returned to the party. In my absence, the crew advised the waiter that I was on my last flight before retirement and asked if the restaurant could provide a small cake for me. It arrived complete with a lit candle. Songs were sung, and one and all thoroughly enjoyed the evening.

The next day, we operated back to Vancouver. Jim joined me on my last walk around Stanley Park, a place I always enjoyed. As we prepared for takeoff in the morning, the tower called and asked if Captain McKay was on board. Jim answered in the affirmative. The tower wished me a very long and happy retirement. I answered and thanked them for their kind sentiments and for all their assistance over the years. I then opened the throttles and we were on our way to Toronto; my last leg.

As we passed Winnipeg, the air traffic control tower, again, asked if Captain McKay was on board. They wished me a good retirement as well. I was beginning to suspect that flight dispatch had put out the word about my last flight. I have to admit I was grateful for their remarks and a little sad as well.

We started our descent into Toronto, and Air Traffic Control asked, "Confirm Captain McKay is on board." Jim answered yes. Air Traffic Control said, "Cleared number one." On handover, I again thanked them for their years of help. We were cleared to the tower, and then the tower controller asked if I was on board as well and Jim confirmed. He was enjoying himself at my expense as I was becoming a bit self-conscious. The tower then said, "Confirm full stop or touch and go." I advised that I knew what I would like to do but I requested a full stop.

Unknown to me, the back-end crew had advised the passengers that I was on my last trip. We approached the gate and shut down the engines for the last time. The cabin door opened and the purser advised that the passengers would not leave until they had shaken my hand. I had a grin that lasted until the last passenger and crew left the aircraft. I really appreciated the remarks from everyone.

I joined Jim in the cockpit, looked around, gathered my gear, and we walked up the gangway to the terminal. I said good bye to Jim and thanked him for all his help on my last flight. I wished him well with the rest of his career.

I proceeded to the Rapidair gate and boarded a flight to Ottawa. Sitting in first class, I was asked what I would like to drink. Although we were not supposed to drink in uniform, I asked the flight attendant for a glass of red wine. I told her it was all right to serve me in uniform as I had just completed my last flight and was heading for home and retirement. She said, "In that case, I will open a bottle of French wine."

Memories started to fill my mind, particularly of those who did not make it. I could not help but think of all the friends I had lost in accidents while in the military. On my drive home, although elated to be retired, I shed a tear or two. I had completed forty-three years of flying, from flying clubs to the RCAF and Air Canada.

Judy greeted me with a kiss and a glass of wine.

During a small gathering of friends that Judy had arranged to help me celebrate my retirement, one neighbour asked how many hours I had flown. I told him I had accumulated 25,000 hours of flying time. He arrived back with his computer and said, "Do you realize you spent nearly three years in the air?"

Dad lived to see me in "one of those."

About the Author

Don McKay was born in Sydney, Nova Scotia, on October 5, 1937. He had a fascination with flying from a very early age and never lost his desire to be a pilot. He grew up in the Maritimes and calls Saint John, New Brunswick, home. Don is married to his high school sweetheart, Judy. They will be celebrating fifty-three years of marriage in October 2012. They have three boys, four grandsons, and one great-grandson. Don and Judy live in Carleton Place, Ontario.

My Dream and Beyond
A Pilot's Journey
Don McKay